On Feeding the Masses

China's food safety system is in crisis. Egregious scandals, as varied as the sale of liquor laced with Viagra and the distribution of fake eggs, reveal how regulatory practices have been stretched to their limit in the world's largest food production system. *On Feeding the Masses* focuses on the oft-cited but ultimately overlooked concept of scale to identify the root causes of China's regulatory failures in food safety. The "politics of scale" framework highlights how regulators disagree on which level of government is best suited to regulate ("the scale of governance"), struggle to address multilevel tensions ("multidimensional scale integration"), and fail to understand how policies at one level of government can affect other levels of government in unexpected and costly ways ("scale externalities"). Drawing from more than 200 interviews with food safety regulators and producers, the study provides one of the most comprehensive accounts of China's food safety crisis to date.

John K. Yasuda is Assistant Professor of East Asian Languages and Cultures at Indiana University, Bloomington. Yasuda's research includes the study of regulatory reform in China, governance, and the politics of regulatory failure. He has published in the *China Quarterly*, *Journal of Politics*, and *Regulation and Governance*. Yasuda has commented on food safety issues for *The Guardian*, *The New York Times*, and *China Dialogue*. He received his PhD in Political Science from the University of California, Berkeley, and his MPhil from Oxford University.

On Feeding the Masses

An Anatomy of Regulatory Failure in China

JOHN K. YASUDA

Indiana University, Bloomington

CAMBRIDGE
UNIVERSITY PRESS

CAMBRIDGE
UNIVERSITY PRESS

University Printing House, Cambridge CB2 8BS, United Kingdom

One Liberty Plaza, 20th Floor, New York, NY 10006, USA

477 Williamstown Road, Port Melbourne, VIC 3207, Australia

314-321, 3rd Floor, Plot 3, Splendor Forum, Jasola District Centre, New Delhi - 110025, India

79 Anson Road, #06-04/06, Singapore 079906

Cambridge University Press is part of the University of Cambridge.

It furthers the University's mission by disseminating knowledge in the pursuit of education, learning and research at the highest international levels of excellence.

www.cambridge.org
Information on this title: www.cambridge.org/9781316648971
DOI: 10.1017/9781108185851

© John K. Yasuda 2018

First published 2018
First paperback edition 2021

A catalogue record for this publication is available from the British Library

ISBN 978-1-107-19964-4 Hardback
ISBN 978-1-316-64897-1 Paperback

For

My Parents, Thomas, and Annabelle Yasuda

Contents

Figures

Tables

Boxes

Acknowledgments

The crafting of this book faced its own "scale problem": it was large, unwieldy, with multiple moving parts. I must thank the many individuals who helped bring into focus my thoughts on food safety and scale. I am deeply grateful to my committee members—Kevin O'Brien, Chris Ansell, Peter Lorentzen, Rachel Stern, and Kevin Chen—that provided many of the seminal ideas contained in this book. The committee chair, Kevin O'Brien, has been a first-rate mentor. I am thankful for his insightful perspective on Chinese politics, sage advice on conducting fieldwork, and editorial expertise. I will always be grateful for our frequent chats in his office, home, and walk-and-talks in Walnut Creek. When I lost my way, Kevin always pointed me in the right direction. Chris Ansell introduced me to new literatures that have fundamentally changed the way I think about governance and scale. It is largely due to Chris's influence that I turned to Europe in search of solutions to China's scale problem. Peter Lorentzen added a much-needed political economic perspective to the project. I must thank Rachel Stern for her comments on the overall framing of the book and for helpful discussions on the development of risk regulation in China. Kevin Chen provided invaluable in-country support, sharing his contacts and guiding my research design in China.

The University of Pennsylvania's Center for the Study of Contemporary China served as my base of operations during the initial drafting process. I am incredibly grateful for the advice of my directors, Avery Goldstein and Jacques Delisle, who provided significant intellectual, institutional, and moral support during the writing process. Yuhua Wang offered excellent advice on how to structure the manuscript, and helped focus my arguments on scale into a coherent narrative. Neysun Mahboubi kindly introduced me to a number of legal scholars working on food safety. Devesh Kapur, my friend and advisor, provided much needed insight on India and helped me tease out the similar struggles that both India and China face in governance. Yuanyuan Zeng played a crucial role in helping organize my book conference. My book conference discussants, Andrew Mertha and Tim Buthe, helped me clarify my arguments and encouraged me to tell "my side of the story" about food safety in China. I must also thank many others at Penn, particularly Regina Abrami, Emily Hannum, Marshall Meyer, and Guobin Yang, who have offered advice and various degrees of support for this project.

I was extraordinarily fortunate to meet a number of individuals in China who provided me with their expertise and time. To Roger Skinner, who took interest in this project and taught me my first lessons on the state of food safety in China—thank you. I am indebted to Philippa Jones, director of China Policy, who introduced me to a network of food safety experts in the diplomatic community in Beijing. John Chapple, who is fighting the good fight for food safety in China, provided technical expertise and organized interviews with exporters throughout Shandong. Yuehua Zhang at Zhejiang University shared his research site in Zhejiang province where I was able to conduct a number of important interviews. Donghui Yang and Suping Shen at Yunnan Normal University played an instrumental role in organizing my fieldwork in Yunnan. I am also thankful for my colleagues at the International Center for Agricultural and Rural Development at the Chinese Academy of Agricultural Sciences for fruitful discussions on rural issues, methodology, and survey research. My research on China's fascinating Community-Supported Agriculture (CSA) movement would not have been possible without the support of individuals at the Social Resources Institute, specifically Chen Wu. Tianle Chang also played an important role in introducing me to a host of CSA producers in Beijing, Shanghai, and Chengdu. I am also thankful to BLW Sunn, a fellow foodie, for the fantastic photo, which has been used for the book's cover.

I must also thank the countless individuals who agreed to be interviewed for this project. While all interviews are referenced by code, each represents someone who has been working tirelessly to address the food safety crisis in China. To the government officials, who invited me to their localities to conduct research on a politically sensitive topic, I cannot express my gratitude enough. Without their substantial support and sponsorship I would not have been able to meet the producers, processors, and state regulators whose words fill the pages of this book. I will not forget the countless conversations shared over meals throughout China with food processing executives, farmers, and NGO leaders. To reporters and diplomats who have been covering food safety developments in China for the past decade, I hope this book will aid you in your efforts to ensure that all people in China have access to safe food.

Research for the dissertation that preceded this book project was made possible through funding from several grant organizations. The Center for Chinese Studies at UC Berkeley provided summer funding, which enabled me to conduct much of the preparatory work for this project. The Fulbright-Hays Fellowship, NSEP Boren Fellowship, and NSF provided substantial funding for more than fifteen months of fieldwork and many additional trips from 2009 to 2016.

This project is a culmination of my academic experiences to date. I was fortunate to be surrounded by a nurturing academic community. Laura Stoker provided comments on my grant proposals and initial research design. Tom Gold, Stanley Lubman, and Rosie Hsueh gave useful feedback on chapters of the book. I must also thank Lynn White who read early drafts of the entire manuscript and provided excellent critiques of each of my chapters. It was Lynn who first gave me the idea of thinking of scale as "degrees-of-zoom." Lynn also kindly introduced me to Evan Lieberman who provided guidance on my use of the nested analysis framework. To my former classmates, Seungyoun Oh, Rongbin Han, Daniel Mattingly, Sara Newland, Denise van der Kamp, Julia Chuang, Alexsia Chan, and Suzanne Scoggins, who read and commented on earlier drafts of chapters—I cannot thank you enough. At Oxford, Vivienne Shue provided guidance on thinking through the conceptual implications of this study, particularly regarding fragmented authoritarianism. I must also acknowledge my former teacher Elizabeth Perry, whose intellect and wisdom have been a source of much inspiration over the years. Most of all, I wish to thank William Kirby for convincing me to start studying Chinese politics all those years ago during my freshman year at Harvard.

Here, at Indiana University, I have been extremely lucky to work closely with a number of China scholars who have advised me on the finer points of the book publication process. Many thanks to Gardiner Bovingdon, Sara Friedman, Adam Liff, Yan Long, and Ethan Michelson, who have read and commented on various aspects of the book.

A final note of appreciation must also go to Robert Dreesen at Cambridge University Press, who helped shepherd this manuscript from start to finish and solicited excellent reviews for this book. I have benefited greatly from the counsel of many, but, of course, all errors contained in this study are strictly my own.

I dedicate this book to my loving family who provided emotional and intellectual support. My father, my first teacher and editor, read every single page I have written on the subject of food safety. Some of our many late-night chats have been included in this study. To my mother, who fed me and prayed for me during dark turns in the writing process—I would not have survived without you. Jeff and Celeste plied me with good food and drink, and opened their home to me. To my niece Sophie and my nephews Cole and Zach, whom Uncle John has neglected for far too long—I will be coming over to play soon. S.D.G.

Abbreviations

APB	Agricultural Production Base
AQSIQ	General Administration for Quality Inspection and Supervision
BRC	British Retail Consortium
CFDA	China Food and Drug Administration
CIQ	China Entry-Exit Inspection and Quarantine Bureau
CNCA	China Certification and Accreditation Administration
CSA	Community-Supported Agriculture
CURA	Chengdu Urban River Association
DGSANCO	Directorate-General for Health and Consumer Protection
EUCTP	EU-China Trade Project
FDA	United States Food and Drug Administration
FSC	Food Safety Committee
FSL	Food Safety Law
GAP	Good Agricultural Practice
GMP	Good Manufacturing Practice
HACCP	Hazard Analysis Critical Control Point System
ISO	International Standards Organization
MOA	Ministry of Agriculture
MOC	Ministry of Commerce
MOH	Ministry of Health
QS	Quality Safe Certification
QTSB	Quality Technical Supervision Bureau
SAIC	State Administration for Industry and Commerce
SFDA	State Food and Drug Administration

Food Safety and China's Scale Problem

"If OUR party can't even handle food safety issues properly, and keeps mishandling them, then people will ask whether we are fit to keep ruling China."

— Xi Jinping, President of the People's Republic of China, 2013[1]

In the last decade, China has experienced a number of grim food safety scandals: melamine in infant formula (La Franier 2009); soy sauce made out of human hair (Tran 2014); heavy metals in rice (Buckley 2013); feces in tofu (Zhang 2014). Concerted policy initiatives and a new Food Safety Law in 2009 did not avert the sale of recycled cooking oil siphoned from sewers in 2010 (Barboza 2010) or the reemergence in 2011 of pork contaminated with clenbuterol that poisons the cardiovascular system (Barclay 2011). And despite the establishment of numerous new regulatory agencies, and the launching of increasingly aggressive campaigns, images of thousands of diseased pork carcasses floating in Shanghai's main waterways were seen globally in 2013 (Davison 2013). In the following year, a US-owned food processor in China was reported to be responsible for a widespread rotten meat scandal that affected major internationally branded food outlets throughout the country (Polansek 2014). A few knowledgeable insiders even suggest that China is on the brink of the world's worst *E. coli* outbreak, with widespread and devastating consequences. On an organic vegetable farm in Shanghai, one auditor explained that if duck feces from the nearby canal found its way into prepackaged salads, tens of thousands could fall seriously ill (EX 4).

[1] As quoted in the Economist (2016). The quote is translated from Xi Jinping's speech at the Central Rural Work Conference on December 23, 2013.

The political consequences of the country's decades-long regulatory failures in food safety have not escaped the attention of the Chinese Communist Party (CCP) leadership: as President Xi Jinping ominously suggests, in the epigraph to this chapter, if the party continues to mishandle its food safety issues, the Chinese people will begin to ask more fundamental questions about whether the CCP is fit to govern a complex market society.

Interviews with food safety experts reveal a system in disarray: microbiological hazards remain unchecked, supply chain management is weak, and policies are uncoordinated. Informed observers predict that, even though China has made significant strides in food safety reform, China's food safety disasters are likely to continue unabated. It should be noted that most experts do not believe that the entire Chinese food supply system is unsafe. Indeed, such an overly broad perspective often clouds objective analysis of the complexity of China's food safety issues. However, investigators of the country's existing food safety failures, including myself, are concerned over the *persistent recurrence* of major food safety scandals despite the government's many reforms undertaken to date. And the broader concern is that the state's continuing inability to cope with the increased risks posed by complex supply chains, accelerated market growth, and policy uncertainty ominously portends regulatory failure in other sectors.

In supermarkets, corner stores, and specialty shops, fearful consumers desperately examine food packaging for signs of tampering and the use of illegal additives, often to no avail. The number of adulterated food complaints recorded by the China Consumer Association in 2011 increased by 22% from 2010 (Zhou 2011). A 2012 Pew survey shows that 41% of respondents identified food safety as a "serious problem," which was up from only 12% in 2008 (Wike 2013). A more recent poll in 2015 reports that 53% of its respondents still believe food safety to be one of the top five governance challenges facing their country (Pew 2015).

Chinese regulators, foreign experts, and academics are all at a loss regarding how to solve China's food safety problems. Tested regulatory best practices have produced only lackluster results; European and American technical assistance programs have had limited success; and global third-party food safety auditors have failed to coax producers into compliance. With the lives of 1.3 billion people at stake and the threat of massive social unrest, food safety has now become a major political issue. This book seeks to examine why China's food safety system is failing and, in a broader context, to gain analytical leverage to better understand the roots of regulatory failure.

The extant literature on China's food safety crisis has largely focused on the country's level of economic development, its lack of state capacity, high levels of corruption, and fundamental flaws in authoritarian governance. As I show in the pages that follow, China massively underperforms in its provision of food safety with respect to each of these factors. Moreover, other studies focusing on local obstructionism or a lack of political will to address food safety also appear insufficient. This is not to say that economic development, state capacity, corruption, and democratic governance have no effect on China's level of food safety, but rather that the lack of explanatory power of these factors points to a deeper dynamic at work.

At the crux of China's ongoing food safety problems is the formidable political challenge of designing a regulatory framework that effectively integrates more than 240 million farms and millions of processors and distributors with vastly different capacities to provide safe food. Few countries in the world have had to address food safety on an order of this magnitude. Even India, with its sizable agricultural industry, only boasts 137 million farms (Lowder et al. 2014). John King Fairbank (1988), one of the world's preeminent sinologists, described well the governance challenge posed by the sheer *scale* of the Chinese polity:

How can so big a polity cohere? The scale is beyond our experience if not imagination. We may grow accustomed to imagining gene-splicing at one end of the material scene and whole clusters of galaxies at the other, but the Chinese behemoth visible every day just across the Pacific remains an equal mystery of a psychopolitical kind.

To the country's own officials working at ground level, the daunting reality of China's size and heterogeneity is regularly featured in their exasperated diagnosis of their problems. Local regulators often simply and directly say that China is just "too big and too populous." China's immense size and population, they claim, are why it is impossible to monitor and prevent the thousands of diseased pigs circulating in the market, the countless numbers of backyard workshops producing gutter oil, and unscrupulous vegetable vendors who use dangerous chemical treatments to increase the shelf life of their produce.

This book seeks to explore the *political* challenges inherent in developing a large-scale regulatory system. Following Fairbank's descriptive pronouncement on the subject, we must develop an analytical framework about how scale affects governance that moves beyond basic considerations of cost and manpower. In order to do this, we must first unpack the concept of scale itself. It should be noted at the start that the way "scale" is defined in this book is more closely related to how the concept is introduced in the fields of political geography, sociology, and anthropology than it is currently applied in the study of political science, which has yet to fully embrace the concept of scale (Hochschild 2009; Marston 2000; O'Lear & Diehl 2007; Gibson et al. 2000).[2] Scholars continue to debate the exact meaning of scale, but the general consensus is that scale entails far more than a measure of a system's geographic expanse or its population. Rather than mere size, scale is fundamentally a *relational* concept, a critical distinction to be discussed in greater detail in the following chapter (Howitt 1998). The scale of a system explores how size *interacts* with the way individuals perceive and relate to space, jurisdiction, knowledge, time, networks, and management styles.

In matters of governance, the scale, or "degree-of-zoom," in which regulators are situated, affects the way they view their political world: how they define problems, craft solutions, and design institutions to address governance challenges. The ability to identify certain patterns, for example, is often highly dependent on the scale at which one is operating. Big, slow-moving processes are sometimes only identifiable on a large-scale and go virtually unnoticed on a small-scale. What may appear to be an isolated bout of cold weather, or a heat wave, in a local village or county could actually reflect a continuous pattern of climate change occurring at a larger, even global, scale.

"Scale politics," the focus of this book, refers to the fierce conflicts that emerge when policy communities operating at different scales—national, provincial, municipal, prefectural, county, and township—are forced to integrate to develop a unified regulatory system. In large, heterogeneous polities like China, where millions of actors are operating at varying scales in diverse economic and geographical settings, scale politics are particularly fierce due to stretched regulatory capacity, mismatched standards among political subunits, and principal-agent problems between center

---

[2] Hochschild (2009) notes that political science would benefit from a more systematic study of scale. She outlines a number of potential avenues for research on the politics of scale: (1) understanding the processes by which scale is constructed; (2) analyzing the relationship between units of different size; (3) exploring the political strategies that revolve around scale; and, (4) considering the different governance processes that arise due to differences in scale.

and periphery. The extreme differences in governance from the largest-scale to smallest-scale system in China make it difficult to align interests about how to coordinate policies across scales. Moreover, in China, resolving interests under a common framework of governance becomes exponentially difficult at each increasing level of scale given the food system's heterogeneity. The Chinese state has the unenviable task of developing a coherent safety system for a food sector in which production conditions (such as soil quality, pest pressures, and availability of water) vary widely from province to province, infrastructural support and economic conditions are highly different, and the industrial composition of the sector includes producers that span the range from small farmers to large agro-processors.

A predictable and particularly catastrophic pattern unfolds as scale politics intensify: (1) regulators cannot agree on the appropriate "scale" of the problem; (2) multidimensional differences across scales cannot be adequately reconciled; and (3) ignorance of processes and procedures occurring at other scales lead to systemic failures.

Learning to cope with scale is not a uniquely Chinese problem. Other large, heterogeneous polities have had to consider how to integrate multiple systems concurrently operating at different scales. In the United States, the development of federalism can be considered a response to scale, distinguishing between state's rights and national concerns for security, interstate commerce, and fiscal control. In India, there has been a constant debate as to whether the national or state governments degree-of-zoom is better equipped to handle issues of governance (Sinha 2003). For more than 50 years, the EU has tried to develop a system of governance that respects the sovereignty of member states while establishing common ground to deal with "European problems" (Jacoby 2004; Ansell & Vogel 2006). Indeed, later on in this book, we will take a closer look at how these other regulatory giants have fared in managing the politics of scale.

Despite similar processes at work in other large, heterogeneous countries, the context in which China's scale politics in food safety have played out differs in important ways. China's production base is more extensive and less developed than its Western counterparts (Gale & Buzby 2009). Production practices vary significantly from province to province when compared with the EU and the United States (EX 4; USDA Interview). Moreover, unlike the United States and India, China lacks a federal or multilevel framework that provides a clearer template for regulatory integration (Alemanno 2009). Finally, and perhaps with pivotal significance,

TABLE 1.1 *Selected Food Safety Incidents by Year*

Major Food Safety Incidents by Year

2003	Jinhua Ham Soaked in Pesticides	2008	Infant Melamine Incident
2004	Fuyang Baby Formula Incident		Insecticide-Laced Dumplings
	Carcinogenic Pickled Vegetables		Contaminated Ginger
	Soy Sauce Made from Human Hair		Contaminated Eggs
2005	Sudan Red Dye in Foods	2009	Plastic Tapioca
2006	Turbot Fish Antibiotic Scandal		Pesticide-Laced Buns
	Illegal Pesticides on Vegetables	2010	Gutter Oil
	Meningitis Snail Meat		Fake Green Peas
	Poisonous Mushrooms	2011	Clenbuterol Poisoning
2007	Carcinogenic Cooking Oil		Glowing Pork Scandal
	Melamine-Laced Wheat Gluten	2012	Chlorine-Tainted Cola
	Sewage-Laced Tofu	2013	Cadmium-Laced Rice

Note: This list represents only a selection of the most egregious food safety incidents reported in the mainstream foreign and Chinese media.

faced with chronic food shortages in the 1980s, China was forced to rapidly expand production and distribution networks to feed its population with little regard given to food safety as a large-scale governance challenge.

Prior to the 1990s, food safety issues in China were largely problems to be addressed and resolved locally. Common problems related to issues of hygiene at canteens and restaurants, the misapplication of pesticides, and the sale of expired foods (Yan 2012). But in the last three decades, the rapid scaling up of China's food production system achieved through industrialization and the lengthening of supply chains has led to a fundamental change in food safety risk; local food safety incidents could now quickly erupt to become national, if not global, food safety scandals. As local markets were integrated with national distribution networks, major food safety incidents occurred frequently, and grew increasingly more disturbing to a fearful public: media reports on pork glowing in the dark, peas painted green, and cured meat soaked in pesticides created widespread panic. This called for the creation of a new comprehensive national system to deal with regulatory challenges emerging at multiple scales.

In this study, I show how fierce, and ultimately dysfunctional, scale politics emerged in the Chinese food safety system as the government attempted to build a new integrated regulatory regime. Regulators, distributors, and producers at the local, provincial, and national levels contested who was best positioned to address immediate or anticipated longer-term problems, the speed of implementation, and the methods employed. Unresolved scale politics led to fundamental and observable coordination problems in regulatory management. Stakeholders persistently defined their own terms for food safety management that best reflected their parochial interests, resources, and expertise based on the scale at which they governed; and they expected other agencies to adjust their routines accordingly. Few officials were willing to risk scarce resources to cooperate with agencies that they did not trust or believe to be competent to address food safety regulation. As a result, China's food safety crisis continues unabated.

WHY FOOD SAFETY?

The grave implications flowing from a consideration of the "food safety question" in China are manifold. As noted, the immense public health issues are clear, and as President Xi has directly and candidly acknowledged, the CCP's very right to govern is at stake if food safety issues are not properly handled. Moreover, and with specific regard to the implications of scale and governance, examination of the food sector provides a useful lens to better understand the dynamics of scale politics because of the sector's (1) high degree of decentralization, (2) low level of industrial concentration, and (3) high interdependence among scales. Due to the combined effect of these defining characteristics, which we will explore in more detail in Chapter 11, China's food sector represents an "extreme case" of scale politics at work where the confluence and interaction of these factors have a noteworthy effect on regulatory politics (Seawright & Gerring 2004).

First, because the food product sector is highly decentralized to local levels, it is challenging to develop a comprehensive framework of governance that can adequately manage the often conflicting pressures emanating from local village production networks and the broader national market. Decentralization refers to what extent a sector is embedded in local political economies. During the 1980s, as the food production and distribution system was liberalized, local governments became actively engaged in the promotion of local agribusinesses and markets (Hsueh 2011). When food production networks in China became deeply entrenched in local political economies and developed institutions and practices best suited to that scale of operation, these local networks became highly resilient to change even as they were nominally absorbed into larger scale systems. In addition, these localized production networks often had little regard for how their own parochial operations could affect other production networks of the same scale (e.g., market town to market town), or broader systems (e.g., market town to regional supply chains). The extraordinary decentralization of the food sector in China created a strong local bias that made it difficult for these localized, market-driven systems to partner with governing communities operating at broader scales.

Second, low levels of industrial concentration also pose severe problems when attempting to integrate a multiscalar system. Industrial concentration refers to the degree to which a sector is dominated by a few large producers (high concentration) or, in marked contrast, is populated by numerous small- to medium-sized producers (low concentration). In China, large, vertically integrated agro-processors are but a small part of a vast production landscape that includes millions of small-scale farmers, cooperatives, and processors. Distribution channels are also characterized as being of low concentration. Distribution networks often involve millions of local traders, thousands of wholesale markets, and numerous regional logistics centers. This study discusses how and why it is difficult to translate and enforce policies from global to local scales across a highly diffuse sector. By contrast, in Europe, where food production is concentrated in a select number of large producers, policy can be more readily transmitted and accepted from the global to the local degree-of-zoom.

Third, the interdependence among scales in the food sector is high, requiring high levels of coordination across scales to achieve food safety. As we will see in later pages, interdependence among scales is determined by the extent to which failure at one scale can lead to system-wide failure. In China, as local production distribution networks link to regional and global supply chains, small-scale contagion can rapidly cascade to become national disasters. Food supply chains are notoriously difficult to manage because each step in the chain represents a potential entry point for contamination. If even a single farmer fails to comply with food safety regulations, adulterated food produced at the local scale can quickly enter into interconnected distribution networks that are linked to processors at the regional scale, and then ultimately affect consumers on the national scale. In effect, governing systems of different scales are highly dependent on one another in order to prevent a food safety failure for the interconnected whole.

By selecting a sector of such extremes, we can observe political dynamics at work that may be less evident when interaction of the sectoral characteristics of centralization, industrial concentration, and interdependence are more benign. In the concluding chapter, we will examine the environmental protection and fishery resource governance systems that share underlying similarities with the food sector and exhibit severe scale politics. The civil aviation sector will also be explored to provide useful contrast, highlighting how sectoral characteristics can, in some cases, present a more favorable baseline set of conditions for scale politics.

In summary, the urgent study of safety regulation in the food sector in China is an ideal case to examine the pathologies of governance stemming from "the problem of scale" and its attendant politics. While the combined effect of sectoral characteristics may make scale politics more or less likely, how a system develops effective governing approaches to *manage* scale politics is the focus of this study. In the chapters ahead, we will explore why some policy approaches exacerbate scale politics while other approaches are more effective at solving the problems of integrating policies at various scales. In order to understand China's governance failures, scholars, regulators, and consumers must take a deeper look at the challenges large-scale countries face in terms of scale externalities, multilevel coordination challenges, and problem identification.

PLAN OF THE BOOK

The study draws on more than 200 interviews conducted in China from 2009 to 2016. To develop a broad perspective about the problem of scale and scale politics in food safety, I engaged regulators, technical experts, corporate executives, and producers at central, provincial, county, and township scales. The study focused on nine study sites with varying geographic and economic conditions in Jiangsu, Sichuan, Zhejiang, Shandong, Yunnan, Ningxia, Beijing, and Shanghai. At each research site, I examined three types of production: pork, vegetable, and aquatic. In addition to interviews, I also consulted publicly available material on food safety in Chinese newspapers, academic journal articles, and county yearbooks. Government officials provided more than 600 pages of internal food safety documents, which discuss the major food safety activities conducted in each county, provide information on government strengths and capacities, and identify food safety problems. These records lend perspectives about food safety governance and assessments from inside of the state. In addition, food producers provided farming records, food safety manuals and procedural handbooks, and annual reports where possible.

A note should be made on the use of variation and generalizable patterns in this book. In large part, this book uses variation only to examine the contours of a new concept, "scale politics." When looking at sectors or various policies, I focus on the striking similarities that emerge across cases to identify patterns of scale politics. For example, when studying China's export sector food safety practices, I highlight similar practices and outcomes that are observable in different provinces, among different firms, and at different times. Likewise, agricultural production bases may not all fail, but when these projects appear to fail in a predictable way in a variety of circumstances, that would suggest an important pattern at work. I leave other important issues of variation to future scholars, who may be able to find within-sector differences, policy distinctions, or regional variations of scale politics.

The book employs a multimethod research design using inferences from comparative case studies, within-case analyses, and cross-national statistical analyses to examine China's food safety failures and politics of scale.

In Part I, I further explain the relationship between scale and scale politics, showing how scale politics is the causal mechanism that explains why managing large, heterogeneous polities is so challenging. The book then examines the baseline levels of food safety in three different markets, highlighting the link between a market's development, scale, and food safety. I focus on three food markets and their distinct regulatory systems: the domestic sector, the export sector, and the community-supported agriculture market.

China's domestic food production sector is vast. The food safety regulatory system attempts to monitor food production that was valued at US$1.6 trillion in 2013 (EU SME 2013). The range of government oversight includes millions of individual farmers who cultivate less than one hectare of land each and are typically older and less educated, as well as large, well-managed farms familiar with international food safety best practices. Production practices and crop yields are different from province to province, hindering the development of safe cultivation standards that can be broadly applied. Moreover, the stretched regulatory system seeks to integrate hundreds of rules and standards issued by townships, county, municipal, provincial, and the national governments.[3]

---

[3] Note that following the 2015 amendment to the Food Safety Law, locally issued standards will be annulled upon release of relevant national food safety standards.

The export sector presents a markedly different food safety template. As of 2009, China became the fourth-largest exporter of food in the world. The General Administration for Quality Inspection and Supervision (AQSIQ) estimated that 99% of exported food products are safe (State Council 2007). Food production networks are limited to large agro-processors (referred to as dragonhead enterprises) that manage their own production bases and are geographically concentrated in coastal provinces, especially Shandong. Food safety in the export sector is managed by AQSIQ, which restricts the number of exporters by a strict licensing system and subjects exporting plants to additional monitoring. As of 2007, only 12,714 enterprises were formally registered with the AQSIQ registration system (State Council 2007). Selected enterprises are assisted in attaining Good Agricultural Practice (GAP), Hazard-Access Critical Control Point System (HACCP), and Good Manufacturing Practice (GMP) certifications.

The community-supported agriculture (CSA) market is a new emerging sector that emphasizes production of local, organic, and safe food. While comprising a small proportion of China's overall food production system, its influence on regulatory governance has been far-reaching. With no more than 1,000 production sites throughout the country, these organic CSA farmers are primarily located around major urban areas including Beijing, Shanghai, Guangzhou, Chengdu, and Chongqing, but they have garnered significant attention from the press and local governments. Many producers are drawn from the local community and supported by an NGO-trained leader who is typically younger and well-educated. CSA networks are delimited to the local community and their direct consumers, who engage in face-to-face exchanges. Producers focus on localized, traditional food production practices, disregarding more advanced production methods and rejecting national certification programs.

The assessment of regulatory effectiveness of food safety across sectors, policies, and countries focuses primarily on *observable* scale problems: (1) the inability to determine the scale of the problem; (2) persistent mismatches across scales of governance; and (3) the willful lack of sensitivity to scalar externalities. Severe scale problems are highly likely to translate into poorer food safety outcomes. Understandably, these assessments are only a proxy for the level of food safety, and some reservations should be noted. Due to spotty data collection, it is difficult to assess the actual level of food safety in these sectors. The study thus relies on expert opinion from food safety auditors, academic surveys of the levels of food safety in different markets, and food safety reports by foreign government auditors and nongovernmental organizations. Notwithstanding the problem of data collection due to limited access, I expect that, where food safety scale politics are severe, the provision of food safety is likely to be low.

Part II of the book then focuses on comparing the various governance strategies employed in the export, CSA, and domestic sectors. The export sector considers how a centralized, hierarchical framework of governance can coordinate actors across scales to achieve a high degree of food safety. By contrast, the CSA sector will highlight how a decentralized, collaborative regime driven by informal politics can also provide a high degree of regulatory coordination across scales.

Governance strategies in the domestic sector are then explored. The domestic sector shows how a partially centralizing and partially decentralizing policy leads to severe scale politics, and, consequently, disappointing levels of food safety. The scale implications of food safety policies are explored to consider how coordinating bodies, food safety campaigns, and the use of model production zones have fragmented regulatory policy implementation in the domestic sector. I also show how different coregulatory efforts that use "dragonhead" enterprises struggle to cooperate with local producers, while farmers' cooperatives have failed to interface with more advanced supply chains.

Part III focuses on what happens when successful policies in the export sector and CSA sector are then applied to large, heterogeneous circumstances. In the export sector, I observe how a centralized, hierarchical mode of governance encounters problems in the domestic sector due to policy sinkhole effects and scale mismatches. Similarly, I find that successful community governance solutions based on social trust in the CSA market cannot always be scaled up to serve as the basis for a national food safety system.

Part IV considers the cross-national implications of this book's findings. A large-N analysis frames a structured comparison of the United States, the EU, India, and China, holding level of development, corruption, and other factors constant. The EU, in particular, stands out as a significant outlier with its strong food safety performance. I then assess the costs and benefits of the EU's multilevel food safety system, India and the United States' federal approach, and China's unitary regulatory model. My concluding chapter, Chapter 11, offers some parting thoughts about the applicability of my developed concepts of scale and scale politics to other regulatory sectors in China, other areas of multilevel governance, and the political and social implications of China's unresolved food safety governance.

Together, the chapters demonstrate how China's food safety problems are rooted in its fundamental scale problem and attendant scale politics. Since national systems must contend with the free flow of food products, diverse markets, and the globalization of standards, development of food safety policies that can align the interests of stakeholders across multiple scales becomes ever more important. China's food safety failures must be corrected because an estimated 300 million of its people are affected by contaminated food products each year (ADB 2005). Research on how to address the scale problem in governance is pressing, and this book seeks to make a contribution to that important effort.

2

Revisiting Scale

China's food safety failures present students of regulation and governance with a rich puzzle. Food safety problems are typically viewed as part of the regulatory growing pains of a developing country. Accordingly, studies have explained China's poor food safety outcomes as stemming from its low level of economic development, lack of state capacity and problematic levels of corruption (Tam & Yang 2005; Yang 2008; Calvin et al. 2006; Han 2007). From a cross-national perspective, however, we shall see that China does not appear to be following the familiar path of regulatory development observed in other countries. For China scholars, still another common set of explanations typically used to explain China's governance deficits—local obstructionism, weak accountability mechanisms, and authoritarian politics—are also found to be insufficient upon closer examination. Compounding the puzzle is the central government's decade-long, comprehensive series of regulatory reforms to resolve the food safety problems with little success.

Before presenting my own scale politics framework to study these puzzles, I first consider in more detail these aforementioned alternative explanations of China's regulatory shortfalls. I then proceed to explain the analytical leverage that the concept of scale and its attendant politics provides to the study of China's food safety governance. Finally, I consider how scale politics relate to and draw from other concepts that have preceded it, and how the expanded framework of scale engages debate in the broader field of comparative politics.

ALTERNATIVE EXPLANATIONS

For the China scholar, a natural starting point for any inquiry into governance failures is local obstructionism. In previous studies of food safety in China, local officials have been shown to disregard central food safety directives due to a lack of funding (Tam & Yang 2005), the weak oversight of a fragmented bureaucracy (Liu 2010, Huang 2012), and a lack of fit between central and local regulations (Yan 2012). This behavior is consonant with broader research on governance in China that focuses on the disconnect between central and local authorities; this research shows that local bureaucrats are largely uninterested in central policy mandates that are not directly tied to their own advancement in the government hierarchy or their own personal enrichment (Gobel 2011; Edin 2003; O'Brien & Li 1999).

However, these studies do not take into account new imperatives in local governance regarding food safety. Whether or not local officials agree with central government mandates, a series of centralizing reforms have streamlined accountability, and local officials are increasingly facing strong pressures from the top as they are evaluated on their record of food safety. Under current food-focused assessments, a major food safety outbreak can effectively wipe out an official's evaluation score, eliminating any chance of moving up in the bureaucracy. In the instance of more egregious food safety failures, officials can be arrested or summarily disciplined by higher level party authorities. Local officials are also encountering equally strong pressure from the bottom, from NGOs, media, and regular citizens reacting to widely reported food safety scandals (State Council 2012; Roberts 2012; Greenpeace 2010). And, while overall food safety budgets remain low, the state has invested the equivalent of over US$800 million to upgrade laboratories and train personnel (Meador & Ma 2013). These changes would at least predict a neutral-to-positive effect on food safety outcomes, and cannot explain China's persistent food safety deficit.

Some observers have argued that the crisis reflects a lack of political will by the central government to address food safety(Hsueh 2011; Tam & Yang 2005). However, over the last decade, mounting food scandals have increasingly incentivized central government officials to address food safety. Government officials are vitally concerned by growing social unrest caused by food safety incidents. Moreover, recent well-publicized problems with Chinese products in the global food trade have placed enormous pressures on central officials to ensure that China is not exporting its regulatory problems abroad. The State Council has already created five special commissions led by senior leaders to address the issue. In 2013, the central government established a new food safety super ministry—the China Food and Drug Administration. Also, in 2015, food safety was the major focus of the party's "Document Number 1" that outlines the policy priorities for the year. Yet, the question remains, why has China's food safety situation seen little improvement?

Others contend that China's food safety problem has less to do with its domestic politics and is instead simply a reflection of the regulatory problems typically attendant to developing countries. As a familiar precedent, they point to the food safety scandals in the United States at the turn of the 20th century—graphically portrayed in Upton Sinclair's *The Jungle*—as evidence that all industrializing countries encounter food quality and safety problems at some stage in their regulatory evolution. Indeed, it could be generally observed that beyond this initially problematic stage, economic development eventually leads to production of goods of higher quality. Similarly, some suggest that China's poor food safety outcomes could simply be the result of a lack of state capacity (Han 2007). These assertions suggest that as China becomes richer, its food safety problems will moderate and resolve themselves naturally in the course of its economic development.

Still other commentators give prominent consideration to corruption, which has plagued developing regulatory systems, to explain China's food safety failures. To be sure, in China, pervasive corruption in the food regulation system has involved collusion between officials and local noncompliant entrepreneurs, the buying of safety certifications, and the manipulation of food safety audit reports (Tam & Yang 2005; Yang 2008; Huang 2012; Calvin et al. 2006). Indeed, in 2007, Zheng Xiaoyu, former commissioner of China's State Food and Drug Administration, was charged with corruption and sentenced to death.

From a cross-national perspective, however, China does not appear to be following the familiar path of regulatory development that we have seen in other countries. It should be noted that the cross-national data on food safety only covers the period from 2005 to 2008. However, China's food safety situation has not improved, and, by some measures is becoming worse (Huang 2012). China has a far poorer record of food safety than other countries with similar levels of economic development, state capacity, and corruption. Cross-national comparisons of food safety suggest a strong correlation between GDP per capita and a country's food safety score in general (see (a) in Figure 2.1). However, China ($3,412 per

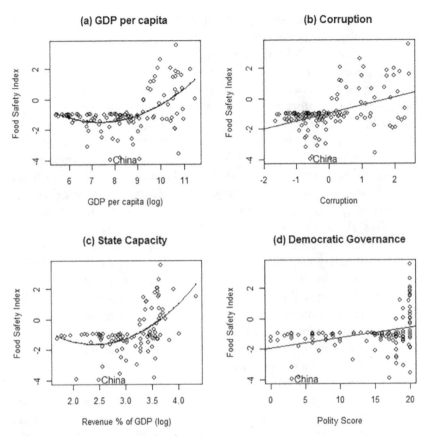

FIGURE 2.1 Explaining Food Safety Outcomes
Source: Food Safety Index developed according to Convertino & Liang (2014);
(a) GDP per capita (World Bank Database); (b) Corruption (Worldwide Governance Indicators World Bank Database); (c) Revenue % GDP as proxy for state capacity (World Bank Database); (d) Openness (Polity IV Database).

capita) performs worse in food safety relative to Thailand ($4,124), Egypt ($2,159), and even Guatemala ($2,867). Corruption, too, is significantly associated with lower levels of food safety (see (b)). But China (−0.54 corruption index), again, is worse off in its food safety record compared to Egypt (−0.71), and Paraguay (−1.0), countries that have similar or poorer World Bank corruption scores. Likewise, in terms of state capacity, despite the strong and significant association between budget revenue and food safety outcomes globally, China still performs weaker relative to countries with similar levels of state capacity (see (c)).

Beyond issues concerning economic development, corruption, and state capacity, another possible explanation for poor food safety performance is China's authoritarian regime, which could negatively affect regulatory governance in a number of ways. Scholars have broadly pointed to the regime's lack of transparency, and its inability to establish the independence of regulatory agencies as problematic for effective regulatory oversight and governance (Pearson 2007; Liu 2010). Thus, a more fundamental issue not to be overlooked in explaining poor food safety outcomes may be related to the polity's lack of democratic accountability. The basic argument would posit that in authoritarian regimes like China, the electoral accountability mechanisms are attenuated, political consequences of government inaction to resolve food safety are less severe, and, thus, there is less regulation, and as a result, more bad outcomes. By contrast, in democracies, such as India, Europe, and the United States, major food safety scandals led to significant losses at the polls, and governments consequently responded with major regulatory reforms. Moreover, another potential problem for regulatory governance in authoritarian regimes concerns the suppression of the media. In democratic regimes, the media plays an important role as a watchdog over public and private actors. Also, in authoritarian systems, the press, if not directly controlled by the state, is often coerced into not reporting on government failures that could reflect badly on the regime.

Consistent with the foregoing hypotheses, when looking cross-nationally, food safety is indeed negatively associated with authoritarianism, as measured by a country's polity score. However, China significantly underperforms in its provision of food safety relative to countries with similar levels of openness, or, lack thereof (Figure 2.1d). As the scatterplot shows, China is an outlier.

The hypothesized link between authoritarianism and poor regulatory outcomes is also problematic in other ways. An attenuated electoral accountability mechanism and the suppression of press freedom may prove to be serious impediments to effective governance more generally. But, in the case of China, the political salience of food safety is high, and the media has been given substantial latitude to report on food safety scandals. Although Chinese government officials do not face electoral pressures, scholars have shown that authoritarian governments are highly responsive to policy demands if problems could lead to social unrest or threaten regime legitimacy (Chen et al. 2016). Moreover, authoritarian regimes like China have adopted a number of quasi-democratic institutions that respond to citizen demands, such as mayor's inboxes (Hou

& Distelhorst 2014) and internet portals (Truex 2014), although official receptivity to such demands varies across institutions (Meng et al. 2014). The central government leadership is well aware of the widespread food safety concerns of its populace; and addressing the food safety challenge has featured prominently in major policy pronouncements. In 2015, following the revised Food Safety Law, Li Keqiang emphasized that a "zero tolerance" attitude must be adopted in regard to food safety (State Council 2015).

In describing the authoritarian state's relationship with the media, scholars have shown that the press in China is not necessarily viewed as an adversary of the state. Because a significant governance challenge in authoritarian regimes is the lack of quality information, these regimes increasingly rely on the media to report on local cases of noncompliance (Repnikova 2015, Egorov et al. 2009). Scholarly work has revealed that in China, the state permits protests and adverse media reports insofar as such outlets provide information to the central government on the activities of local officials (Lorentzen 2014). Notably referred to as the "sandwich theory" of Chinese politics, the central government uses bottom-up forces (media and social protest) to induce local officials to comply with central government regulations (Lorentzen et al. 2014). Throughout the 2000s, at the height of the food safety crisis, reporting on food safety scandals in China increased in frequency from 277 articles in 2000 to 28,515 articles in 2011 despite the presence of a strong censorship apparatus (Yang 2013).

Journalists reporting on food safety are permitted significant leeway provided the scandal is limited to a locality. In fact, many mainstream media channels have news and documentary features focusing entirely on such emerging food safety problems (Yang 2013). Furthermore, Chinese netizens are quick to post news of a dangerous eating establishment or food item; and these manifestations of local discontent are allowed. However, once a scandal has emerged with broader or national implications, such as in the case of the melamine infant milk scandal, media coverage quickly falls under the control of government censors as the political leadership seeks to frame the issue in terms of government responsiveness. In other instances, where food safety scandals could lead to adverse economic consequences for an entire region, journalists are instructed to tread carefully. When food safety scandals trigger protests, or online media call for collective action, the government is swift to respond (King et al. 2013). Diffuse dissent, however, in the form of "airing grievances," "venting," and even critiques of failed government responses are largely tolerated by the state and its agents of censorship (Yang 2013, Repnikova 2015). Within this bounded area, investigative journalists in China have successfully negotiated a space for limited governance.[1] Authoritarianism certainly plays a role in the food safety crisis, but it alone cannot explain China's strikingly poor performance in food safety.

The purpose of examining alternative explanations is not to say that corruption, local obstruction, deficient state capacity, and lack of democratic governance have nothing to do with China's ongoing food safety crisis, but rather that there is likely to be a broader dynamic at work. In fact, I suggest that these factors in explaining poor governance outcomes themselves may well be an important, but *collateral*, consequence of China's scale, and the inability of the system to effectively govern across multiple degrees-of-zoom in a large, heterogeneous context. The food safety crisis, and regulatory failures in other sectors, may be less a function of "growing pains" and more the result of a more structural issue that will plague Chinese governance for years to come.

REVISITING SCALE

References to China's complexity, vast geographical landscape, enormous population, and sizable markets as major impediments to governance are commonplace. Indeed, social scientists have shown that bigger bureaucracies are harder to govern, longer borders more difficult to monitor, and larger populations more problematic for coordinated action. But, what do we mean exactly by the term *scale*? Scale is not simply a measure of size. As introduced in the previous chapter, scale involves more than size, and is a relational concept. And, as we shall see, failing to recognize the distinction between scale and size is analytically critical.

To establish the scale of a governing system, one must adduce the effect of three intertwined elements: size, limits, and relations (Howitt 1998). The *size* of a system refers to any quantity whether it is the number of individuals or firms or the expanse of its land mass. If the size of a system remains under a certain threshold, a system is said to be of a certain scale.

---

[1] Repnikova (2015) highlights a number of tactics that journalists have used to carve out a space for more critical reporting: (1) local newspapers report on governance failures outside their own home province; (2) utilizing the government's endorsement of the media in its role as "public opinion supervision" to criticize the government without challenging the legitimacy of the party state; (3) adopting a balanced, constructive tone rather than a negative, adversarial one; (4) avoiding critiques of the central state.

This threshold can be usefully conceived as a scale *limit*, or boundary. Actors within a certain scale should be seen as subject to a set pattern of *relations* between individuals and institutions, in terms of politics, transactions, and communication. Beyond a certain size, a village, for example, is no longer subject to processes that typically unfold at that scale. Scale dictates whether individuals communicate on a face-to-face basis, or if relations are more formalized and distant.

Economists and political scientists have largely conflated a country's "scale" with the size of its landmass, population, or markets. This is not so much an oversight as it is a question of disciplinary focus. Economists study scale in terms of the marginal cost advantages that accrue due to size or production output as fixed costs are spread out for each additional unit. They examine how certain industries must increase output to operate efficiently, rely on foreign trade to exploit economies of scale, or examine the advantages of sharing infrastructure (Perkins & Syrquin 1989). For example, as the size of a country increases, per capita costs of goods are lowered, large militaries are more easily maintained, and regional insurance coverage becomes more feasible (Alesina & Spolaore 2005). But, as size increases, heterogeneity of preferences also increases, making it more difficult and costly to effectively implement central government policies (Alesina & Spolaore 2005). Given these trade-offs, economists contend that there are "optimal" sizes for cities, nations, or regions (Gibson et al. 2000).

In political science, population and geographic size have long been seen as pivotal in helping us analyze political activity. Population plays a crucial role in shaping the nature of political representation. Studies showing the relationship of population size and the quality of democracy demonstrate how population size makes it more difficult for citizens to voice their concerns, explain the trade-offs among different types of representative assemblies, and identify the challenges of collective action and interest articulation in populous countries (Dahl 1994). Small states are more likely to be democratic than large states due to increased face-to-face interactions (Srebrnik 2004; Sutton 2007; Oliver 2000). For other political scientists, a key question is how size and population affect state capacity. In Africa, nations have often struggled to project authority over inhospitable territories that contain relatively low densities of people (Herbst 2000).

Geographers, sociologists, and anthropologists, however, contend that the scale of a system is more than its mere size, focusing on the relational implications of size and space. A system's degree-of-zoom is a useful metaphor employed by sociologists and geographers that intuitively highlights the concept of scale as a function of size, limits, and relations, and will be used throughout this book (Gibson et al. 2000). Much like the operation of the zoom lens of a camera or a microscope, governing systems may operate at a "smaller" scale (for example, a village), or "larger" scale (a nation), depending on the focus of analysis. For example, the degree-of-zoom in governance dictates whether one focuses on local laws, community markets, and community governance, or national policies, national supply chains, and national institutions.

Defining scale as a function of size, limits, and relations provides additional analytical leverage in the study of political science that is often absent when simply focusing on the "size" of a system. In my study, I explore how an expanded treatment of scale can help us identify governance challenges that are typically overlooked, and how consideration of three important scale dynamics leads to better understanding of regulatory politics: (1) scale is socially constructed; (2) systems are subject to multiscalar processes; and (3) scales are nonlinearly related. It is these properties of scale that can lead to severe political tensions, and, if poorly managed, result in regulatory failure.

Scale as Socially Constructed

First, the aggregate size of a system tells us little about how a population is organized (e.g., a single large-scale population or numerous small-scale populations). In fishery management, for example, ecologists may determine that there are tens of billions of fish in a particular body of water. But, it is only through the lens of scale that we can determine whether these fish should be managed as a single large-scale population, or as many populations of fish existing at a smaller scale (see Figure 2.2A). In large, heterogeneous polities, it is often difficult to determine, as a matter of policy, at what scale a regulatory problem is most likely to emerge. In the case of food safety, do problems typically arise in China's villages, or its provinces, or across jurisdictions? Such calculations determine whether to design governance systems that regulate on a nationwide basis, or to set up smaller regional authorities; how resources are deployed throughout a system; and how monitoring stations should be established.

However, determining the scale of a governing system is a highly contested process, because, unlike size, scale is a social construct (Marston 2000; Smith 2008). The scale of a system is often mistakenly accepted ex-ante as an objective, immutable reality. However, as O'Lear (2010)

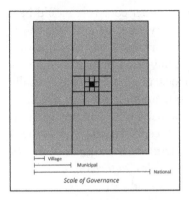

Figure A. Scale as a Social Construct: Regulators must decide on the appropriate "degree-of-zoom" when addressing a problem. For example, should a problem be framed at the national, municipal, or village scale? Such decisions affect whether to establish a national authority, or to set up several regional agencies. The size of a system remains the same, but the "scale of governance" is an outcome of a political process.

Figure B. Scalar Externalities: Because systems of governance are nested (e.g., villages are nested in municipal systems), decisions made at certain scales of governance have significant consequences for the other scale levels of a system.

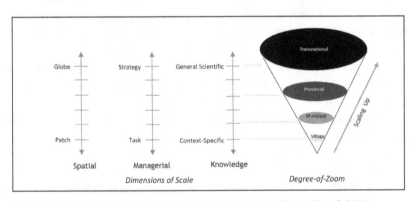

Figure C. Scaling Up as Non-Linear Process: To scale up governance is to increase one's "degree-of-zoom," which has implications across multiple dimensions (e.g., spatial, managerial, knowledge-related). For example, moving from a village scale to a transnational scale implies a non-linear transformation, altering a governance system's spatial concerns (patch to globe), managerial modes (tasks to strategy), and knowledge (contextual to general scientific).

FIGURE 2.2 Rethinking Scale and Governance
Note: Figure C adapted in part from Cash et al. (2006) on multiple dimensions of scale, p. 3.

succinctly and elegantly states, "[scale] is the spatial product of human activity" (p. 7). She posits that jurisdictional scales (e.g., national, provincial, townships) are a negotiated outcome—a reflection of human processes and activity. Moreover, scale need not be bounded by physical jurisdiction or space. For example, when considering the "scale" of a university, individuals may be inclined to denote the size of its campus, or its student population. But, O'Lear suggests either construct would be a reductive rendering of scale because university students and faculty are regularly embedded in global research networks and relationships that extend far beyond the physical reach of the university or its student body. Whether the scale of a system is defined in local or global terms, physically or otherwise, is a negotiated outcome among multiple actors.

Powerful interests determine that a certain size of population or landmass constitutes a "township" or a "province." Marston et al. (2005) assert that "scale is a result of marking territories horizontally through boundaries and enclosures, documents and rules, *enforcing agents and their authoritative resources*" (420; emphasis added). Scales are self-reinforcing constructs as institutions and individuals develop systems that operate most effectively at a socially determined and enumerated scale. Politicians, bureaucrats, and experts involved in these determinations reinforce these scalar logics through resource allocation, authorization, and legitimation. In some cases, officials may insist that policies should be conceived and implemented based on the perspectives of regulators operating at one scale. In welfare governance, for example, the Keynesian state was largely conceptualized at the national scale in which polices are formed at the national level, and local and regional subnational units were tasked with implementing them. The "Keynesian coalition" depended on support for the national economy, national state, and national society by policy communities at lower scales (Jessop 1999).

Regulators may push for a *rescaling* of governance to another scale as political conditions shift. For example, the forces of globalization are leading many to rethink the geographical scale at which political power and authority are located. The politics of the EU highlight a reconfiguration of power in certain policy arenas to centralized EU institutions (Leitner 2008). This process can be contentious as new scale boundaries are redrawn, determining a new set of relationships among individuals. When municipalities are absorbed into regional entities, old institutional relationships have to be refashioned, resources must be reallocated, and new metrics for assessment (at higher levels of aggregation) are adopted.

The critical point to be made about the dynamics of scale politics is that precisely because scale is a social construct, actors existing throughout a multiscalar system have differing and strong views about their place and role in the system. When regulators cannot clearly define and fix the appropriate scale of a regulatory system to resolve outstanding issues, major coordination problems can arise. Regulators operating at different scales may refuse to cooperate, or actively resist the implementation of policies developed at other scales. Regulatory priorities are difficult to set, as governance systems at varying scales define the regulatory challenge differently. And, without a clear consensus on the scale of governance it becomes impossible to efficiently allocate resources, design institutions, and develop regulatory standards.

Multiscalar Effects and Scale Externalities

Second, the challenge of managing scale is that systems typically operate at *multiple* scales simultaneously (Ansell & Torfing 2015; Buizer et al. 2011). Focusing on size alone does not permit us to see that reality. China's food safety system operates at the national, provincial, prefectural, municipal, county, and township scales. Nesting these systems effectively involves aligning the views of these systems, which all have different degrees-of-zoom. The critical necessity in effective governance is to develop the mechanisms and institutions to coordinate the actions of regulators, producers, and consumers across scales. Thus, rather than to speak of the challenge of managing scale, it is more appropriate to highlight the difficulty of simultaneously managing a host of *scales*—nesting smaller scale systems within larger scale systems.

Given the nested nature of a system, a major challenge presented by multiscalar governance are scale externalities—in which decisions at certain scales can spill over and affect governance at other scales (see Figure 2.2B). In broad terms, an "externality" is defined as a cost or benefit that affects a party who did not choose to incur such cost or benefit. Changes in a system's resource base, population, technology, infrastructural access, and human values at one scale (degree-of-zoom) have important consequences for a system's operations at another scale. In my analysis of scale politics, such scale externalities will be seen to manifest themselves politically in (1) ignorance or (2) minimizing.

Ignorance in the context of this analysis describes commonly occurring conditions where participants in a nested system ignore how processes at other scales of governance can affect them directly (Cash et al. 2006). Actors often disregard scale externalities to the detriment of the system as a whole. Some actors may ignore scale externalities because they consider them irrelevant, beyond their purview, or because they are simply uninformed. However, ignorance of developments at other scales can be severely adverse. For example, ignoring regional climate change patterns may lead to poor preparedness for local flood management, which could decimate local communities (Cash et al. 2006). Ignorance in the context of this study can also refer to how individuals operating at one scale fail to consider how decisions will unfold at other scales of governance. For example, as we shall see in the chapters that follow, and particularly when considering the fiscal aspects of scale, cost-cutting decisions at larger scales can have extraordinarily deleterious effects as they trickle down to lower scales.

Minimizing is another problematic response to scale externalities in which regulators disregard small-scale problems because they perceive a problem as only affecting a delimited group of individuals. However, as we will note, for example, in the now infamous infant powder milk scandal described further on, a series of small outbreaks of food contamination at the lower scales can quickly cascade to become a provincial problem, then a national problem, with even transnational implications. The problem of minimizing is compounded when small-scale systems internalize and rationalize their own local problems as unimportant in relation to higher level "broad-scale" directives. As a result, local actors often fail to see the aggregate effects of their own small-scale problems as an important and integral part of a nested system of multiple scales.

Nonlinear Relationship between Scales

Third, increasing the size of a system, and "scaling up" a system, operate according to different dynamics. The transition from one scale to another implies a *nonlinear* transformation. A new scale dictates establishing an entirely new set of boundaries and relations, imposing different cost-benefit structures, institutions, and rules (see Figure 2.2C). Governing a population of, say, 10,000 as opposed to 1,000 individuals is not simply a matter of a linear tenfold increase in state capacity represented by more manpower and money, public infrastructure, and the like. New institutions must be built, different modes of communication must be employed, and institutional rules must be modified. As many who have tried to apply small policy experiments to a national context can attest, this nonlinear process of transformation is highly challenging, and is the reason why integrating governing systems operating at different scales is so problematic.

James Scott's (1999) pathbreaking work on "seeing like a state" high-lights how those governing at a national scale view the world very differently from local officials operating on the ground. In much the same way, the scale of a system has implications across multiple dimensions: space, jurisdiction, time, management, knowledge, and networks (Cash et al. 2006).[2] The *spatial* dimension of scale ranges from patches (smallest) to the globe (largest). The *jurisdictional* dimension of scale ranges from villages to transnational systems of governance. *Time*, too, can be thought to exist on a range of temporal frames from the short term to the long term. The *knowledge* dimension of scale highlights the scale at which knowledge is developed and transmitted: at the "smallest" scale, know-how is traditional and context specific, and at its "largest" scale, knowledge is scientific and generalizable. *Networks* exist at different scales, ranging from local markets to multinational distribution chains. *Managerial* practices can also be conceived to operate at different scales, from tasks (smallest) to strategies (largest). Moreover, because each dimension of scale interacts with one another, a change in one dimension of scale often implies a change across each of these dimensions (Figure 2.3).

The politics involved in integrating policy communities of different scale emerges during two processes: scaling up and scaling down. Scaling up a governance system describes the process of assimilating systems operating at smaller degrees-of-zoom into larger systems. It is an integrative process of political contestation and accommodation—give and take—in which smaller scale systems are subsumed under the operations of a larger scale system. Systems may need to scale up, for example, when local products enter into broader distribution networks and circulate on a national scale. As a system scales up it must address how local concerns, preferences, practices, and knowledge are effectively aggregated at a larger scale.

The process of scaling down represents a mirror-image of scaling up. Scaling down involves transmitting, translating, and integrating policies from larger scale systems to smaller scale systems. Uvin (1995) describes scaling down as a process whereby global organizations alter their

---

[2] A number of scholars of scale have pointed to scale as a multidimensional concept. As an alternative, Ansell & Torfing (2015), for example, focus on the following dimensions: (1) membership; (2) interaction; and (3) strategic horizon. Under this conception of scale, membership refers to the number of individuals, interaction refers to the scale at which these members' interact (i.e., local, national, or global) and strategic horizon refers to the scale of applicability and production.

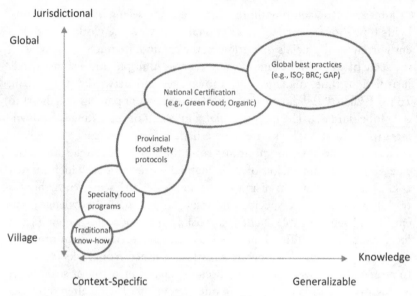

Jurisdictional

Global

Global best practices
(e.g., ISO; BRC; GAP)

National Certification
(e.g., Green Food; Organic)

Provincial
food safety
protocols

Specialty food
programs

Traditional
know-how

Village

Knowledge

Context-Specific   Generalizable

FIGURE 2.3 Interaction between Dimensions of Scale
Note: Adapted in part from Cash et al. (2006), p. 7.

structure and modes of operation to allow for meaningful interaction and integration with actors on lower scales. For example, the scaling down of the national food safety law entails making it understandable at each degree-of-zoom throughout the system. That is, in China the food safety law needs to be understood by regulators operating in the national system, 32 provincial systems, 332 prefectural systems, 2,853 county systems, and 40,666 township systems. National regulatory strategies need to be dis-aggregated into plans, projects, and tasks. Global food safety knowledge must be scaled down to be transmitted and practically applied to address regulatory problems at lower scales. During this process significant challenges can emerge, including the loss of information and a lack of sensitivity to on-the-ground conditions.

When developing a nationally integrated regulatory system, aligning the governing processes across scales must occur across multiple dimensions, which often generates political conflict. Technocratic challenges can quickly develop into scale-based political conflicts. How does one create political coalitions across governing systems of different scale to facilitate policy coordination? How do scientists and standard setters operating at different scales of knowledge (i.e., traditional know-how or generalizable scientific knowledge) function in concert to generate and disseminate knowledge readily accepted by actors at all scales? Managerially, how do you disaggregate a national strategy into the day-to-day tasks to be implemented at lower scales? I will explore how the multidimensional nature of scale (space, jurisdiction, time, knowledge, networks, and management) poses significant challenges when trying to integrate a multiscalar system.

As scale politics emerge, regulatory coordination falters. Subsequent chapters will examine in more detail the consequences of the following types of scale politics: (1) when regulators cannot determine the appropriate scale of the problem, resources are misallocated and interests are misaligned (scale is socially constructed); (2) scale externalities either through ignorance or minimization are not addressed, resulting in failed coordination (governing systems are nested); (3) multiscalar, multidimensional conflicts lead to fundamental disagreements about how food safety policy should be implemented across scales (scales are nonlinearly related). Suffice it to observe and conclude at this point in our analysis on revisiting and redefining scale—if scale politics are not addressed, system-wide failure results.

WHY IS MY MILK BLUE?

China's infamous infant formula scandal serves as an instructive example of how scale politics can produce coordination problems that result in severe food safety mishaps. By 2008, melamine-tainted infant formula had poisoned more than 300,000 infants in China, and precipitated a global food safety crisis leading to import bans of Chinese food in more than 30 countries.

The genesis of China's scale problem in dairy production began in the early 2000s, as the dairy sector began to incorporate local dairy production networks into national distribution systems. From 2001 to 2009, China's consumption of milk quadrupled from 10 million metric tons to 39 million tons, making China the third largest milk producer in the world (Xiu & Klein 2010). The government concentrated production in four firms, which eventually developed into regional monopolies that together sold nearly half of China's dairy production in 2008. The sheer size and reach of these companies created a dense network of government officials, milk collection stations, dairy farmers, and distributors operating at multiple scales.

As a matter of scale politics, little attention was given to determine the scale at which problems were likely to emerge, and the appropriate scale of governance that could address these problems. What is often considered the first misstep in the management of dairy safety was the failure of the national government to develop a regulatory framework to integrate regulatory activities and to understand the various processes unfolding at multiple scales. Food safety standards began to proliferate at each level of government, which were all developed to suit their scale of governance, leading to increasingly divergent interests regarding food safety management. At the national scale, the government chose a noninterventionist approach to regulation, which they felt would facilitate the development of the dairy sector. No national standards for raw milk and its products were developed. At the regional and provincial scales, local governments proceeded to develop their own regulations in close consultation with their own dairy processors, and what made sense given the scale of their distribution networks.

As supply chains integrated systems of various scale, multidimensional conflicts emerged regarding how to implement food safety. Many of the managerial practices and much of the food safety knowledge employed were developed with a particular scale of operation in mind. National corporations, such as Sanlu, sought to redirect the sector toward industrialized dairy production, employing advanced supply chain management techniques and quality assurance protocols. These enterprises engaged in aggressive recruitment by offering loans to dairy farmers to purchase their own cows and the enterprises would initially provide technical assistance for free (Xiu & Klein 2010). The rollout of modern dairy production practices to encompass small-scale farms, however, proved to be challenging: production protocols that made sense for corporations enmeshed in national supply chains were often unintelligible to farmers with one or two cows on small plots of land. Farmers resisted the imposition of new techniques and lacked the technical know-how and capital to invest in dairy quality and safety, leading to the deterioration of quality and quantity of milk production over time.

Exacerbating problems in the rapidly growing dairy industry was the lack of feedback mechanisms to highlight the deteriorating conditions, and to sensitize actors to processes unfolding at other scales (i.e., ignorance of scale externalities). Producers operating at the lower scales of the system were far removed from directives issued by corporate headquarters. Corporations unilaterally imposed new quality and pricing guidelines that appeared rational from their national vantage point. However, these new policies did not consider the delimiting cost structures and practices of producers at lower scales. Given their lack of economic clout, producers in the countryside had little recourse to protest these centrally mandated changes. The rising costs of inputs, increased competition, and demand for higher volumes placed smaller farmers in a severely disadvantageous position. These producers were forced to develop numerous ad hoc and extralegal techniques to cut costs, the most common of which was the use of melamine in milk production.

Government regulators were largely unaware of developments at other scales of governance. This ignorance of multiscalar processes was fueled by a lack of uniform recall protocols and the lack of monitoring and surveillance systems. As scattered reports about the use of melamine circulated at lower scales, few individuals knew how or were adequately vested with the authority to respond. Due to the highly fragmented nature of the regulatory system, it was unclear which operating or supervisory unit was in charge of responding to reports of infant formula contamination (Xiu & Klein 2010). Had information been channeled to the appropriate scale, officials would have been able to realize that the use of melamine was not a series of isolated small-scale incidents, but suggested a phenomenon developing at a much broader scale. Moreover, Pei et al. (2011) assert that freezing-point depression tests, specific gravity analysis, and fat content analysis would have been able to detect substandard milk, but that government officials were simply unaware of the scale of the problem.

The confluence of the mishandling of scale included an inability to define the scale of governance, a lack of attention to the multidimensional aspects of scale, and poor sensitivity to standards and processes at various scales. As scale politics continued unabated, severe regulatory coordination problems emerged that directly led to the melamine disaster. This widespread disaster was not simply the result of deliberate corporate malfeasance, but, rather, stemmed from a fundamental inability to manage scale. Throughout the pages of this book this frightening scenario of regulatory failure is played out over and over. China's bewildered consumers have endured a monthly onslaught of food scandals involving disturbingly innovative food adulterations. As one observer of the food safety crisis despairingly and tellingly exclaimed, "I wonder when my milk will be blue?"

SOLVING THE PROBLEM OF SCALE

To address the problems brought on by scale, regulators have developed at least three different modes of governance: centralized, hierarchical; decentralized, collaborative; and multilevel. Each mode of governance defines

TABLE 2.1 *Three Different Approaches to Managing Scale*

	Centralized/ Hierarchical	Decentralized/ Collaborative	Multilevel
Scale Problem	Fragmentation across scales	Lack of fit between national regulations and local conditions	Scales are not optimized for governance
Scale Solution	Top-down, emphasize national scale	Bottom-up, emphasize local scale	Delegation of authority to each scale of governance
Costs	Costly; lack of fit between regulations and locality; cannot detect emerging small-scale problems	No clear plan for integration; high coordination costs	High coordination costs; decisive action is difficult
Benefits	Single reference point; clear accountability; policy standardized	Policies fit local conditions; no need for overarching regulatory framework	Sensitive at all scales; policy is well fit

and addresses scale politics in different ways, and consequently encounters a distinctive set of trade-offs (see Table 2.1).[3]

A centralized, hierarchical mode of governance reflects a top-down approach to addressing the scale problem. Under this approach, the primary problem is defined as a lack of coordination across scales due to entrenched parochial scale interests. This in turn leads to the following problems: (1) each level of government pursues policies that place undue burdens on other levels of government; (2) too many regulators issue conflicting regulations across a range of dimensions; and (3) a lack of a clear reference point promotes incoherence for the system as a whole.

The centralized, hierarchical response to these problems is to impose uniformity on the system from the top-down, whereby the national scale dominates policy making and implementation. Under this mode of governance, the national degree-of-zoom is understood to be the only scale that can take into account the needs of the entire system. To promote policy

[3] This analysis builds of a framework developed by Termeer et al. (2010), which assesses trade-offs in monocentric, multilevel, and adaptive governance.

standardization, a single body of regulations developed at the national scale is then implemented either by the center's agents, or by local governments that are given limited discretion to modify policies.

There are a number of drawbacks to this approach to addressing scale politics. First, centralized, hierarchical governance can be prohibitively expensive. Significant manpower must be deployed to ensure that local agents are following central government policies. Second, the imposition of the national degree-of-zoom can foment tensions across scales due to lack of fit of imposed policies, or bureaucratic turf wars. Finally, the national scale often does not accurately target the problems and processes unfolding at smaller scales. Treating all producers as part of a single population, when in fact producers are organized in smaller populations, can lead to severe policy distortions.

In contrast, a decentralized, collaborative mode of governance is an approach that seeks to build regulatory coherence from the bottom-up. Rather than placing an emphasis on the national scale, the governance template empowers governments operating at a local scale to develop regulatory solutions and address problems emerging on-the-ground. The contention is that national policies cannot account for the regulatory needs of actors that exist and operate in diverse circumstances. Aggregating policies at larger scales often fails to recognize the localized dynamics that both produce and address localized problems. Instead, effective governance should focus on the lowest scale to ensure the best fit of policies with local conditions. For example, in the case of food production, it is argued that food should be regulated where food is actually produced.

This mode of governance does not require a costly and burdensome overarching regulatory apparatus, but relies instead on smaller scale regulatory agencies and monitoring networks. Since smaller scale systems address on-the-ground regulatory problems on their own, the larger market gradually improves over time. Decentralizing governance to the local scale utilizes local knowledge and the close social ties between regulator and regulated to improve compliance.

This decentralized approach to governance, however, can pose significant problems for standardization. As each locality develops its own sets of regulations, it becomes increasingly difficult to negotiate and achieve regulatory equivalence across subunits. Coordination costs can be prohibitively high, as products move across thousands of small-scale governance systems. Also, developing unifying regulatory standards at higher levels involves a tortuous process of negotiations between numerous subunits.

A multilevel approach to governance emphasizes the delegation of regulatory authority across multiple scales of government (Hooghe & Marks 2003). The overall architecture is designed to enable each level of government to perform certain regulatory tasks that are feasible and effective given the scale of each jurisdiction. Those championing a multilevel approach contend that the primary problem in effective governance is lack of attention to processes occurring at other scales, and a failure to optimize government functions given their scale. Specific rulemaking is normally delegated to lower levels of government to ensure a better fit with local conditions, while higher levels of government are responsible for providing broader rulemaking guidelines to ensure harmonization across jurisdictions. Monitoring is the delegated responsibility of local governments where proximity and dense social networks can aid local inspectors, whereas regulatory actors at higher level governments can audit the regulators of subnational units.

At its best, a multilevel framework enables actors at each level of government to perform the tasks that they are optimized for given their scale. Higher levels of government can intervene when lower levels of government fail to perform their delegated tasks. As regulatory autonomy is delegated to each level of government, rules are better suited to local conditions, leading to higher levels of compliance. However, the coordination costs in this mode of governance are high. And, in times of crisis, when decisive action is required, a multilevel approach is often unable to generate consensus across scales in a timely fashion.

In sum, polities may use any number of regulatory modalities and strategies to coordinate policies across scales. What is important is that a regulatory approach actively seeks to identify and then address scale-related tensions. Failing to recognize and resolve scale politics will lead to poor regulatory coordination, and, ultimately, regulatory failure. In the chapters that follow, I will explore the costs and benefits of these various approaches to address scale politics in China's complex food production sector. Before moving on to that discussion, I conclude with a review of how the introduced concept of scale politics relates, in broad terms, to existing studies in Chinese politics and comparative politics.

SCALE, CHINESE POLITICS, AND COMPARATIVE POLITICS

The concept of scale politics builds on and informs a number of literatures that extend beyond a discussion of China's food safety crisis.

Scale Politics and the Study of China

In the study of Chinese politics, the scale politics framework offers a different analytic vantage point from which to understand bureaucratic politics. Lieberthal and Oksenberg's (1988) classic work on China's fragmented authoritarianism (FA) highlights how actors responding to China's fragmented governance system alter central policies to suit their particular institutional interests and emphasizes how policy implementation is a result of intense bargaining among multiple actors that leverage different resources and strategies to gain an advantage. The scale politics framework, however, approaches analysis of bureaucratic politics with a different set of assumptions regarding the goals, incentives, and challenges of policy making in China.

First, scale politics emphasizes the overarching *shared* interests of actors rather than the parochial interests of various bureaucratic participants. Scale politics considers the conflicts that emerge as regulators seek to build an integrated system. Government regulators, local officials, and producers in China realize that they cannot go it alone because of the sheer magnitude of the food safety undertaking and the interconnected nature of the market. However, conflict emerges due to an inability to agree on how to integrate different systems of governance. By contrast, in the FA framework, bureaucrats manipulate policies to achieve their own institutional goals with less concern given, in relative terms, to how this activity will affect the overarching coherence of the system. The resulting "system" is in ultimate effect the incoherent outcome of an ad hoc bargaining process.

Thus, this book departs from the perspective that regulators are narrowly self-interested, rent-seeking individuals solely focused on creating their own bureaucratic fiefdoms or climbing the administrative ladder. In the articulated FA framework, "bargains are struck over revenue sources, budgets, personnel, organizational jurisdictions, market shares, production rights, subsidy levels, investment allocations and jobs" (Lieberthal & Lampton 1992:44) However, as one food safety expert commented, "if the average bureaucrat is as bad as people make him out to be, you would expect China's food safety situation to be far worse." Regulators can and do have strong views about what type of regulatory system can best solve the country's food safety problems (Balleisen & Moss 2010; Ansell & Vogel 2006). Moreover, as Yeh et al. (2013) notes in describing the governance processes at work, scholars of Chinese politics are sometimes given to developing a "fetishism of targets," narrowly modeling bureaucrats as *homo economicus*, when bureaucrats are in reality motivated by a far more complex range of factors. Paradoxically, the bureaucratic and technocratic conflicts that arise among officials acting in the interests of the common good can still lead to fundamental regulatory failure when interests across scales are not aligned.

Second, the emphasis on "scale" moves our analysis and actions beyond narrow conflicts about jurisdiction, funding, or the need to protect local economic interests among levels of government, and forces us to consider disagreements about knowledge, timing, managerial methods, and spatial understandings that are driven by a governance system's varying levels of scale. Central, regional, provincial, prefectural, county, and township levels operating according to different degrees-of-zoom have to be carefully aligned across multiple dimensions in order to operate effectively.

Finally, while the FA framework of analysis usefully describes the complex bargaining processes that result from the nested nature of the Chinese political system, this book seeks to explore the implications of the varying "scales" of the nested system. To be sure, the notion of the Chinese polity as a nested system has long been a cornerstone of our understanding of Chinese politics (Skinner 1964; Shue 1988; Hsing 2010).[4] But, I suggest that we have not considered how regulatory outcomes are affected by the nesting of systems of different *scale*. We understand far less about scale externalities, the nonlinear relationship between scales, and the processes of scaling up and scaling down these embedded systems.

Scale politics turns our attention to the challenges of administrative integration as pressures for standardization and routinization grow. As Naughton and Yang (2004) argue, China has remade institutions and enacted a series of new policies to increase the capacity of the administrative state, counteracting much of the centrifugal dynamics in state development. The scale politics framework thus provides an additional analytical lens to understand why significant political obstacles persist even when bureaucrats have a shared interest to develop coherent national systems of governance.

---

[4] Skinner (1964) explores the relationships of embedded market towns and villages, and Shue (1988) describes the impact of honeycombed systems within the body politic that limit the reach of the central state. Hsing (2010) explores the complexity of nestedness within a municipality, showing how centrally empowered "socialist land masters," municipal leaders, and submunicipal units compete for control of land.

Beyond the FA framework, the notion of scale politics permits us to reinterpret other notable characteristics of the Chinese polity. The frequent cycles of centralization and decentralization that are endemic to Chinese politics can also be re-examined in terms of scale. That is, these evanescing forces can be understood as the "rescaling" of the powerful vectors of governance to a single scale at any given time, be it the center or localities. In either scenario, the views of actors at a single scale in the governance system are imposed on all other actors at different scales. In food safety, prior to the 2000s, local governments were in control of food safety, but currently the recentralization of regulatory authority has delimited local food safety standards in favor of a unified food safety law developed by Beijing.

Understanding the alternating processes of centralization and decentralization as a "single scale" solution gives us insight about why both approaches have been less successful at integrating actors at multiple scales. The framework of multiscale governance and ensuing scale politics described in this book suggests that what is now required to resolve China's food safety deficiencies is not to secure control by the center, but to see that policies can be understood, implemented, and coordinated across all scales of government. This perspective, at least insofar as it relates to China as a large and heterogeneous polity, represents a departure from broader comparative politics debates outside of China on the relative merits of decentralization and centralization in addressing governance problems (Treisman 2007). Instead, characterization of China's regulatory failures as a scale problem points to the need for novel multiscale risk management solutions that are driven by neither the center nor the locality (Hooghe & Marks 2003; Ostrom 2005).

Understanding the implications of rescaling governance is particularly important in the current climate of dramatic change in China. Several scholars of public administration have shown that the CCP is experimenting with developing new subprovincial units to deal with perceived challenges. While the basic provincial structure in China has remained stable since 1954, subprovincial units have been highly fluid in modifying their jurisdictional configuration and reach, being reshaped to suit the needs of an increasingly complex system. Prefectures have been replaced by prefectural cities, new county level units have been established, townships are being empowered and given county-level responsibilities, and new special zones are emerging throughout China (Chung & Lam 2009). "Comprehensive integrated reform experiment zones" have been tasked with designing new institutions to cope with fast population growth and

rapid economic development (Lam 2010). In other areas, such as the Pearl
River Delta, China is experiencing a "reterritorialization," in which a
new geography of overlapping and previously unstable territorial scales
of governance and regulation are coming together as regional relations
are being re-forged (Yang 2006). Central government initiatives—such
as the "Develop the West" and "Revive the Northeast" programs—are
leading to the establishment of new macro-regions in order to combat
adverse trends developing across the region, including the rise in peti-
tions, economic malaise, and uneven development (Chung et al. 2009).
This wholesale refashioning of governance in China requires us to better
understand how scale will affect the coordination of policies across and
between these new subunits.

Scholars of policy diffusion and policy experimentation in China will
also find the concept of scale politics instructive. Teets & Hurst (2014)
examine how and why policies are diffused throughout the polity. Building upon the work of Heilmann (2009), they identify four modes of diffusion: (1) top-down (center to subnational); (2) bottom-up; (3) provincial
to township; and (4) provincial-to-provincial. Policy entrepreneurs face
significant challenges as they innovate to develop new solutions within
these identified frames. Here, the processes of scaling up or scaling down
can shed additional light on why policy diffusion is particularly difficult.
Policies that appear to operate smoothly at the local scale are more problematic when applied at the county or provincial levels because scaling
up is a nonlinear transformation. Also, diffusing national policies to local
contexts requires the translation of multiple dimensions of scale, including strategies, knowledge, and managerial know-how that were developed
for the national scale.

Moreover, due to vested interests among numerous actors, new policies sometimes face opposition at certain scales of governance. As Skinner (1964) has shown, the spatial and temporal patterning of economic,
social, and political life is deeply rooted even when facing strong political pressures from the center. Regional dynamics are created over time,
leading to unique regional identities that affect a broad range of governance outcomes (Hurst 2009). Also, important regional variation in how
regulatory, social, and market forces are converging in an institutional
environment has led to persistent regulatory patterns regardless of new
policy innovations (Van Rooij & Lo 2010). Building upon this scholarship, in the chapters that follow, old dynamics in China's central-local
relations will be recast and reinterpreted in terms of scale politics for new
insight.

Scale Politics and the Study of Comparative Politics

Revisiting the implications of scale on governance is also consistent with the developing literature encouraging subnational analysis in comparative politics. Both the notion of scale politics and the subnational turn recognize that polities operate concurrently at multiple levels and that governance at each level operates according to distinctive logics. Snyder's (2001) proposition that the overemphasis of the national scale—what Rokkan referred to as "whole nation bias"—has led to a number of methodological problems: (1) national comparisons do not account for high degrees of internal heterogeneity; (2) studies overlook the variegated policy outcomes across different levels of government; and (3) the interconnectedness between national and subnational politics is often ignored. To avoid these methodological shortfalls, subnational studies argue that theories that apply to the nation-state should not be applied to that state's subnational units (Gervasconi 2010). Also, subnational units must be recognized as operating differently due to different jurisdictions, regimes, rules, and practices (Gibson 2005). In addition, the national scale often misses important dynamics at work at the subnational level. For example, causal processes, such as clientelism, are observable only at finer scales (Moncada & Snyder 2012).

This book extends the foregoing analysis to argue that it is not enough to engage in subnational comparisons, but that it is equally essential to compare units of similar *scale*. Cross-national studies have too often lumped together countries of different scale, such as Sweden and China, without critically assessing how the scale of these polities operating under distinctive scale politics (social constructs, scalar externalities, and nonlinear dimensions) would affect comparative inferences. Comparing subnational units might be problematic as well since countries use vastly different criteria to define jurisdictions—a municipality in one country may resemble a state in another (Moncada & Snyder 2012). Moreover, in making subnational comparisons, consideration should be given to how different scales of governance relate to one another within a single polity. For example, given the different relationship between subnational and national governments in the United States (where the federal government is strong) and in India (where the state governments hold greater sway), dynamics at the state level are likely to be different.

In many respects, the concept of scale politics builds on the work of comparative federalism and intergovernmental relations (IGR), which examines the relationship between subnational and national governments. Studies in comparative federalism have focused on the sharing and division of powers or competencies, institutional design, political representation, and symmetrical and asymmetrical arrangements (Elazar 1993). Scale politics provides another, but distinctive, analytical frame to advance scholarship in these areas.

Despite the similarity of focus with scale politics, most of the literature on comparative federalism and intergovernmental relations is framed in terms of a discussion of "levels" rather than "scales." This has several important implications for these studies because the "scale of government" is a more expansive concept than a "level of government." Whereas level speaks to the jurisdiction and position of a system within the overall hierarchy, scale also addresses how size, space, and its relations affect the way policy is conducted, framed, and discussed by government officials and leads to scale politics. The emphasis on jurisdictional level rather than scale is perhaps not surprising given that the original bargain struck in most federal polities is an agreement about the composition and powers of central government and the rules between it and its subunits (Rodden 2004; Auel 2014). However, unlike studies involving "levels of government," scale is a multidimensional concept concerned not only with jurisdictional issues, but the temporal, spatial, managerial, and knowledge base of a nested system. As such, creating linkages between different levels of government is not simply a matter of accommodating jurisdictional interests, but also of translating "scaled" understandings. Significantly, scale also recognizes that many governance systems do not cleave to the jurisdictional structures of the formal government hierarchy. Thus, for example, a dense network of food producers may be connected spatially in ways that do not neatly conform to a system's regulatory structure, bringing together actors, institutions, and norms that may exist outside the traditional jurisdictional hierarchy, but constitute an important component of intergovernmental relations.

Taking a brief tour to complete the picture, it should be noted that, despite these differences regarding levels and scales, studies in intergovernmental relations and comparative federalism do often implicitly address questions of scale, offering up areas for fruitful cross-fertilization. First, scholars of federalism point to how the delegation of powers does reflect the idea that some levels of government are better suited to certain tasks given their position in the jurisdictional hierarchy, or framing it in terms of scale, what I would refer to as a system's degree-of-zoom. For example, Wibbels (2003) argues that the center is best positioned to provide for the overall economic health of a country. By contrast, Borzel and Hosli (2003) contend that local governments are better positioned to address the question of streetlights and traffic alleviation. Other work highlights the bifurcation of policy making and policy implementation between center and locality on account of different competencies due to scale (Kelemen 2000). Second, similar to studies on scale, IGR literature recognizes that different levels of organization create distinct patterns of governance that are not replicable across other levels. Thus, as common shared knowledge at intermediate levels of any organization accrue and, as these processes are reproduced, persistent differences across multiple levels of government result, which can create problems for organizational coherence (Ostrom & Ostrom 1965, Burke 2014). Third, much like in scale politics, IGR literature also considers the spatial overlap of governing systems. For example, IGR has long focused on the notion that in any governance policy area, national, state, and local perspectives are simultaneously involved in addressing governance concerns. These models can be collaborative (Agranoff 2001), inclusive (Davis 2001), and interdependent (Cameron & Simeon 2002), or emphasize one level of governance over another (Burke 2014). Also, these patterns of engagement are in constant flux (Peters & Pierre 2001). Fourth, studies in comparative federalism can also be viewed as implicitly examining the consequences of scale externalities. For example, in what is known as opportunistic federalism, a breakdown in collaborative federal relations compels subnational actors in the system to pursue immediate interests with little regard for collective consequences (Conlan 2006).

While most issues regarding scale in the foregoing studies are only implicitly applied, one notable strand of the intergovernmental relations literature explicitly addresses issues of scale. Studies on "polycentricity" emphasize multiple centers of authority, highlighting the multilevel, nested nature of a polity (Ostrom 2005). This logic of governance emphasizes multiple centers of authority that can respond to emerging conditions at different scales and leverage appropriate resources throughout a system. Scholars have shown how polycentric governance in policing arrangements in the United States (Ostrom 2010), forestry management systems in Latin America (Andersson & Ostrom 2008), and coastal fishery management solutions in Canada (Dietz et al. 2003) have successfully overcome what are, in effect, problems of scale.

CONCLUSION

Our understanding of scale and its impact on governance has largely been limited to discussions about population, market size, and geographic territory. This chapter has redefined the notion of scale to be framed as a governance system's degree-of-zoom. A comprehensive national regulatory system must integrate governing systems operating at multiple scales. Effective systems must devise strategies, mechanisms, and institutional frameworks to facilitate the scaling up and scaling down of policy. While this book does not purport to frame a general theory of scale, it does aspire to outline building blocks for a renewed focus on the importance of scale in governance, using the subject of food safety in China as a case study.

First, scale determines the interests of regulatory actors across *multiple dimensions*. Local officials are concerned with local cultivation techniques, wholesale market networks, and local consumers. National regulators, by contrast, must focus on standard setting, supply chain management, and a large and diverse consumer base. Their understandings of scale shape the way they believe regulatory funds should be disbursed and how policies should be designed. The key challenge for effective governance relates to how to reconcile and transform these different perspectives of scale, or degrees-of-zoom, into a coherent, functioning system.

Second, regulatory systems must develop governance frameworks that can actively operate across multiple levels and different dimensions of scale. Whether they are government institutions, social networks, or producer supply chains, these linkage mechanisms play an important role in translating and enforcing regulations among different actors across a system. In many ways, these mechanisms must serve as "common carriers" linking the various interests according to scale.[5]

Third, the exclusivity of focus of either central or local government action as a singular scale solution fails to view regulatory activity as part of a *multiscale whole* (Cash et al. 2006: Termeer et al. 2010; Andersson & Ostrom 2008; Hooghe & Marks 2003). Rather than viewing governance as either being centrally or locally driven, we must observe how central and local government activities must work in concert in a nested system to address food safety challenges. More detailed consideration must be given to how policies can be scaled up and scaled down into an integrated whole.

In an era in which global giants play a definitive role in regulatory governance, it is imperative that we have a deeper appreciation of the

---

[5] The concept of a "common carrier" was first developed by Schickler (2001) to describe policies that could successfully bring together supportive coalitions of multiple legislative orders for successful passage.

challenges and techniques of managing scale. Having set forth a framework for how to view scale in governance, I now turn to China's food safety system to explore how scale politics has fueled multilevel conflicts, exacerbated bureaucratic rivalries, and, ultimately, led to regulatory failure.

3

A Short History of China's Food Production

How did China's food safety crisis start? In the 1970s, food poisonings involved basic and largely manageable issues of hygiene and expired food, not the deliberate, widespread, or systemic adulteration featured prominently in headlines today. Severe food violations only began to emerge following the rapid expansion of China's food markets occurring well into the 1980s. A regulator cynically quipped that in the past, "there was too little food to worry about whether it was safe." The tragic irony is that now there is enough food, but too few guarantees for safe consumption.

Media accounts of China's food safety crisis often suggest that problems have emerged throughout the country's food production system without much differentiation. But, China's food production can be divided into at least three different systems, each with different baseline levels of food safety: the domestic sector, the export sector, and the organic, community-supported agricultural (CSA) food markets. A side-by-side comparison of these sectors (see Table 3.2) offers a useful lens to better understand the relationship between market development, scale, and food safety. In the case of the domestic sector, a market can become "too big, too fast" for effective food safety. By contrast, the export and CSA sectors present more rational paths of market development that have resulted in fewer food safety problems.

The sequencing of *market-facilitating* and *market-constraining* policies has played an important role in how food safety problems emerged in the country. Market-facilitating policies are those that rapidly expand the scale of a system by increasing production volumes, the number and type of participants, and the global reach of production. Market-constraining policies slow down this process by imposing stringent food safety standards and market entry requirements.

In China's domestic sector, the urgent need to feed more than a billion people prompted the government to pursue a policy of market facilitation for a 30-year period beginning in 1978, integrating local markets with national supply chains. As the system expanded rapidly, the following problems emerged: (1) producers emphasized practices that increased supply and lowered prices rather than emphasizing quality and safety; (2) as supply chains lengthened, linking local and national markets, there were no protocols in place for monitoring and testing; (3) regulatory gaps formed as governing systems at different scales did not have clear processes in place to harmonize policies and identify emerging problems. By the time the government moved forward with new food safety reforms in 2004, China's food safety system was fundamentally broken.

By contrast, in the export sector, both market-facilitating and market-constraining policies were implemented concurrently, and the integration of governing systems at different scales occurred in step with market expansion. Under this mode of market development, the sector faced countervailing pressures of expansion and contraction. At times, government officials, exporters, and importers did try to capture global market share, but when overexpansion led to food safety problems, the government instituted new measures to slow down growth and better enforce new quality control measures. Because the expansion of the sector was carefully negotiated and policed by the government, the development of a comprehensive regulatory system was less fraught with contentious scale politics and, thus, better food safety outcomes.

In the CSA sector, market-constraining policies were pursued in order to facilitate the realization of regulatory goals. Capturing market share, lowering production costs, and increasing revenues were less of a concern than ensuring food was safe. Unlike the domestic sector, in which regulations chased after the market, in the CSA sector, strict regulations were developed first and only producers capable of meeting those requirements were permitted to participate. Not only was the sector limited to a small, homogeneous set of actors, but the system also had rules in place that limited the scaling up of the market. As a result, high levels of food safety were maintained.

This chapter identifies the origins of many of the important scale dynamics at work for three distinct food production sectors, and provides a brief history of these markets before exploring in greater detail in later chapters the governance strategies employed to address the food safety crisis. I first explore the origins of failed regulatory coordination in the domestic sector. I then examine the development of the export sector and show how a robust food safety regulatory regime could be maintained by balancing market-facilitating and market-constraining forces. Finally, I show how the CSA sector's baseline regulatory coordination arose out of the benign conditions of market development that placed an emphasis on market constraint.

THE DOMESTIC SECTOR

The specter of famine has long haunted the collective memory of the Chinese people. From 1959 to 1961, 30 to 45 million people died of starvation due to a series of failed policies during the Great Leap Forward (Bernstein 2006; Dikotter 2010). Even after the agricultural sector recovered from the trauma of that period, China still faced constant food shortages. In 1978, China's average per capita food availability was as low as that experienced by an entire generation before it, and more than 100 million people did not have access to a stable supply of food (Smil 1995). In Sichuan from 1965 to 1976, for example, the annual rate of food output growth was at 0.7%, whereas annual population growth was close to 3%, leading to a decline in per capita agricultural output (Bramall 1995). Even as late as the early 1990s, tens of millions of people in China's poorest provinces still did not have access to the suggested minimal caloric intake (Smil 1995). China's leadership had been aware that food productivity was well behind other nations. Chen Yun, party elder and senior economic specialist, warned that if food shortages were not addressed, a massive wave of peasants would flood into the cities to demand food (Fewsmith 1994). As a result of these conditions, food security—ensuring the *supply* of food for the masses, not food safety—was the order of the day.

As Deng Xiaoping, Zhao Ziyang, and Wan Li, the major architects for rural reform, consolidated their power base in Beijing, government ministries were put to the task of expanding food production. A key component of China's food production strategy was the implementation of the household responsibility system, which decollectivized agriculture, triggering the spectacular growth in agricultural production. Beginning in 1978, a new policy line was developed in agricultural production, which would link income to productivity in order to increase the quantity of agricultural output. Other senior officials in the party hierarchy, such as Wan Li, party secretary of Anhui province, introduced the use of

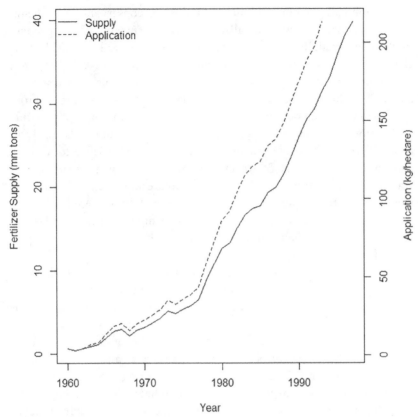

FIGURE 3.1 Supply and Application of Fertilizer, 1975–1997
Source: Data from Hellig (2011). Accessed July 28, 2017 at www.china-food-security.org/data/tech/tech_5.htm

household contracts in lieu of the previous ideologically driven forms of remuneration. Under the new system, peasants were required to sell a specified amount of their production to the state and any output above established quotas could be sold on the market. Leaders permitted reforms to advance more rapidly in more mountainous and remote areas of the country (Weersink & Rozelle 1997). By 1984, 99% of rural households had adopted the household responsibility system, and the number of products required for state procurement was reduced from 113 to 38. By 1993, 90% of all agricultural produce was sold at market-determined prices (Fan 1997).

China also made substantial investments in agricultural technology and input production. In the 1970s, the state moved investment from steel production and machine building toward water conservancy and chemical fertilizer production (Bramall 1995). Investments in fertilizer production sky rocketed. In 1973–1974, the government moved forward by purchasing 13 large synthetic ammonia and urea factories abroad (Naughton 2006). In Sichuan alone, 130 fertilizer plants were built. Between 1978 and 1996, China's fertilizer supply quadrupled (Naughton 2006). From 1971 to 1975, the government invested RMB 1,350 million in pesticide production, up from RMB 452 million expended from 1966 to 1970 (Bramall 1995). Pesticide was priced below the market value to increase consumption (Weersink & Rozelle 1997). The use of advanced inputs was promoted by agricultural research stations established to disseminate new growing techniques. Agricultural research stations were established across the country to promote the use of a new high-yield variety of seeds. In addition, the mechanization of irrigation helped to provide more precise water control.

Taken together, advancements in irrigation, agricultural chemical inputs, and high-yielding crop cultivation, amounted to a green revolution in China's agricultural development. From 1979 to 1995, agricultural production increased on average 6.5% per annum (Fan 1997). By the mid-1990s, China made the transition from being in short supply of major agricultural products to being self-sufficient and, in some product types, in surplus. During the 1990s, the sowing area for vegetables rose from 10.491 mm hectares to 17.353 mm hectares, averaging 8.75% growth per year (FAO 2004). Vegetable production increased from 223.2 mm tons to 528.6 mm tons (FAO 2004). Fruit output doubled over the same period as did production for aquatic foods (FAO 2004).

The Chinese government also pushed forward a series of initiatives to develop the infrastructure for new food markets, dramatically altering the scale of production and distribution. In an effort to stimulate productivity and innovation in the food sector, during the 1980s, production was decentralized to local governments, spurring local investment in food processing (Hsueh 2011). Producers began to seek customers beyond their immediate locales, linking up to markets operating at larger scales. In 1993, local government farm bureaus were further restructured into integrated agricultural businesses that soon diversified into supermarkets and pharmaceutical companies. In some areas, local governments merged food companies with small-scale livestock and agricultural farms into large-scale vertically integrated companies. New retail outlets replaced or competed with state-owned monopolies and other SOEs in cereals, oils, and food stuffs, and import-export corporations. By 1990, the food

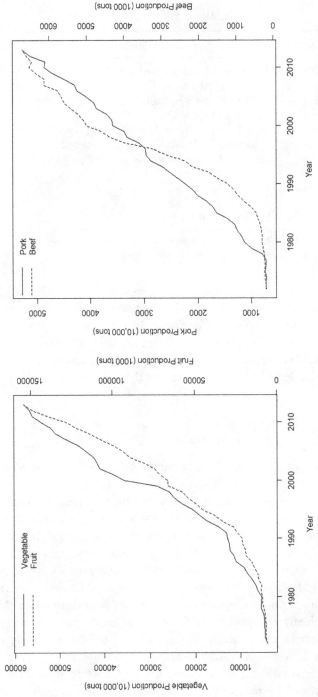

FIGURE 3.2 Agricultural Output of Vegetable, Fruit, and Meat, 1975–2015
Source: FAOSTAT Database.

TABLE 3.1 *Major Food Safety Reforms*

Year	Major Law/Regulatory Innovation
1982	Provisional Food Hygiene Law
1995	Food Hygiene Law
2001	Market Access Regulations
2003	Creation of the SFDA
2004	State Council Decision on Enhancing Food Safety
2006	Agricultural Product Quality and Safety Law
2007	State Council Leading Group on Product Quality and Food Safety
2009	Food Safety Law
2013	Establishment of CFDA
2015	Amended Food Safety Law

Note: This list is only a selection of major food safety reforms, and does not include numerous minor policy initiatives.

industry was the 3rd largest industrial sector in China, valued at RMB 144.7 billion (Liu 2010). In 2001, industrial output of food was valued at RMB 954.6 billion (Wei 2001). In the course of two decades, local markets were integrated with national food commodity markets, and national logistics centers were established to facilitate the transport of food throughout China and the rest of the world.

MARKET-CONSTRAINING POLICIES: BUILDING A FOOD SAFETY SYSTEM

Attempts to establish a food safety regime only began in the mid-1990s, long after the significant scaling up of the food production system. Little thought was given to how to carefully integrate governance in a scaled up food market. As administrative reforms in the broader economy decoupled food production from the state enterprise system, regulatory control began to concentrate in particular nodes in China's vast state bureaucracy (Table 3.1). In 1995, the Food Hygiene Law was promulgated, and the Ministry of Health (MOH) became the leading food safety regulator in a multi-ministry food safety system. The Ministry of Agriculture (MOA) remained chiefly responsible for limits on pesticide residues in agricultural products and the quality of agricultural inputs. The 1993 Product Quality Law gave AQSIQ the authority to regulate food processors and producers with respect to manufacturing, packaging, and labeling. The Ministry of Commerce could amend standards and rules regarding storage, transportation, and sales (Tam & Yang 2005). Other food safety responsibilities were doled out to a wide range of agencies and ministries throughout China's bureaucracy. This fragmented system was replicated at each level of government throughout China.

Due to persistent regulatory gaps, food safety incidents continued to escalate in the early 2000s. Local food safety incidents quickly evolved into national scandals, as contaminated products entered national distribution channels. With no recall protocols in place, a weak market surveillance program, and spotty inspection system, regulators were at a loss as to how to control the problem.

By the time new rules on additives, pesticides, and feed were being discussed, farmers had by then developed a plethora of unsafe methods to expand their production volumes to participate in the growing food market. Farmers often relied on the heavy use of chemicals to produce food (Calvin et al. 2006). To deal with significant pest pressures, some producers apply four times the recommended amount of pesticide to boost yields, thereby increasing the risk of pesticide poisoning (Yan 2012). In 2001, 2,110 samples of produce were inspected in 14 provincial cities in wealthier areas of China and it was found that 31.1% of vegetables had pesticide residues violating established maximum residue limits (Han 2007). Similarly, in meat production, farmers have administered significant amounts of antibiotics to prevent the spread of disease. In one study of 60 pig farming households, only 55.8% of households were found to comply with food safety laws (Yan 2012).

Developing a comprehensive food safety plan that could accurately reflect the capacities of all producers operating at different scales of production and distribution was challenging. By the time officials began to tackle the food safety problem in earnest, the regulatory system had to oversee a diverse production landscape that included small farmers and traders operating in local markets and national agro-processors linked to global supply chains. Within local markets, the vast majority of food processors were small, ill-equipped, and nonlicensed (Han 2007; Liu 2010; Yan 2012). Also, many producers lacked even basic food safety knowledge or the willingness to observe sound practices. For example, more than 10,000 Chinese farmers died of pesticide poisoning every year in the 1990s (Yan 2012). In the 2000s, studies continued to show how farmers had little knowledge regarding how to use chemical inputs properly. Thus, many still failed to observe the technically specified waiting period following the application of pesticides before harvest (Calvin et al. 2006). In 75.4% of municipalities surveyed, fewer than 100 processors kept production records, and only 1 in 7 complied with food production rules (Yang et al. 2012). These local risks quickly spread to distribution and production systems at larger scales as producers were linked to regional logistics centers that supplied the national market. At broader scales, the notable absence of infrastructure for distribution, packaging, storage, and transportation contributed to the risk of microbial contamination (Han 2007). Also, large agro-processors were increasingly developing new, sophisticated methods of food production that were unsafe in order to lower costs. Regulators were presented with a host of problems emerging at different scales of governance.

The largely unchecked expansion of the food production system has led to significant variation in establishing a comprehensive food safety regulatory regime. In a coherent system, the regulatory apparatus operates on a relatively uniform basis at each scale of governance throughout the polity. At the regional scale in China, however, the implementation of food safety is highly uneven from region to region (Yang et al. 2012). Areas in Eastern China have established the strongest food control systems and have the highest implementation rates in recognized procedures: 80% of municipalities established a certification system, 83.1% conducted quantitative analysis of food safety incidents, and 155 products were managed under the food safety certification system (Yang et al. 2012). By contrast, in areas in the center of China, only 53.9% had established certification systems, 61% conducted quantitative analysis, and only 66 products were managed under the food safety certification system (Yang et al. 2012). Results in Northeastern China and Western China were worse.

As food safety problems continued to mount, in 2004, the State Council moved forward with plans to develop an integrated system from the local to the national scale. These new initiatives, however, produced significant scale politics, which will be examined in the proceeding chapters.

THE EXPORT SECTOR: BUILDING A MARKET AND REGULATORY SYSTEM CONCURRENTLY

In its export sector, China has sought to develop its food and agricultural product market cautiously, seeking to prevent massive food safety incidents that could trigger an erosion of consumer confidence in the "Made in China" label. Incidences of food poisoning involving Chinese exports include insecticide found in frozen dumplings in Japan, the deaths of pets due to melamine-laced food in the United States, and traces of carcinogenic antibiotics in shrimp in Europe, all of which have led to global bans on Chinese products. As such, market-facilitating pressures to capture global market share are counterbalanced by equally strong constraining pressures to ensure food safety. In contrast to the domestic sector, in the export market, the Chinese government has sought to carefully address issues emerging at different scales of production and governance in an integrated fashion.

The Chinese government has sought to preserve the small, homogeneous characteristics of the sector, which has facilitated the linking of producers at the global and local scales. Implementing a closed, segmented system to regulate food exporters helps to preserve the elite nature of the food export sector. As such, the system should be considered to be distinct from the domestic regulatory system (Gale & Buzby 2009). Local producers seeking access to the global market must subject themselves to a strict licensing system and extra inspections. As of 2007, only 12,714 enterprises had been formally registered with the China Entry-Exit Inspection and Quarantine Bureau (CIQ) registration system (State Council 2007).

Best practices developed by standard-setting bodies at the global scale have been carefully scaled down to be comprehensible to local producers. The 11th Five-Year Development Plan highlights the government's strategy to promote China's comparative advantage in the export of low-cost and labor-intensive agricultural products. Selected enterprises are assisted in attaining Good Agricultural Practice (GAP), Hazard-Access Critical Control Point System (HACCP), and Good Manufacturing Practice (GMP) certifications. Support is offered to those firms who invest in new production technologies and conduct research and development. The government established a "Development Fund for Export Brands," which subsidizes firms in their marketing efforts abroad and helps them to solicit professional assistance in brand development. Training is offered to all export enterprises in a range of areas including technical standards, food safety monitoring, and the attainment of international certifications, among others. For the enterprises deemed viable, the government offers significant support.

Over time, producers have become sensitized to the food safety demands of the global market. In the export sector, producers are policed by government officials and third-party actors, which help to preserve general confidence and keep prices high. The development of an export credit system—in which food enterprises discovered to be violating food safety standards or whose shipments are rejected by importing countries are penalized—also preserves the integrity of the market. Companies are thus more inclined to invest in food safety and food quality.

Distinctions between the global and national scales of governance are blurred as foreign actors actively participate in the export food safety system. EU companies work directly within China's export licensing system, refusing any product that does not comply with AQSIQ's stringent food safety requirements. An EU food safety official in Beijing asserted that the EU would prefer the volume of trade from China be reduced in order to ensure higher levels of food safety (EU Interview). Japanese food safety officials permit only a subset of China's export-licensed enterprises to export food to Japan. Also, importers from Hong Kong and Singapore only conduct business with those firms that have been certified by both China and their respective governments.

In recent years, the Chinese government and producers have achieved a shared understanding that the overexpansion of the export system introduces significant food safety risks, which could damage the reputation of the "Made in China" brand. Food safety scandals have reduced importer confidence in Chinese food exports. These major scandals prompted Chinese officials to create additional safeguards for Chinese food exports, and to initiate a nationwide campaign on food safety in 2009.

When food safety incidents do occur, market-constraining pressures operate to recalibrate the export sector toward safety. Additional measures are taken to ensure global and local actors are in regulatory sync. In some instances, the government will adopt new standards from its major global partners. For example, China adopted Japanese labeling requirements and also employed Japan's quality standards for product size, shape, and color for producers shipping products to Japan (Chen et al. 2005). Other times, AQSIQ further limits the number of producers eligible to export food, or revokes licenses of previously approved establishments.

The careful management of the export system has led to a more uniform implementation of food safety. In 2007, the Chinese government issued a white paper called "China's Food Quality and Safety," which outlines a management framework called "One Pattern and Ten Systems," which emphasizes elite production and strict licensing. The "One-Pattern" structure refers to the inclusion of food enterprises with an industrialized, modern supply chain, effectively excluding over 90% of China's food producers. The typical food export enterprise is a large, government-designated "dragonhead" enterprise, which can attain significant production volume and has substantial registered capital. These enterprises operate their own "production bases" with on-site inspection teams and monitoring facilities. Some firms contract farming to township

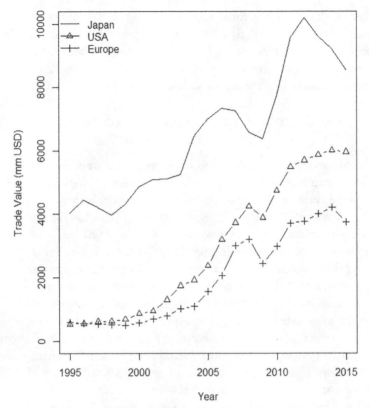

FIGURE 3.3 Trade Value of Food Exports from China by Partner, 2000–2015
Source: World Integrated Trade Solution | World Bank Database (WITS).
Note: Europe also includes trade to Central Asia.

agricultural production bases where township leaders direct farmers under their jurisdiction to produce according to specifications set by the enterprise, and hand over a designated amount of product to the enterprise following harvest. The government asserts that this model "is an important guarantee for the quality of such food ... and the only way for enterprises to aim for scale and intensive development in the international market" (State Council 2007).

By carefully calibrating market-facilitating and market-constraining policies, the export sector has managed to avoid the regulatory chaos observed in the domestic market. Maintaining a small, homogeneous sector in which scales of governance have been carefully linked has enabled better coordination of regulatory policies from the local to the global. While some contaminated food products have emerged from China's export producers, the sector exhibits high food safety pass rates. Foreign border inspections have also reported that less than 1% of total food imports from China are rejected.[1] This is not to say that Chinese food exports are not problematic, but only to contrast the sector's strong performance relative to its domestic sector.

CSA SECTOR: MARKET CONSTRAINT FOLLOWED BY MARKET FACILITATION

The community-supported agriculture sector is a system that emphasizes market constraint before facilitation, and exhibits a high level of food safety coordination. The scale of the system was deliberately constrained to facilitate the realization of regulatory goals. In addition, the system has largely operated on a scale no larger than the municipal, even though its ambitions are national in scope. The CSA market is an initiative that brings urban consumers and rural producers together in a mutually beneficial relationship. CSA farms are typically located around major urban areas and commit to organic production principles, and sell their goods in farmer's markets or through farm-direct sales to the consumer.

The market evolved in response to the failures of the broader food safety system, and developed according to a self-regulating, self-constraining logic. The architecture of the CSA market provides ideal baseline conditions for a system that orients all actors in the system to maximize food safety outcomes. Farmers in this niche sector emphasize the importance of limited production, which they believe to be the critical factor to overall ecological sustainability and maintenance of food safety (Yang 2011). Most producers believe that food safety problems emerge as farmers seek to artificially increase food production by the heavy application of pesticides and other inputs (Gale & Buzby 2009). When farmers turn to cheaper, more hazardous pesticides to increase their profit margins, the consequences can be lethal. CSA farmers, by contrast, do not seek high levels of production and have a strong aversion to entering markets where high volumes are expected: "we need to develop a rhythm with the land. Once you get too big and it becomes unsustainable and once you become marketized, you have to adapt your farm to the market, which in turn transforms the nature of the farm" (CSA 1).

---

[1] For example, using Japanese food safety statistics in 2010, the rejection rate of Chinese food given its share of total imports (247 rejections/14% of total food imports) is better than other developing countries (Indonesia 44/1.8% and Vietnam 117/1.6%) and comparable to Korea (40/2.9%) (MHLW 2011).

CSA farmers seek to gradually improve the environmental quality of their farms and encourage sustainable production (Dan 2011). Many employ cyclical farming practices, in which animal waste is converted to fertilizer, and methane tanks are used to heat homes and power irrigation pumps. Farms have seen a significant improvement in soil and water quality as a result of these practices: "the overall production conditions have improved since beginning cultivation. The pH level of our water has gone down from 8 to 7 and the humus content of the soil has increased from 1.3 to 2.4" (CSA 3). Improvements in baseline conditions allow farmers to use fewer inputs, which reduce costs and the risk of food safety incidents.

A commitment to sustainable development limits the size and heterogeneity of this market, creating the ideal conditions to develop an effective governance system. Moreover, the emphasis on the local scale—local markets, community ties, and local conditions—helps to establish a consensus among producers to provide safe food. As the market was developed, CSA organizers limited market entry to only "trustworthy" producers. Actors are highly aware of the rules of the game and norms, which are conveyed through charters, standards of conduct, and participatory guidelines: "(1) openness and transparency of information, and a willingness to share all aspects of production with consumers; (2) sustainable production and operation, representing concern for human and environmental health; (3) a commitment to cooperation, among farmers and consumer alike; (4) true product traceability" (Beijing Farmer's Market Guidelines). These informal agreements provide a flexible framework of interaction and support to keep actors focused on responsible, public-oriented behavior.

Dense, local social ties in the system also help to ensure that individuals do not disregard production protocols. While the system is highly informal, and does permit deviations from established practices, CSA participants are quick to sanction individuals who are viewed to violate key aspects of the system. In particular, those who break food safety agreements and engage in competitive marketing behavior are shut out of CSA programs, and face social consequences in their communities.

The CSA system in China is credited with relatively high levels of food safety by scholars (Shi et al. 2011), journalists (Yu 2011 Xu 2012; Macleod 2011), and NGOs. CSA-produced food is low risk due to strict rules prohibiting the use of conventional inputs such as chemical fertilizers, nonorganic pesticides, and growth hormones (Goland 2002; Jarosz 2000; Murdoch & Miele 1999). Compliance with food safety rules is high and Chinese consumers of CSA food view it to be safe (Shi et al. 2011).

TABLE 3.2 *Market Development and Scale Politics by Sector*

	CSA	EXPORT	DOMESTIC
Phase One	Market-Constraining	Market-Constraining and Market-Facilitating	Market-Facilitating
Phase Two	Market-Facilitating		Market-Constraining
Integration of Scales	Constrained to local scales	Careful, deliberate integration of scales	Haphazard, ad hoc integration
Food Safety	High	Medium/High	Low

Although the CSA market constitutes only a tiny fraction of China's food supply, its influence as a model for food safety continues to grow, and perhaps offers another potential solution to China's food safety crisis.

DISCUSSION AND CONCLUSION

Differences in the severity of food safety problems in the CSA sector, export sector, and domestic market are directly linked to how these markets developed (Table 3.2.). As the scale of a market rapidly increases under market-facilitating policies, scales are forced to integrate; and without a clear template for coordinating governance and weak monitoring protocols, food safety problems begin to emerge. In China's domestic sector, severe regulatory coordination problems occurred. But, in markets operating under a logic of constraint, scales are able to integrate more effectively. In the export market, a small elite group of producers and regulators are able to transmit and integrate regulatory processes from the local to the global. And, in the CSA market, producers and regulators have resisted expanding beyond the local scale, and have achieved remarkable levels of food safety.

This chapter shows that the size and heterogeneity of a system and its baseline level of regulatory coordination in food safety are largely a consequence of history. The way in which a system develops has important consequences for the integration of governing systems operating at different scales. In an ideal world, regulatory and market systems would develop alongside one another. However, in most cases regulatory systems markedly lag behind the establishment of markets. Moreover, pressing priorities of governance often are the key determinate in regulatory development.

In this chapter, I have offered a brief history of food safety in the domestic, CSA, and export sectors in China. The resulting differences in the scale dynamics of the sectors outlined provide the baseline framework for food safety governance. We have seen that not all starting points in the massive Chinese food production system are the same. In the following chapters, the book will explore how governance strategies employed in the 2000s address scale politics in food safety with varying degrees of success and failure in China's distinctive food sectors.

4

The Export Sector

The Heavy Hand of Direct Control

How can we design institutions to better address and resolve China's ongoing food safety failures? Turning to China's export sector for a first look at effective regulatory solutions to the country's food safety problems may strike many as odd given the widespread publicity about its food safety mishaps. After all, in the last decade, multiple made-in-China food safety scandals brought the weaknesses of China's food safety system to the world's attention.

From the perspective of its global trading partners, China's apparent lack of control over food safety in its export sector poses significant risks to the inward bound domestic food supplies of other countries (DeLisle 2009). However, while concerns regarding China's food exports are not unfounded, they are often exaggerated. Media coverage of China's food safety failures, without journalistic regard for the differentiation of China's food production system, has caused many observers to take only a cursory view, overlooking the surprising fact that relative to its own domestic sector, food safety in China's export sector is rationally managed, stringently enforced, and responsive to international food safety requirements.

China has emerged as a major participant in the global food trade, ranking as the fourth largest exporter by value at approximately US$63 billion in 2014 (WTO 2015). From 2005 to 2010, the average annual global growth of Chinese food exports has been at 15%. In Japan, China is the second largest external supplier of food, accounting for 13.6% of Japan's food imports in 2010 (JETRO 2011). China's exports to the United States have tripled in the last decade and were valued at approximately US$5 billion in 2010 (Food & Water Watch 2011). China supplies more than 60% of apple juice, 50% of garlic, and 10–15% of fish and shellfish consumed in the United States (Gale & Buzby 2009). Chinese exports to the EU have increased at an average of 15% per year from 2001 to 2010 (UN Comtrade Database).

Experts argue that the level of food safety in the export sector is higher than in its domestic sector for several reasons: (1) food production for export is limited to large, technically proficient enterprises (Gale & Buzby 2009); (2) government regulation and enforcement are more stringent (Asian Development Bank 2005); (3) rates of third-party certification are high (State Council 2007); and (4) foreign governments and enterprises provide technical assistance and disseminate information on best practices (Calvin et al. 2006).

This chapter focuses on the export sector's centralized, hierarchical governance framework, which has enabled China to seamlessly regulate food safety from the global to the local scale for a limited set of producers and regulators. Despite the obvious differences between the domestic and export sectors, examining a well-coordinated system may allow us to develop a few useful clues as to how to develop a more consistently replicable set of "first principles" in regulatory design in multiscale systems. The next sections explore how a centralized and hierarchical governance framework is effective in integrating the degrees-of-zoom of global and local actors. As a result, problematic aspects of scale politics are not an issue for the following reasons: (1) actors can agree on the scale of governance; (2) policies are carefully coordinated across scales in multiple dimensions; and (3) regulators and producers are sensitized to and address scale externalities.

GOVERNANCE IN A CENTRALIZED, HIERARCHICAL SYSTEM

The export sector can be considered *centralized* because regulatory authority is primarily vested in a single agency—the General Administration for Quality Supervision, Inspection, and Quarantine (AQSIQ). It is *hierarchical* because regulators and corporations enforce food safety standards in a top-down fashion through formal, routinized codes of procedure. This governance framework is highly effective at preempting the emergence of scale politics. AQSIQ is charged with control over the licensing, standard setting, and monitoring process of regulatory agents operating at multiple scales. Its dominant position in the regulatory hierarchy in the export sector prevents bureaucratic infighting with other agencies at other levels, which can translate to weak regulatory coordination. Also, because AQSIQ is centralized, it can act as a single contact point between China and its trading partners, effectively interfacing and translating knowledge developed at the transnational scale to domestic actors. AQSIQ staff work closely with foreign regulators who regularly audit the sector's food safety system.[1] As of 2015, AQSIQ dominance in the export sector remains unchallenged despite the major regulatory reforms that have consolidated food safety authority in the CFDA.

This is not to say that AQSIQ's central position in the system is never challenged and that there are few conflicts between the often heavy-handed regulators of AQSIQ and export producers. The risk of a global food safety incident caused by Chinese food exports is a constant concern. As such, sometimes AQSIQ is known to be overly cautious. When problems arise, AQSIQ will sometimes issue a complete ban on a particular product, penalizing all producers. One exporter comments about the monitoring organization: "they are at times scrambling to get up to speed. There are knee-jerk reactions such as these major bans...full stops...a [CYA] operation" (EX 3). The benefits of a centralized, hierarchical system of governance, however, appear to outweigh the costs of occasional rifts caused by AQSIQ's heavy-handed approach. In particular, the hierarchical nature of relationships enables important regulatory information to be quickly transmitted to governing systems across scales, and creates a strong mechanism for accountability.

Within this centralized, hierarchical framework of governance, regulators, producers, and foreign importers enforce a strategy that can be described as "direct adaptable control." Access to markets on the global scale is overseen by AQSIQ, and the practical management of food safety is delegated to transnational private actors and foreign government regulators. Foreign importers prevent noncompliance by *directly controlling* the production process at the farm and factory level, as opposed to solely relying on post hoc testing, providing them with a clear perspective of production conditions at the local scale. The system also places emphasis on institutional flexibility to *adapt* to emerging food safety risks at various scales of production and distribution. In addition to Chinese export producers, Japanese, European, and American importers have established

---

[1] The Japanese, in particular, are highly active in China's export sector. For the Japanese, inspections go beyond issues such as pesticide residues and soil quality, but also, for example, extend to matters of color, shape, and size of an apple. In addition to collaborating with Japan as an import partner, the agency has formed close working relationships with the EU, the United States, and Korea through a series of MOUs.

their own unique approaches to direct, adaptable control driven by consumer demands for food safety in their individual home markets.

The system of direct, adaptable control was established as a way to supplement AQSIQ's regulatory capacity to manage a highly challenging production context (Godfrey 2012). Importers have developed their own systems to manage and ensure food quality that in some cases supersedes AQSIQ's regulatory functions. *Direct control* of the supply chain, as opposed to delegating control to suppliers, is essential to avoid food safety incidents. In an environment of low social trust, and faced with exacting global food safety standards, importers cannot delegate food safety responsibility to intermediaries or farmers. Trust may develop over time, but due to legal liabilities at home requiring importers to show that all means necessary were taken to ensure safe food, tight control remains the norm. Firms that depend on local agents who operate through their personal networks face significant risks. Importing companies contend that local agents often defer to the strength of their relationship with a supplier over an importer's commitment to food safety (EX 4). Even when importers purchase produce directly from farms, there is still a risk that unmonitored suppliers will source from the open market, whose food safety standards are much lower than food specifically produced for export. One importer comments on the widespread practice of sourcing from the open market: "the other alternative is going onto the open market, but there are huge food safety issues. Chinese companies are flying beneath the radar and can get around these rules.... I know for a fact that other Chinese exporters purchase from the open market... and this presents real risks" (EX 3).

Many producers supply food to both the domestic and export markets, and company executives believe that lower quality food produced for the domestic market is likely to be intermingled with food destined for export. "You see guys mixing stuff into dried food products all the time. Aside from the dead rats and other stuff, they add food to get the required volume. So you have to watch these guys," one manufacturing boss said (EX9). Therefore, in order to manage the export supply chain in China, establishing direct control through on-site management at larger production bases is paramount. "It's expensive," he says, "but there's no way around it."

The importance of a strategy that is also adaptable is self-evident given the constantly evolving global food trade environment and dynamic local conditions. A regulatory system that is unable to respond to changes emerging at other scales will quickly fall off the pace with new standards, or fail to address emerging food safety problems. In the early 2000s, an increasing number of international food scandals highlighted the weaknesses of China's food safety monitoring system, but it also showed how quickly the Chinese could restructure and address weaknesses in the sector. In 2002, high levels of pesticide residue were identified on spinach from China after dozens of Japanese consumers fell ill (Fackler 2007). That same year the EU discovered residues of chloramphenicol, an antibiotic with a lethal side effect on humans, in seafood from China, leading to a blanket ban on all imports of animal origin. In 2008, melamine, an additive which causes kidney stones when consumed, was identified in Chinese dairy products. Later, melamine was discovered in products from major food producers such as Heinz, Mars, Unilever, and Cadbury sourcing from China (Food & Water Watch 2011). These widely publicized food safety incidents prompted the Chinese government, importers, and foreign governments to collaborate to strengthen the export control system, reconfigure supply chains, and modify strategies of direct control.

Identifying the Scale of Governance

One of the primary challenges in addressing scale politics is determining the scale of governance capable of delivering optimal outcomes. Actors within a system must determine (1) the degree-of-zoom which is best positioned to address food safety and (2) the scale at which regulatory problems are likely to arise. In the export sector, a centralized, hierarchical framework is enforced by global and national authorities who seek to orient regulators and producers toward the global marketplace. China is well aware that it is an integral part of a broader food trading system that has become increasingly governed by a coherent body of regulations to facilitate trade and ensure food safety at the global scale. As a result, the Chinese government has actively partnered with multinationals, and international quality assurance personnel. Also, transnational third-party certifiers help to train state regulators on new food safety best practices emerging on the global scale, such as GlobalGAP or the BRC (British Retail Consortium) standards. This global scale orientation is reinforced by extensive audits by foreign regulators, testing by independent labs, and spot investigations that occur at each scale of production and distribution (global, national, provincial, and below). And, because producers seek to gain and maintain access to the global market, they pay close attention to changes in international food safety protocols.

For a country that is highly sensitive, and largely opposed to foreign interference in most of its domestic affairs, China has been unusually open toward foreign food safety regulators operating within its borders. Inspectors from Japan, the United States, Europe, and Hong Kong frequently conduct audits of local companies and the regulatory system. Japan and Hong Kong in particular follow stringent monitoring and inspection protocols for Chinese exporters including on-site inspections, certifications, and technical assistance. One pork exporter to Hong Kong notes, "Before selling our pigs to Hong Kong, [Hong Kong inspectors] would check for additives and veterinary drug residues. The Hong Kong government would sometimes send inspectors and they would test each pig even before we could finalize a sale" (ZJ 11).

In terms of determining the scale at which problems are most likely to emerge, actors focus the bulk of their attention on local scale processes and conditions that could lead to a global food safety scandal. Importers understand that farmers in the countryside have only received varying levels of a primary school education, which is often associated with unsafe agricultural practices (Zhou & Jin 2009). Record keeping, carefully monitored pesticide usage, and quality assurance are not well understood. Importers recognize that factory managers are not food production specialists with strong technical expertise: "these factory owners are an interesting lot . . . they are mostly old officials or connected to money . . . they aren't farmers or in the food business. They don't read 'food processor weekly'" (EX 1). Without direct control many exporters believe product quality deteriorates. One auditor shook his head commenting on a major American company seeking to source from China, "They wanted a product at a certain price and volume, and said 'who do you know?' And, they work through faceless agents and don't ask questions. Is it any surprise when something falls through the cracks?" (EX4).

Direct control involves careful management of the entire supply chain from inputs, production, and distribution precisely to prevent these local scale problems from scaling up. On the buy side, importers often provide inputs to their suppliers to mitigate food safety risks. Importers are highly cognizant of local market dynamics. With the widespread availability of substandard seeds, pesticides, and fertilizer in the market, importers believe that controlling or supplying quality inputs is critical to assert their control over production (EX 6; EX 9). Low-cost inputs often prove to be too tempting for their local suppliers, who already face razor thin margins. A major exporter located in Shandong imports all of their inputs from abroad, including seedlings, pesticides, and herbicides (EX 6).

Box 4.1   Liability Concerns in Home Markets

In the EU, the 1996 BSE crisis and subsequent dioxin contamination scare led to a complete loss of consumer confidence in the European food safety system. In response to these problems, the EU changed its policy, placing primary responsibility for producing safe food on the industry and suppliers through the implementation of HAACP (Vos 2000). The move toward increased producer responsibility was pursued earlier in the United Kingdom. The Food Safety Act of 1990 created a due diligence requirement for suppliers, shifting legal responsibility downstream. Prior to the reform, companies could claim the "warranty defense," which only necessitated that the company proves food was safe while under its direct control (Hobbs et al. 2002). The new legislation mandated that a food producer take "all reasonable steps" to ensure that food from upstream suppliers is safe. Upstream suppliers would also bear the burden of demonstrating to downstream buyers that they were handling food correctly (Hobbs et al. 2002). Thus, European importers must apply this same standard to Chinese food imports.

Japanese importers and retailers face significant legal pressures regarding food safety at home. The discovery of pesticide residues on Chinese-imported spinach in 2002 decimated consumer confidence and prompted the government to amend the Food Sanitation Law in late 2002, which imposed a series of stringent food safety regulations and increased the penalties for importers who failed to ensure the food safety of products from abroad. In addition to Japan's food safety laws, Japanese firms are also subject to the 1994 Product Liability Law (Jonker et al. 2004). Although enforcement of the law has been inconsistent, the mere threat of prosecution is considered significant enough to ensure compliance. The law states that importers are absolutely liable for the consequences of a food safety incident and that a retailer is entirely exempt provided contamination does not occur while food is under direct control of the retailer. The importer must pay for the costs of any recall, dispose of any defective food products, and compensate the victims. Companies that are found to violate food safety laws are viewed as high risk and become socially ostracized; suppliers and partners quickly dissociate with violators, often cancelling contracts immediately (Jonkers et al. 2004).

American importers are faced with the least pressures to exert on-site direct control. Prior to major food safety reforms in the United States, importers were not required by law to directly ensure that food imported complied with US food safety standards. Instead, importers could operate through agents who would attest to the compliance of food producers.

The indirect control mechanism coupled with the US FDA's low inspection rate of Chinese food imports was largely ineffective. In 2007, melamine-laced pet food led to more than 6,000 pet deaths and in 2008 melamine was found in rice protein and gluten products, prompting a massive overhaul of the import system.

Importers also examine carefully the initial growing conditions of fields, going from locality to locality to ensure production conditions are ideal. Soil conditions are highly variable throughout China and in some areas the soil has been contaminated by industrial pollution. Lipton, a major tea producer, found traces of toxic rare earths in its tea leaves because of the soil, and had to recall its products (Anderlini 2011). One exporter comments: "our importers conduct soil investigations, examine pesticide usage . . . but our main concern is always with the soil" (EX 9). In order to ensure that soil quality is fit for production, importers invest in expensive soil regeneration programs; one large firm estimates that managing their fields costs nearly RMB 100 to 200 million a year (EX 6). Other firms may partner with external testing laboratories to examine soil and water conditions (EX 6; EX 7).

Larger producers have cleaning and testing facilities on site to establish an additional level of food safety protection. For those exporting higher risk food products, such as freeze-dried food, investment in testing facilities is necessary: "the freeze-dried business is very difficult because it concentrates pesticides as [the] agricultural product is dried . . . we have a large cleaning facility near the port and also a lab (EX 3)."

When methods of prevention fail, importers have a number of tools available to sanction noncompliant food producers. Among them is locking delinquent exporters out of global markets. Noncompliance has been met with requests for outright contraction of the export sector, comprehensive trade bans, and the implementation of even stricter border controls, which substantially raises food safety costs (Calvin et al. 2006). When chloramphenicol was discovered in shrimp exported to the EU in 2002, shrimp exports immediately dropped by nearly 10% (UN Comtrade). The Japanese are particularly notorious for their severe responses toward noncompliant Chinese suppliers (Fackler 2007). A major eel exporter to Japan notes, "During 2006–2008, our [Japanese] clients became incredibly skeptical about the safety of Chinese products in general . . . we had to spend a great deal of time reassuring our products were safe . . . of course we still experienced a significant reduction in sales" (ZJ 19).

At the firm level, the threat of losing their hard-earned export license proves to be a significant deterrent for noncompliance. While investment in food safety management is expensive, one export producer that supplies the Japanese market comments, "We conduct soil investigations, examine pesticide residues, and at the time of purchase we conduct additional inspections. [A lab] conducts five-spot testing. . . . In the end we have to be more strict. I have to do this for the long-term...if one thing happens, I lose my credibility and I'll be shut out of the market" (EX 9).

Until their local food safety teams are adequately trained, foreign QA personnel are in control of the production process. Over time these roles are transitioned to local staff. This heavy-handed management style provides few opportunities for producers to engage in unsafe activities. Importers observe that direct control has led to a change in producer attitudes toward food safety over time (EX 3; EX 4; EX 6). Technical experts would note that initially compliance with protocols was half-hearted: staff would reuse contaminated gloves; hair was never neatly tucked beneath hair nets; and some workers would remove their face masks, complaining of the heat as they coughed on produce. One auditor comments, "Bless their hearts. They have the right idea. But, if you don't have your cap on the whole way, hair can still get into food. They think it's a uniform, and don't realize the food safety reasons behind the articles they wear" (EX4). Over time, however, conditions markedly improved. One vegetable producer notes that after learning how to meet Taiwanese safety standards, he upgraded his production to meet even more stringent Japanese standards (ZJ 17).

A strategy of direct control emphasizes the primacy of the global scale in governance, and actors are sensitized to problems emerging at the local scale. In due course, direct control leads to a change in producer attitudes toward food safety, and facilitates the transmission of food safety knowledge from the global to the local.

Addressing Multilevel/Multidimensional Conflict

Even though regulators and producers are agreed on the appropriate scale of governance, the integration of systems operating at different scales also entails reconciling different scaled understandings of food safety knowledge, jurisdiction, and managerial practice, which is often less straightforward. In the export sector, importers, third-party auditors, and independent labs operate together to facilitate the scaling down of food safety policies from the global to the local.

Third-party certifiers play an important role in ensuring that international food safety standards (knowledge-related dimension) are made comprehensible to China's food producers. In the EU, third-party certification primarily serves as a legal requirement to prove that all procedures were observed to ensure food safety. But, in China, auditors also provide important regulatory advice and technical assistance. Third-party auditors help to navigate local conditions while assisting producers in meeting international food safety standards. Export producers are rarely left to their own devices to achieve compliance, and are often guided step-by-step by auditors. One auditor comments, "In the export sector, we aren't just providing a legal service, we really are the main regulators . . . we bring a unified standard, have standard checks for risk, and are entirely accountable to consumers, which creates a very different dynamic than simply being tied to protecting a government standard" (EX 8).

Independent laboratory testing is also an important mechanism to facilitate the transfer of food safety knowledge from the global to lower scales. Laboratories provide a range of services that include tests for pesticide residues, soil and water quality, veterinary drug residues, microbiological contamination, and food additives. These labs provide assistance to farmers by teaching them how to comply with multiple food safety standards. Laboratories also offer consulting services to farmers when problems are identified through testing.

Scale politics, however, cannot be completely avoided as disagreements between third-party certifiers, independent labs, and national state regulators arise due to uncertain jurisdictional scale boundaries between global and national standard setters. The AQSIQ licensing system coexists uncomfortably with independent testing laboratories and third-party certifiers that are accountable to global authorities. AQSIQ officials view independent testing laboratories to be an unnecessary and burdensome addition to the formal regulatory apparatus. The head of an independent testing laboratory notes, "AQSIQ has always been very skeptical of our work . . . they believe that because they were already here . . . there was no need for anyone else . . . food safety in China must at some level be done by private auditors. It's impossible for a single agency to handle everything" (EX 4). Auditors also complain that global safety standards come into conflict with local AQSIQs that may privilege local food safety standards. One exporter comments, for example, "the AQSIQ system is subject to unhelpful regionalization, with local agencies establishing different protocols for pesticide residues and microbial contamination, being in compliance in one part of the country does not mean you are in compliance everywhere" (EX 8). These tensions can lead to AQSIQ creating restrictions as to how food safety information collected by third-party certifiers can be used and disseminated to the global scientific community, and sometimes even declaring certain types of food safety data to be "state secrets" (EX 4).

However, AQSIQ over time has grown accustomed to the role that third-party certifiers perform in training farmers about international food safety standards. In the last decade, AQSIQ has engaged in productive benchmarking projects with GlobalGAP and the Global Food Safety Initiative (GFSI) to upgrade food safety standards in the export sector (CNCA 2009). In 2003, the China Certification and Accreditation Administration (CNCA) sought to establish its own domestic certification based on GAP principles and began collecting appropriate materials for consultation. Based largely on the GlobalGAP standard, ChinaGAP was established in 2006. CNCA adopted a pilot scheme in 18 provinces, and by 2009 the program had established 552 pilot sites (Song et al. 2010). As of 2009, following a three-year benchmarking process, ChinaGAP had gained recognition by GlobalGAP, 603 ChinaGAP certificates had been issued and 15 certification bodies with 435 inspectors had been approved.

Scaling down on the managerial dimension of scale involves the careful translation of strategies (largest) into plans and then into actionable tasks (smallest). Importers cannot incur the risk that food producers, who are subject to different market pressures and production conditions at various scales will haphazardly, or worse, opportunistically, pick and choose from a menu of food safety standards. Therefore, importers use a system of contracts to ensure that broad food safety protocols and strategies developed in the head offices of agro-processors are translated into concrete tasks that local producers understand. Contracts vary from annual to multiyear commitments. Those who emphasize multiyear contracts believe that stable, long-term relationships encourage producers to invest in training. The multiyear contracts also provide local producers protection from global market fluctuations. Exporters contend that by providing security to producers it incentivizes farmers to produce according to international standards (EX 6). Others believe that shorter term contracts provide importers with greater leverage to manage producers because they can use the threat of cancellation to discipline producers, and have more flexibility to renegotiate contract terms as local production conditions change (EX 5). This system of contracts has the added benefit of teaching suppliers how they fit into the overall supply chain, and how actions further upstream can have significant impact downstream.

In summary, importers, third-party certifiers, and independent testing laboratories impose a system of hierarchical control. These actors work together to teach producers about food safety and to ensure that producers understand food safety practices developed at different scales across various dimensions.

Box 4.2 Case Study: Japanese Importers and Direct Control

Among foreign importers in China, the Japanese model of import management provides an almost ideal typical representation of using direct control to ensure the legibility of standards. Japanese companies are intimately involved in making food safety standards understandable to farmers. Japanese importers follow what is commonly referred to in the Japanese literature as a "development import" strategy, in which an importer attempts to vertically integrate suppliers rather than depend on a system of contracts (Iwata 1995 in Chen et al. 2005:111). Japanese trading companies, for example, regularly provide seeds, spores, and pesticides to farmers in China. Most Japanese food companies monitor the type, quantity, and number of applications of pesticide usage (Jonker et al. 2004). Importers also invest in production facilities to improve food safety monitoring and surveillance capacity. In many cases, Japanese firms will embed resident staff at Chinese farms to manage and oversee production. Often, Japanese importers purchase a supplier's entire production to encourage producers to tailor their entire facility to meet the demands of the importer (EX 3).

Chinese producers note that the Japanese are extraordinarily hands-on in their management of suppliers: "our Japanese buyers come to China often to manage everything. They conduct onsite inspections and teach new techniques. They have standards for everything even for color, shape, and size. They are extremely careful when it comes to quality management" (EX 5). Due to strict requirements, many exporters comment that the Japanese approach serves as a model for "best practice" management of the export sector. However, adopting a Japanese approach is prohibitively expensive, and only supported by a Japanese consumer base willing to pay higher prices. Yet compared to other export management models, one specialist comments, "The Japanese are better in their ability to organize their own production networks . . . most of them send their own technicians that remain on site to supervise their producers and help them to comply with food safety requirements" (EX 1).

Addressing Scale Externalities

To effectively manage scale politics, systems must also sensitize actors to processes unfolding at other scales, and develop appropriate mechanisms to respond to these changes. Specifically, a system must have procedures in place that prevent actors from falling victim to *ignorance*, in which scale externalities are ignored, or *minimization*, where small-scale problems are characterized as isolated events or considered unimportant for the system at large. A high level of adaptability in the export sector optimizes regulatory management, enabling private and public regulators to identify new risks and to close loopholes that develop between the global

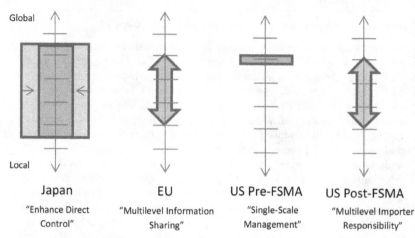

FIGURE 4.1 Different Country Adaptations to Address Food Safety

and local scales. For example, the implementation of BRC and Global-GAP standards are frequently reassessed at the local scale to identify the unintended consequences of applying a "global" standard in a Chinese context. China interacts regularly with its trading partners to renegotiate food safety agreements, seek technical assistance, and legislate new food safety requirements as food safety circumstances change. And, because the export sector is ring-fenced, it enables the government to tailor the sector to the needs of trading partners without overhauling its entire regulatory apparatus.

Perhaps more notably, exporters, importers, and Chinese and foreign regulators have developed specific mechanisms to prevent small-scale problems from going unnoticed or unreported and becoming widespread. These measures vary according to food trade dyad. For example, Japan and China have established procedures to enhance direct control at each scale of governance when food adulteration problems arise. The EU favors a more multilevel, indirect approach by enhancing information flows up and down scales. The United States has a different approach and actively cooperates with China to develop a multilevel system of importer responsibility.

Sino-Japanese Food Safety Relations: Enhance Direct Control
Japan's adaptation strategy involves tightening control over regulatory and production processes at each scale of governance. Following two food

safety crises in 2002 and 2008, Japan and China successfully concluded a series of negotiations to rectify perceived weaknesses in the export sector in China, which ultimately was codified in the Japan-China Food Safety Agreement of 2010. Japan secured more direct involvement in food safety regulation by gaining access to food safety investigations, and selecting export-approved producers.

This style of adaptation is best reflected in the Sino-Japanese spinach crisis of 2002. After Japanese authorities discovered containers of frozen spinach laced with an insecticide barred in Japan, the Japanese moved swiftly to strengthen border controls and directly intervene in China's export management system. To prevent an issue of local noncompliance from China cascading throughout the Japan-China food safety system, the Japanese and Chinese governments immediately developed new measures at each scale of governance. At the transnational scale, the incident prompted the Japanese to amend the Food Sanitation Law in 2002 and implement a more stringent "positive list" system as a means to strengthen inspections at the border, to which the Chinese acquiesced. In addition to new border controls, at the national scale in China, the Japanese government demanded that the Chinese strengthen their closed agricultural export system by instituting a health certification program and further restricting the number of export certificates issued to firms seeking to export to Japan (Jonker et al. 2004). At the local scale of production, Chinese and Japanese authorities approved a scheme in which the Japanese government conducted a series of yearly inspections of all processing plants for certain foods produced in China (USHRCEC 2007). For spinach, the Japanese and Chinese agreed to license 45 Chinese companies, and specified that these farmers could only grow spinach on their own plots and not buy from other producers (Fackler 2007). Spinach producers were subject to additional inspections by Japanese officials prior to gaining export approval.

Sino-EU Food Safety Relations: Multilevel Information Flows

Compared to the Japanese, the EU has adapted its food production and distribution system to prevent food safety problems from cascading through a multilevel approach that facilitates the transfer of information to multiple scales of governance. The EU-China food safety system experienced two major shocks: in 2002, when EU member states discovered residues of the antibiotic chloramphenicol in several products from China, and in 2008, following the identification of melamine in a number of dairy products. Consultation between both governments occurred immediately

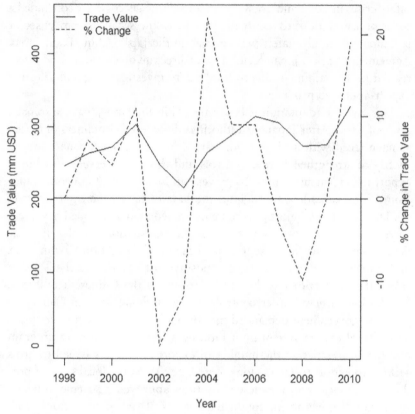

FIGURE 4.2 Sino-Japanese Frozen Spinach Trade, 1998–2010
Source: UN COMSTAT Database.

after both incidents, and the EU and Chinese authorities formed a joint study group to address European food safety concerns.

In response to the crises, the EU began facilitating the transfer of information regarding food safety through the EU-China Trade Project (EUCTP), an ongoing European commitment to China to assist China's entry to the WTO. The food safety office of the EUCTP held workshops with Chinese officials and producers at various levels of the Chinese government on food safety best practices and the development of food safety standards. From 2004 to 2009, the EU conducted 10 training programs with officials and food producers, 3 workshops and conferences, 2 study visits to the EU, published 3 manuals and guidance papers, and a joint study on the organic food and seafood product safety (EUCTP 2009). A majority of these activities focused on local scale issues. Phase II of the

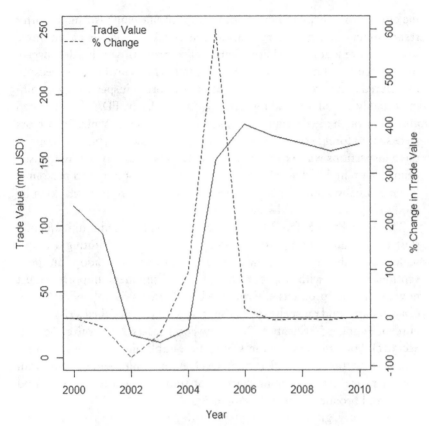

FIGURE 4.3 Sino-European Shrimp Trade, 2000–2010
Source: UN COMSTAT Database.

EUCTP was targeted at issues concerning the national market, and provided support to help the Chinese develop their traceability system, pesticide controls, and scientific risk assessment mechanisms. At the transnational scale, a memorandum of understanding (MOU) on administrative cooperation was also signed between AQSIQ and DG SANCO in 2006 (DGSANCO 2006). The MOU details an agreement to exchange information, to conduct annual working meetings, to create contact points, and to keep shared information on unsafe products confidential.

Sino-US Food Safety Relations: From Single Level to Multilevel Solutions

The bilateral US-China food safety relationship is particularly instructive because the United States has changed its strategy from one focused on the global scale through border inspections to one emphasizing importer responsibility and private regulation that engages producers at multiple scales. Before 2011, the United States relied primarily on border inspections as the frontline of its food safety regime. This is problematic because the United States conducts a low number of border inspections, examining roughly 1% of all food imports (GAO 2008). The FDA also operated abroad through the Foreign Food Inspection Program, in which inspectors were sent to foreign countries to inspect food production, but the scope of these inspections was extremely narrow. The inspection program focused primarily on high risk establishments due to a lack of qualified personnel (Gale & Buzby 2009). This regime was found extraordinarily lacking by food safety experts worldwide.

The 2011 Food Safety Modernization Act represented a fundamental shift in the American approach to import safety by instituting a multi-scale approach. The FDA now mandates that importers adopt an interventionist stance with respect to their Chinese suppliers. Importers must now certify that products entering the United States comply with American standards and must ensure that suppliers have established a risk-based Foreign Supplier Verification Program (Food Safety Modernization Act, Sec 301). Foreign importers in China are establishing quality assurance programs at the farm and factory level. As a result, leading American importers are now stationing permanent staff in China to monitor food safety, and broader market developments.

In summary, given the changing nature of food safety risks as global food trade expands, regulatory systems based on control must continually adjust to respond to new conditions at multiple scales in order to prevent small-scale problems from cascading throughout the ever-growing system. Global, national, provincial, and local scales of governance work in concert to accommodate different adaptive strategies based on national preferences of regulatory style. As new food safety risks surface, new solutions can be devised and implemented.

CONCLUSION

In this chapter, we have seen that a centralized, hierarchical regulatory system emphasizing direct, adaptable control skillfully integrates regulators, importers, and producers operating at the global, national, and local scales. Because the export sector is limited to China's best food producers, who aim to gain market access in global markets, producers and regulators are oriented toward following food safety best practices developed at the global scale. As food safety standards and practices are scaled down, actors are attuned to the multiscalar, multidimensional implications of scale. Also, each trading dyad has developed institutionalized mechanisms to address negative scale externalities.

Direct, adaptable control is a pragmatic response to China's poor food safety record in its broader domestic sector and its deepening integration in the global food trading system. In recent years, there has been an internationalization of food safety practices through the WTO's Codex Alimentarius Commission (Ansell & Vogel 2006). Also, the increased food trade between developed and developing countries has resulted in the diffusion of food safety "best practices" worldwide and harmonization of food safety standards. Chinese authorities are acutely aware that countries that fail to meet global food safety standards are unable to sustain a robust and growing food export sector.

China's experience in establishing an effective food safety regime in its export sector will prove instructive for other developing countries that seek to increase their share of the global food trade. Nigeria has worked tirelessly to establish export safety practices in their fishery sectors (Maclaren et al. 2006; Bagumire et al. 2009). Brazil and India have bifurcated food production into export and domestic sectors, using stringent licensing or specialized trading firms to manage food exports. Taking note of China's employment of a strategy of direct, adaptable control may help to improve food safety performance.

Centralized, hierarchical modes of control, however, are costly and require high levels of technical expertise. While China's elite export sector may offer useful benchmarks regarding how to effectively govern in a multiscale context, we must consider to what extent this model needs to be modified to operate effectively in the country's more unwieldy domestic market—a subject to be dealt with in greater detail in Chapter 8. In the next chapter, we turn to a more bottom-up strategy, and examine another model of governing across scales that operates according to a decentralized, collaborative framework of governance.

5

CSA Markets

"I Don't Sell Vegetables, I Sell Trust"

In September 2010, vendors from local farms surrounding Beijing arrived at a small venue in Chaoyang District to sell "safe, healthy, and local food." A small group of 160 food safety-conscious consumers, distressed by increasing scandals, anxiously shopped at the various vendor stalls. Unlike organic food consumers in the United States who visit farmer's markets to avoid unspecified, long-term health effects from consuming conventionally produced food, China's CSA consumers fear falling victim to one of China's oft-reported food safety scandals. Alarmed by regulatory failures and modern agricultural methods, these consumers took food safety into their own hands: buyers questioned farmers on pesticide usage, they requested production site visits, and inquired about planting conditions and the types of seed and fertilizer administered. Produce and meat prices were on average three times the price of products that could be purchased at supermarkets, but there was little haggling. Consumers were willing to pay high prices due to the severity of the food safety problems in the broader market. Relationships continued beyond the physical marketplace as consumers traveled outside Beijing to inspect production, to help farmers with the harvest, or to donate much-needed equipment. Two months later, over 2000 individuals attended the second farmer's market.

The Beijing Farmer's Market is but a small part of a growing CSA movement in China aimed at ensuring food safety outside the usual regulatory system for food production (Yu 2011; Xu 2012). Currently, due to significantly higher prices and geographical constraints, most consumers are upper-middle-class urbanites. The CSA movement seeks to develop an alternative food market that emphasizes safety, sustainable development, and close ties between producers and consumers. Unofficial estimates of the number of CSA projects, which include multiple producers, range from less than 100 (Gale 2011) to several hundred (CSA 2). They are primarily concentrated around large metropolitan centers such as Beijing, Shanghai, Tianjin, Chongqing, Chengdu, and Guangzhou (Gale 2011). Other, smaller sites are located in Henan and Anhui (Day 2008). Farmer's markets, the primary distribution channel for CSA producers, are growing in popularity. In 2010, the Beijing Farmer's Market convened more than 40 times, with an average of 4,000 individuals in attendance (Wu 2012). Shanghai's farmer's markets began operating soon afterward, in May 2011. Markets have since spread throughout the country.

China's CSA sector, which has also been credited with a high level of food safety, provides another example of an effective governance strategy that mitigates scale politics. In contrast to the export sector, the CSA sector's governance framework is decentralized and collaborative. Where governance in the export sector is centralized in a single regulatory authority (AQSIQ), the CSA sector is governed by local councils at the municipal, county, and township levels, and is loosely affiliated with provincial associations. Where the export sector is hierarchical, governance in the CSA sector is collaborative, with local producers, government, and NGOs negotiating food safety processes and production protocols that are sensitive to processes emerging at each scale.

Social trust, as opposed to direct, adaptable control, plays a crucial role in this decentralized, collaborative system of governance. Social trust explains why individuals submit to regulatory authority, how the system is maintained, and why compliance is high. This dynamic is best captured by a statement made by a market organizer: "I don't sell vegetables, I sell trust" (CSA 11). The CSA market represents more than simple commodity exchange; it offers producers and consumers a guarantee of food safety. The fact that the cost of CSA-produced food can be 3 to 10 times higher than that sold at other convenient retail outlets (Gale 2011) indicates that the monetary value of trust is high.[1] The system is reinforced by a self-regulating, dense network of actors with strong mutual obligations, high levels of reciprocity, and a shared identity across scales (Brown & Miller 2008; Goland 2002).

---

[1] Gale (2011) shows how a CSA farm's cabbage costs nearly 10 times that of cabbage in regular produce markets, and that the price of pork is 3 times that of pork in supermarkets.

In the broadest sense, the CSA sector can be seen as an experiment in self-regulation. Self-regulation refers to the use of "internal control systems that assure product quality where the system participants set, monitor, and self-certify the control parameters" (Henson & Caswell 1999: 594). Scholars assert that as the state transitions out of its central role in coordinating governance (Braithwaite 2008), informal, self-regulation provides a way forward to address market failures and common pool resource problems (Ostrom 2006). Self-regulation leads to the development of systems that are flexible (Coglianese & Lazer 2003), and better utilize expert knowledge (Provost 2010). Some critics argue that self-regulation leads to a "hollowing out of the state," weakening a central state's ability to coordinate policy, standardize regulation, and maintain public oversight of private actors (Bevir 2007; Klijn 2002). However, an examination of CSA governance of food safety suggests that self-regulation performs a much-needed function when state food regulation has been viewed to be ineffective.

The CSA governance framework should not be viewed as a panacea to China's food safety problems. The CSA system is effective in achieving the regulatory objectives it sets for itself. However, as we shall see, these are relatively simplistic safety goals, and do not address the panoply of food safety problems that producers face in the broader market. Another point of concern is that food safety auditors argue that most CSA producers still face risks of microbial contamination. Individuals in the CSA farm focus primarily on reducing pesticides, growth hormones, and chemical fertilizers. But, few are familiar with the intricacies of microbiological contamination or the proper use of chemical additives. One auditor commented, "You might have products that are pesticide-free. But, if you don't understand microbiological contamination, you might have a terrible outbreak of E. coli poisoning" (EX 18). Finally, CSA production volumes cannot approximate that of conventional agriculture. As several food safety auditors note, "We tried 'organic' farming for hundreds of years, and we had periods of starvation. Organic production can't solve our country's problems" (EX 1).

This chapter focuses on CSA sites that are considered to be "successful" models of the CSA experiment in China, and is not meant to portray what *all* CSA producers are like. As in the case of the export sector, I seek to explore governance frameworks and strategies that may serve as models for better understanding scale politics. In this case, we take a deeper look at how a decentralized, collaborative mode of governance can prevent and preempt coordination problems due to scale politics.

A DECENTRALIZED, COLLABORATIVE FRAMEWORK OF GOVERNANCE

The CSA governance system operates through a decentralized network of farmers, markets, and local councils that together ensure the quality of food. Local organic farmer's markets play an important role as institutional purveyors of trust by nominating knowledgeable and independent gatekeepers to establish conditions of entry. As in the case of traditional local butchers in Europe, the farmer's markets are relied upon as institutions to help to distinguish food quality and safety on behalf of consumers. The embedded participants are relied upon for their specialized expertise and familiarity with producers (Brown & Miller 2008). The organic market committee in Beijing, for example, helps select producer participants on the basis of the committee members' personal experiences with these producers, and the extent to which these producers could be considered "ethical," "trustworthy," and "not entirely driven by a profit motive" (CSA 11). The CSA organizers seek to develop the market at a measured pace free from the influence of large corporations and focus on building relationships between local farmers and consumers: "right now the system is built on trust and that must be garnered over time. We don't want to get too close to big companies because they will want to try to control us. We enjoy our independence. We will continue to work with individuals who want to establish friendships with sellers, and build trust networks" (CSA 11).

Local councils involving farmers and their consumers operate within a collaborative framework of governance. CSA farms have some form of "open surveillance" (*kaifang jiandu* 开放监督) in which consumers are invited to inspect production and participate at significant junctures in the agricultural season, such as planting and harvest. This practice helps to reinforce the connection between consumers and producers and to sensitize them to developments at the local scale. Farms are typically on the periphery of major cities, and consumers need only to drive a few hours to visit their supplier farms. Farms commit to transparency, providing customers with information on seed type, plant management, production volumes, cost structures, and their personal finances. The Dreamland Eco-Farm in Chongming County, Shanghai, for example, states in its governing manifesto that "during the delivery period, the customer has the right to bring [his or her] family to observe farm production" (Ecoland). Consumers are invited to monthly town-hall-style meetings in which producers present information on new developments on their farms. Some farms also run educational activities with nearby schools. Another CSA farm, Biofarm has organized a program called "roots and shoots" to teach students about organic farming and community farming (BioFarm website). By opening the black box of production, local producers seek to engender trust with their municipal consumers: "we work hard to publicize our efforts through our newsletter and we have a network of farms and an online forum about farming. We build social capital by engaging the public through multiple partnerships," (CSA 10).

Local CSA projects are embedded within a broader social movement (社会运动 *shehui yundong*), which promotes a high level of local solidarity and enhances collaboration. While there is no overarching governing body, a common set of principles undergird the system. First, CSA farmers state explicitly that they oppose conventional agriculture. Second, the movement brings together social groupings that are on the periphery of mainstream agriculture. The CSA movement in China brings together wealthy urbanites, farmers, and NGOs united by a clear set of values. Academics and policy makers affiliated with the Rural Reconstruction Movement have also expressed their support of CSA agriculture. Third, CSA farmers in China commit themselves to sustainable agriculture, organic production, and safe food. The ultimate goal for many CSA farms is to facilitate a shift in consumer preferences for sustainable agriculture. In Sichuan, CSA farms and organizations have helped to develop the "green consumer alliance" to promote the ideal of limited production. A leader in the association presents this view most clearly: "a large part of the CSA movement is to promote an idea of 'restricted consumerism.' People need to be alright with less. [The food industry] has created an unhealthy atmosphere where everyone feels like it is their right to purchase and eat all that they want" (CSA 2).

The CSA movement is not monolithic. While CSA participants broadly espouse the values of sustainable agriculture and limited production, three distinct groups have emerged as sponsors of CSA initiatives. Corporations, government, and NGOs play an important role in the movement's development and have different objectives. Corporations strive to develop the CSA movement into a profitable business model, while the government has tried to co-opt the CSA movement to operate within its own formal organic certification system. NGOs seek to integrate CSA farms into broader transnational networks while preserving the market's local nature.

We now explore how this decentralized, collaborative framework is effective in mitigating scale politics by defining the scale of governance for its participants, addressing multidimensional conflict across scales, and mitigating scale externalities.

Local Governance, Local Challenges, and Local Solutions

In the CSA system, the scale of governance is focused on the local degree-of-zoom, and actors go to great lengths to preserve the local orientation of the system. In direct contrast to the export sector, producers contend that the vast majority of food safety problems emerge due to highly competitive market pressures at the national and global scales of production and distribution.

The strong emphasis on the local scale of governance is reinforced by a collaborative system of shared regulatory responsibility focused on pressures and processes unfolding at the local scale. First, CSA farms participate in *risk-sharing* in the interests of local producers. Consumers must commit to purchasing a certain volume of produce before the planting season. A portion of the purchase money is paid up front. In the event of a poor harvest due to weather conditions, consumers pay for a portion of the farmer's loss. Second, food prices are not simply determined by the market, but also account for the challenges that exist in the local production context, including the amount of labor invested and the welfare of the farmer, reflecting a sense of *shared burdens*. In the case of small CSA farmers, organic production can be extremely labor intensive— consumer labor contributions are absolutely necessary: "my produce is still the cheapest in the organic market. We really need to build good relations with consumers . . . we depend on them to come out to help at harvest so things can be cheaper" (CSA 4). Third, farmers depend on their customers that operate in larger scale social networks to help them find additional buyers in the cities, which evidences a sense of *shared opportunity*. Despite operating at a continuous loss for three years, for example, one farmer observed that it was the social network that was important: "we really like the CSA model. It's good for business and I get to meet a lot of new people . . . and my customers come and take care of my farm" (CSA 6).

Farmers feel a sense of obligation toward other producers in their local community, which prevents excessive competition and tampers the need to expand the scale of the CSA market. There is a generally accepted consensus among CSA producers that they are building an alternative market, which is collaborative and geared toward the preservation of food safety, and not increasing production. Many realize that if any individual CSA producer sells unsafe food, the broader CSA market will be discredited (CSA 3; CSA 6; CSA 8). The failure of China's formal organic certification scheme serves as a cautionary tale to CSA producers who understand that it only takes one cheater to destroy the market (Macleod 2011).

Producers view other farmers as collaborators rather than as competitors. CSA farms do not have corporate secrets, or try to poach consumers from other producers. They form local associations and share best practices with one another: "we formed a little producer association and there are about six of us that go and tour other farms and we try to learn from one another. We need to break through the isolation. We need to increase trust between ourselves so we can then impart that same feeling of trust to our consumers" (CSA 1). This high level of social trust enables local farms to work together during difficult times, such as market downturns or inclement weather.

Due to the primacy given to the local scale of production, CSA farmers do not drive other producers out of the market by increasing production to unsustainable levels, or through aggressive pricing. In China, most producers do not view the organic market as being oversaturated, and are confident in the market's potential for orderly growth (Zhao 2011; CSA 8; CSA 16). Since producers have a committed group of consumers, most are not concerned about or driven by competition. In fact, CSA farms of all sizes—those with customer bases of more than 8,000 clients as well as others with less than 100—view the introduction of additional players as a positive development for the organic market. In Sichuan, CSA farms and organizers have helped spread the concept of sustainable local farming to Yuantian, Yunqiao, and Jianyang villages and to Chifeng and Xuankan townships (CSA 2). Collaborative efforts seek to effect a change in consumer culture, attract new customers, and encourage the spread of the CSA concept throughout the country (Jiang 2011).

The overarching social nature of the local CSA food system "softens" the economic incentives of producers, but does not altogether eliminate the desire to scale up production, or link to the broader market. Hinrichs (2000) cautions that researchers should not become too enamored by the strong sense of community and quaintness of localized exchange and overlook the demands of the market. Notwithstanding broad consensus about the desirability of cooperative, trusting market behavior, producers, consumers, and distributors face significant pressures to lower costs, expand production, and engage in destructive overcompetitive behavior.

The localized market ecosystem is still fragile. A bad harvest or difficult season may induce producers to seek shortcuts in production and use unauthorized inputs. Producers mentioned that many seek to return to conventional farming if they feel that consumers are not paying a "fair price" for their products. On the demand side, consumers also face strong pressures to leave the CSA system for the convenience of the broader food market. A common grievance among consumers is that the CSA market is inconvenient due to a lack of choice in the CSA food supply. Certain foods are only available during a particular growing season. Supply can also be erratic. Depending on growing conditions, consumers may be supplied with too much or too little food. As a result, some consumers lose interest in CSA production and may renege on commitments to purchase food from farmers.

Other pressures for leaving the local CSA production network for the industrialized production and distribution system involve the high start-up costs in organic farming. Farms previously under conventional agricultural cultivation must first go through "withdrawal." Over time, chemical fertilizers cause soil to lose its ability to retain water and nutrients. Prolonged pesticide usage results in highly resistant pests that can overwhelm entire fields when stronger dosages or new pesticides are not administered. The withdrawal process can take as long as two to three years, which is prohibitively costly for small farmers: "in 2007, when I started out, we faced a number of significant challenges in ecological farming. The pests ate everything... the soil was in the process of changing. I couldn't grow anything" (CSA 6). For some, the use of pesticides and chemical fertilizers was a necessary compensation for the chronic agricultural labor shortage in the countryside: "for a lot of homes around here... everyone is working in the city. The high use of inputs helps to cut down on the amount of work" (CSA 6). Many farmers have to return to conventional agriculture because CSA farming is not economically feasible. Only the most ideologically committed can survive.

The local scale of the sector, which promotes frequent interactions with their consumers and support from NGOs and other CSA farmers, helps orient them toward providing safe food. Given countervailing market pressures, an overriding norm of social trust is necessary and serves as a collaborative dynamic to realign interests that need continual reinforcement.

Addressing Multidimensional Issues

When participants in local CSA systems engage with actors operating at larger scales, the primary focus and intent of such interaction is to provide greater access to knowledge and resources while preserving the multidimensional coherence of the local scale system. The local scale of the food safety system is reflected across multiple dimensions: knowledge-related, jurisdictional, and managerial. Actors within this decentralized system emphasize the importance of local knowledge, local certification, and local management. CSA farming standards are developed by trusted fellow producers and thus standards are viewed as rational and well-suited to the demands of ecological farming. Also, the CSA system has been able to develop its own standards independent of central food safety directives.

In terms of the knowledge dimension of scale, most CSA farmers actively resist practices pushed by businesses focused on broader scales of distribution. They are particularly resistant to multinational interests that seek to co-opt CSA farms into their own supply chains and promote technically complex food safety standards. Attempts to impose advanced, modern agricultural techniques on CSA farmers, such as hydroponics or drip irrigation, failed because farmers considered them to be unsuitable due to the high input costs and the technical know-how required. "We do not want to work with new, high technology techniques. It's an admission that sustainable, traditional agriculture is not possible" (CSA 2). Instead, CSA farms invest in techniques that are "traditional" and that "seek balance with nature" (CSA 3). CSA farms place major emphasis on creating cyclical economies in which water is reused, fertilizer is produced locally, and bio-diversity is utilized as a means to combat pests and disease. CSA farmers assert that they must revive techniques that have been underemphasized during the era of industrialized agricultural production and combat what some NGO supporters have called "agricultural illiteracy" (*nongmang*). CSA farms seek to recover "traditional" techniques: "our methods are old. People who are 40–50 years old are familiar with these old methods. Remember, China has a 4,000 to 5,000–year history of agricultural production" (CSA 13).

This is not to say that operatives within the CSA system are precluded from the global discourse about organic production. Transnational CSA organizations actively provide support to CSA producers (Luo, email communication, 2011). For example, the Japan Organic Society and International Federation of Agricultural Movements regularly engage with local CSA programs and provide technical assistance to farms and promote dialogue among CSA farms. However, while this assistance informs local producers about new best practices developed across the globe, CSA producers are highly selective as they apply these techniques to a local system.

In jurisdictional terms, CSA farmers prefer locally based, informally enforced standards contributing to group solidarity and enhancing social trust. Local CSA councils develop new food safety standards to fit local circumstances. The national government's attempts to integrate the CSA system into its formal "organic" certification program among CSA farmers have largely failed. Farmers believe that the state system of regulation actively disempowers farmers, and farmers prefer informal, ad hoc approaches to address food safety as problems emerge. Most importantly, they believe that it is most important that these standards are developed by other farmers whom they trust.

China established its first organic standard in 1992, the "green food AA standard," which was managed by the Ministry of Agriculture. In 1994, organic certification responsibility was moved to the National Bureau of Environmental Protection. In 2005, China established its most detailed standards and rules for organic production, which were set by the General Administration for Quality, Supervision, Inspection and Quarantine (AQSIQ). The government has actively promoted its organic certification scheme, seeing organic farming as a significant area for growth in agriculture. In 2006, China's organic exports were valued at US$350 million, less than 0.05% of global market share. By 2015, Chinese experts hoped to capture nearly 5% of global market share in organic produce (EUCTP 2008: 5). Domestically, in 2007, domestic sales of organic production were approximately US$1.13 billion. As of 2007, 2,500 producers were certified to market their products as organic.

The main objection to the state-sponsored certification system is that many CSA farmers consider the formal organic provisions to be slanted toward the development of modernized agriculture, which would effectively bar CSA producers from the standard-setting process and move the CSA system away from its localized focus. In effect, formalized state action actively seeks to alter the system's reliance on social trust and transition it to industrialized, depersonalized agricultural production. The organic certification program, for example, involves the use of techniques that cannot be employed by most farmers and creates a dependence on expensive state-certified "organic" inputs.

Instead of formal organic certification, CSA farmers prefer to use the terms "ecological (*shengtai* 生态)," "natural (*ziran* 自然)," or "biodynamic (*shengwuhuoli* 生物活力)" to describe their farming practices.[2] This is not to suggest that the CSA movement's agricultural policies are diametrically opposed to the formal organic standard. Both the CSA system and the formal organic certification program seek the production of safe food on a sustainable basis. For example, the organic regulations and CSA provisions both encourage the use of dried rice husks to cover fallow soil to preserve nutrients and discourage monoculture. Many CSA farmers, however, suggest that the profit motive becomes paramount in the state-sponsored organic system and thus reject the state's regulatory authority: "our development models are too different. We want to expand slowly and [the official organic cooperatives] want big production and aren't concerned about the negative consequences of their production style" (CSA 5).

CSA farmers believe that an overriding profit motive is the root cause of a rash of scandals related to the state's organic certification system. Farmers have used a number of underhanded or illegal tactics to market their products as organic: (1) using expired organic labels (Wang 2012); (2) gaining certification for one particular production base, but using organic labels on all produce (Gale & Buzby 2009); (3) using counterfeit labels (Kim 2011); (4) bribing certifiers and auditors (Neumann & Barboza 2010). Supermarkets have also been known to place nonorganic items on organic shelves to confuse consumers (Bradsher 2011). CSA farmers do not want to be affiliated with the certification scheme because they fear that their reputation will become tainted by association.

Thus, an increasingly competitive relationship has emerged between the national government and local networks of CSA farmers. Some state officials do not support the emergence of the CSA movement as a viable alternative system. They charge that CSA farmers are inappropriately using the term "organic" to market their food, and that farmer's markets are "getting dangerously close to the edge" of legality (Xinhua 2012). However, thus far, the state has made no overt attempts to regulate the emerging sector.

In terms of management, CSA farms are largely focused on developing their own operating rules tailored to their specific local conditions, rather than following a fixed standard operating procedure designed to manage

---

[2] These terms were used on the websites of the Phoenix Hills Commune, Dream Land Eco-Farm, and Little Donkey Farm.

production in a large-scale system. There is no "model" of CSA development: farms across the country exhibit different management structures, ownership models, emphasis on work shares, levels of employment of local farmers, and integration with the local economy. One farm in Shanghai is operated by three investors who operate an e-commerce platform. Another CSA project in Beijing is managed by a consortium of academics and NGOs. The Anlong Village Project in Chengdu operates as part of an environmental sustainability program of an NGO. CSA farms are designed to complement the local communities to which they supply food.

CSA farms are encouraged to experiment with a mix of incentive-based reward systems and enforcement mechanisms based on their local conditions, which helps to empower enlisted members to be proactive in monitoring food safety. In turn, these schemes further induce producers and consumers to preserve the CSA's local scales. For example, on one CSA farm in Pudong, production is monitored by locally nominated production team leaders. Other CSA projects incentivize farmers through novel reward schemes: at a farm in Haidian, Beijing, farmers are rewarded for their level of participation in community activities as well as the quality of their produce. Individuals who have worked with the farm receive a small subsidy for length of service. Those who use good cultivation techniques are awarded a larger subsidy. The highest reward, a rent-free parcel of land, is given to those who contribute and train other CSA members.

Flexibility is built into the operating system. First, the horizontal nature of CSA producer relationships promotes a dynamic, collaborative framework for enforcement. CSA producers understand that conditions may change. There are no contracts or binding legal agreements, which facilitates flexibility (CSA 3; CSA 11). Second, leaders within the system rotate positions of authority in order to prevent the accumulation of power by a single participant and to encourage cooperative decision-making. In one producer association, the leadership structure was even changed to have two rather than one team leader to prevent uneven development among producers (CSA 2).

CSA farms are only loosely affiliated through national CSA conferences or transnational NGOs. For example, one farm helps organize conferences among CSA farms around Beijing, and the CSA Green Alliance organizes farmers in southern Sichuan (CSA 2; CSA 10). Farmer's markets do view themselves as being part of a network, but different cities adopt different standards for their suppliers. The Shanghai market has a stronger anticapitalist orientation, refusing to allow larger, more corporate farms from participating (CSA 11). Producers interpret what constitutes "community-supported agriculture" differently. For example, some contend that a CSA farm that is formally associated with the government organic certification scheme should not be viewed as a traditional CSA farm.

The CSA governing system preserves its local orientation across multiple dimensions of scale. Knowledge is locally derived. Pressures to conform to the national organic production standards are rejected in favor of local eco-friendly techniques. And, management techniques are developed in line with local conditions.

Addressing Scale Externalities from Below and Above

Local participants understand the consequences of scalar externalities in which small-scale noncompliance results in large-scale consequences, or large-scale processes adversely affect small-scale systems. As a result, CSA farmers have developed self-enforcement mechanisms to prevent dynamics "from below and above" from spiraling out of control.

Noncompliance at the local scale can quickly destroy the trust that prevails throughout the entire system. "We have to be responsible for our neighbors. You can't let them get away with stuff, otherwise it will come back to haunt you, too (CSA 6)." Because trust is at the core of the system, a single food safety incident on one farm can lead to the collapse of the system. There is no "certification" system in place. Producers are willing to disclose as much information as necessary to engender consumer trust in their product (CSA 13). Also, they believe that their "face-to-face" interactions serve as their guarantee of food safety (CSA 11). If one person decides to cut corners, the entire system is called into question.

A vigilant system of self-enforcement and monitoring has been set in place. In the broader literature, self-enforcement arrangements are viewed as effective because inspectors share the same attitudes and understanding of production as those whom they inspect (Provost 2010; Rees 1988), and because they are viewed as problem-solvers rather than enforcement officials (Prakash 2000). In the CSA context in China, producers have formed "green associations" in which farmers visit other members in CSA networks at the provincial scale on a monthly basis to observe production and to offer advice. This roving group of local participants in the self-regulated system disseminates best practices, updates production standards to evolving local conditions, and enforces food safety rules.

CSA farmers have also tried to shield themselves from scale externalities generated by larger scale production and distribution systems. Private and state-owned companies alike endorse the Enterprise + Base + Farmer model. Yet, farmers who participate in this model complain about the significant power asymmetry between downstream buyers and farms. That is, head offices of large-scale enterprises are ignorant of how decisions made at their scale of operation affect producers operating at smaller scales. CSA farmers believe that standardization programs set by head offices means less sensitivity to conditions on the ground, leaving farmers with little leeway to make necessary adjustments to how farms are managed.

The common belief among CSA farmers is that a unilateral control structure often places unreasonable demands on farmers, which inevitably leads to food safety problems. For example, a common complaint is that dragonhead enterprises operate as monopsonies, arbitrarily setting prices for products and having unrealistic expectations for controlling costs, which drive many farmers to cheat: "the basic premise is that a company has some of its own production under their direct control, but a decent portion of it is sent out to other smaller finders and other production units. These units are often less capable of maintaining quality/safety in their food production processes. The large producer often unilaterally decides that they want to sell the product at a lower price, which is transmitted down this unmanaged chain in the form of cost cutting in every way possible, which results in illegal food safety behavior" (*NYT* Interview).

While isolation from agro-processing supply chains shields them from scale externalities of the broader market, this decision is not without consequences. The high cost of CSA food is irrational from the perspective of the national food market, and precludes expansion to populations with lower incomes. In addition, CSA farms, by rejecting the official organic food scheme, have also eliminated the possibility of reshaping the certification program in favor of the CSA model. For now, access to safe CSA-produced food is limited to isolated pockets of privileged consumers possessing the means to purchase safe food.

CONCLUSION: SOME IMPLICATIONS AND QUESTIONS

A decentralized, collaborative mode of governance facilitates definition of a unified scale of governance, coordinates food safety activities across multiple dimensions of scale, and leads to the development of enforcement strategies that are dynamic and sensitive to emerging conditions at the local scale.

The literature on self-regulatory systems generally hypothesizes that successful self-regulation is dependent upon the presence of a well-functioning state that can intervene if such regulation fails (Heritier & Lehmkuhl 2008). However, this chapter shows that successful self-regulation can take hold under certain scale conditions without state action and, in fact, the CSA food production system eschews most formal governmental support. A self-regulatory system can utilize strong local norms to improve food safety outcomes.

I will now turn to consider China's large and heterogeneous domestic sector, with its myriad food safety problems. Up to this point in the analysis of food safety in China, we have seen that the centralized, hierarchical system of governance in the export sector, and decentralized, collaborative governance in the CSA market were both systems that could integrate and manage well the pressures emanating from different scales. China's export sector was largely dependent upon state-led or state-supported policies, while the CSA sector was aggressively self-regulated. By observing these different, but successful, models, we have useful referential frames to identify why China's domestic food sector seems to fail so spectacularly by comparison. Indeed, we will see that in many instructive contexts, food safety governance in the domestic sector tries to approximates certain aspects of both of these models, resulting in a conflicted mix of governance logics that confound and confuse and leads, invariably and ultimately, to regulatory failure.

6

Failed State Policies

Scale and Its Discontents

During the early 2000s, an unending spectacle of food scandals involving chemical additives erupted on an almost weekly basis. Consumers darkly joked that "because of food safety the Chinese people have successfully eradicated illiteracy in chemistry (*zhongguorenzai shipinzhong wanchengle huaxue saomang* 中国人食品中完成了化学扫盲)." Concerned Chinese citizens would assiduously pore over packaging in supermarkets, read between the lines in official news reports, or tap into the rumor mill of neighbors and other unofficial sources, trying to identify potential additives that could harm or possibly kill one of their family members.

Despite efforts to reassure the public through state-led initiatives, such as the establishment of coordinating bodies, model production zones, and frequent campaigns, scandals involving poisonous and counterfeit food continue to emerge. Pundits in the popular press now openly discuss how China's food safety crisis is challenging the very credibility of its new leaders. What was once viewed as a technical regulatory problem has evolved into a more serious critique—the Chinese state's inability to govern a complex market society.

The failures of China's state-led approaches to food safety would not surprise scholars who have long highlighted the shortcomings of state-centered regulation (Sinclair 1997; Bevir & Rhodes 2004; Greer 2011). Those favoring "new governance" approaches based upon non-state-centered regulation have argued that state-led initiatives are costly, ineffective, focused on end-of-the-pipe solutions, and lack sufficient flexibility to address complex regulatory situations (Nash & Ehrenfield 1996). One should accept, however, that China's experience with state-led governance has been largely positive in many sectors calling for needed oversight, such as financial regulation (Heilmann 2005) and aviation safety (Chung 2003; Suttmeier 2008).

In fact, food safety specialists and scholars who have highlighted the effectiveness of China's state-led initiatives to address major governance challenges throughout the 1990s and 2000 remain puzzled by the country's continuing policy shortfalls in food safety management. Coordinating bodies, food safety campaigns, and model production zones, which have formed the core of China's food safety strategy, have all proven ineffective. The prediction that increased centralization and the establishment of coordinating bodies would enhance regulatory control (Tam & Yang 2005) is yet to be borne out. Unlike the successful "managed campaigns" noted by scholars in other sectors (Heilmann & Perry 2011), China's food safety campaigns have so far done little to invigorate the bureaucracy or reduce the frequency of food safety incidents. Moreover, using model production zones to diffuse food safety best practices (Han 2007) has not yet proven to be effective.

Often the lackluster performance of state policies is generally viewed to be a consequence of obstructionism or a lack of technical capacity at the local level (Li 2010). Yet, local officials in China have been diligent in their attempts to address food safety through extensive monitoring, market surveillance, and the upgrading of food safety facilities. Townships have worked tirelessly to establish new food safety protocols. The "Gengmin" Township Food Safety Plan, for example, directs officials to "ensure 100% vaccination, 100% disinfection of production sites, and no major disease outbreak," "advance the 'Four No's and One Clean-up,'" "prepare reports on major campaigns against swine flu, rabies, H1N1," among a comprehensive series of other activities (FSDOC 29). Township officials in another county explain that each food safety official manages a docket of well over 20 processing firms (YL 11). While food safety experts report on disturbing levels of corruption, most assert that local governments at all levels are *obsessed* with preventing a food safety incident (EX 8; EX 1).

Particularly, since such state-led initiatives are career defining, after the institution of explicit food safety evaluation measures, officials have been increasingly incentivized to meet targets specified in their responsibility contracts with higher levels of government. For 2010, officials in "Zhuguang" County were instructed to make certain that "100% of producers did not use melamine," "the use of clenbuterol was at 0%," and "inspection pass rates increased by 0.35%" (FSDOC 44). Implementing measures of the 2009 Food Safety Law state clear penalties for food safety incidents:

> When the local people's government at or above county level fails to perform its statutory duty for food safety supervision and management and gives rise to severe food safety incident or causes serious social impact in the region, the responsible office and other directly responsible personnel *shall be punished by a special demerit, demotion, removal from office or dismissal.* (Article 61, emphasis added)

As of 2013, food safety now serves as a veto point in cadre evaluations in which a single food safety incident cancels accrued points in other areas of the evaluation. (State Council 2013).[1]

This chapter will show that current state policies fail to address severe scale politics due to built-in shortcomings in the overall governance framework. We have seen how centralized, hierarchical governance has been effective in the export sector, and how community-oriented, collaborative governance has improved food safety in the CSA market. The domestic sector governance framework, however, is neither centralized and hierarchical nor decentralized and collaborative. Instead, food safety governance in the domestic sector is a conflicting mix of centralizing and decentralizing mechanisms that have exacerbated scale politics.

As a threshold matter, when assessing the major food safety reforms in the domestic sector, one is struck by the lack of a consistent governance logic. Policies are only *partially* centralizing or decentralizing. The establishment of coordinating bodies is a prime example of a partially centralizing initiative. Rather than consolidating food safety management in a single ministry and granting it clear hierarchical control of the apparatus from the national scale, the government established a centralized coordinating agency but left a fragmented regulatory apparatus intact. Food safety campaigns are yet another incomplete centralizing initiative—creating bursts of centralized control to restore confidence in the food safety system, but failing to develop institutional measures to reinforce central oversight of local food safety activities. The state's use of model production zones reflects a partially decentralizing policy that

---

[1] A number of provinces were instituting food safety as a veto point in cadre evaluations prior to 2013, such as Gansu and Sichuan in 2012, and Liaoning in 2011.

allows local governments to develop their own food production bases to produce a better fit between local regulations and agricultural conditions. However, these bases are developed with the aim to attract central government approval and typically follow a uniform template of industrialized agriculture favored by the central government.

As a matter of scale politics, partially decentralizing and partially centralizing policies lead to an inability to identify the primary scale of governance, produce conflicts across multiple dimensions of scale, and foster an inability to address scale externalities. The chapter proceeds as follows: first, it will examine the failure of coordinating bodies in their management of food safety; second, the problems of food safety campaigns will be explored; and, third, China's model production zones will be analyzed. The chapter will then conclude with some observations about the challenges of state-led initiatives and the scale problem.

COORDINATING BODIES

In a system in which there are a significant number of government agencies, a multitude of food safety standards, and unclear lines of accountability, the central government established coordination bodies as a centralizing measure to ensure that all regulatory players operating at different scales follow a national food safety plan. "Coordination" (*xietiao* 协调) entails setting annual work plans for all ministries involved in food safety, facilitating communication between different ministries and levels of government, and resolving disputes arising from bureaucratic turf wars.

Since the early 2000s, China has created several coordination bodies to clarify jurisdictional conflicts in its massive food safety bureaucracy. A coordination body at each level of government is meant to harmonize food safety policies at their scale of governance, and respond directly to a coordination body at a higher level. In 2003, the State Food and Drug Administration (SFDA) was formed to coordinate China's food safety regulatory bodies from the top-down. Due to a series of failures involving information flow problems, bureaucratic competition, and corruption, the SFDA was swept away in favor of other coordinating bodies (Tam & Yang 2005). In 2007, the State Council formed a special committee to address food safety challenges led by Vice Premier Wu Yi. Then, in 2009, the Ministry of Health (MOH) was appointed as the new lead ministry in charge of coordinating regulatory activity. Later in 2010, a National Food

Safety Commission was established and led by Vice Premier Li Keqiang, which would lead Food Safety Committees (FSC) established at each level of government to coordinate regulatory actions. As China's food safety crisis worsened, the central government announced plans in early 2013 to establish another super ministry, the China Food and Drug Administration (CFDA), which would strip food safety portfolios from other ministries, and serve as the new nexus in food safety management, reprioritizing the national scale in policy formation and implementation (Haas & Wang 2013).

In reality, coordinating bodies reflect a logic of partial centralization. These new agencies serve only as an organizational palliative laid on top of a poorly integrated regulatory system. To avoid significant bureaucratic conflict, the state eschewed comprehensive regulatory reform in favor of establishing a coordinating body, often without the research and infrastructural support necessary to succeed. The SFDA served as the primary coordinating unit that was to oversee a fragmented bureaucracy, including the SAIC, Ministry of Environment, Ministry of Agriculture, Ministry of Health, and the Administration for Quality and Technical Supervision at each level of government. The contention was that the SFDA could address the numerous regulatory gaps that had emerged in a system where each ministry was in charge of a specific link of the food production process (e.g., production, retail, and distribution), and enforce central directives from the top-down through local-level SFDAs. But, coordinating bodies were effectively sidelined in the regulatory process, and failed to pursue their regulatory mandate to "coordinate."

Who Shall Govern?

Coordinating bodies have more often led to the increased fragmentation of interests across scales rather than integrating them on the basis of a uniform, nationally scaled approach to food safety. The partial centralization of the food safety bureaucracy leaves unclear as to which scale should dominate the food safety policy making process. From the purview of the central government, the primary problem in food safety management is the system's fragmentation. In a series of food safety notifications, plans, and circulars, local governments were instructed by central government ministries to form "leading small groups" and "coordinating bodies" in the hopes of unifying the system according to a national food safety template. Food safety authorities were to develop "organizational strength

TABLE 6.1 *Provincial Food Safety Evaluation Point Allocation*

National Food Safety Work and Reorganization Assessment (Provincial Level)

Evaluation Item	Points
Organization and System Building	15 Points
Government-Restructuring Measures	55 Points
Develop Corporate Responsibility	20 Points
Effect of Government-Restructuring Measures	10 Points
Extra Credit	10 Points
Penalties (Major Food Safety Incident)	−20 Points

Source: Author's Fieldwork.

and leadership" and set "clear responsibility arrangements" through coordinating bodies. In the central government's annual food safety assessment of food safety work at the provincial level, more than 70 out of 100 points were related to forming a coordinating body and restructuring food safety management in line with central policy aims (Table 6.1). This mandate is echoed in county-level assessments of food safety management at the township level, in which the formation of an operating coordinating body represented 50 out of 100 points of its evaluation (Table 6.2).[2]

TABLE 6.2 *Township Food Safety Evaluation Point Allocation*

Food Safety Assessment (Township Level)	
Leadership/Organization Evaluation	
Leadership Committee Formed/Research	10 Points
Districts Have FSC	20 Points
FSC Targets Established	20 Points
Work Situation	
Coordination	10 Points
Education Work	10 Points
Monitoring Work	10 Points
Meets County FSC Plan Targets	10 Points
Launch Wholesale Market Clean-Up	10 Points
TOTAL	**100 Points**

Source: Author's Fieldwork.

[2] For in-depth discussions of the cadre evaluation system and its effect on policy implementation, see Landry (2008), Edin (2003), Whiting (2000).

Officials operating at the county and township levels, however, disagree with the central government's assessment and view government restructuring as an irrelevant, burdensome reform. Most officials argue that the 2009 Food Safety Law, which established the FSCs, reflected national bureaucratic struggles rather than local food safety concerns (ZJ 3). As local officials surveyed the food safety challenge from their degree-of-zoom, they perceived that the real business of food safety involved the constant monitoring of thousands of small farmers and trader markets, transitioning to modern forms of agricultural production, and training local farmers—not establishing coordination bodies (ZZ FSC, YL11).

The establishment of an additional organizational unit only created significant paperwork and reporting requirements for officials. County officials commented that the reports that they prepare for coordinating bodies are largely "politically driven," emphasizing targets and development goals established by agencies that are irrelevant at their degree-of-zoom (ZZ 56). For example, local officials often mentioned how they would be charged with searching for a nonexistent, illegal additive in the local market, simply because the noxious substance had emerged as an issue in the national media (ZJ 15).

Time and again local officials of husbandry, agricultural, and fishery bureaus confessed that they refused to cooperate with a coordinating body focused on policy objectives that made sense only at the national scale. For example, a major goal of the central government was to promote new food safety certifications, as a means to strengthen the position of the food sector in international markets. But, local officials would openly discuss how targets for the percentage of land meeting organic and green certification requirements hardly seemed rational given that a majority of the farmers under their purview could not even keep records of their agricultural inputs (ZZ 21; ZZ 38).

SFDA agents with an unclear mandate to "coordinate" food safety activities at the local scale felt disempowered relative to their local counterparts who had deep ties to local production networks. Local agency heads questioned the new coordinating bodies' legitimacy: "What experience do these guys even have? What can they do?" (YL 11) A nationwide survey of food safety systems in municipalities showed that most coordinating bodies have been sidelined in the regulatory system: while 60% of cities had established a new food safety coordination body, 85% of these cities continued to manage food safety through individual local agencies (Yang et al. 2012).

From National Strategies to Day-to-Day Tasks

A major problem in the coordinating body–led system has been that regulators failed to consider how policies scaled down on the managerial dimension of scale (from strategies to tasks). Coordinating bodies must harmonize regulatory management across scales in a way that effectively balances interests, reallocates resources, and re-establishes standards. In theory, a national food safety strategy is developed by the center, provinces are then to develop plans with actionable items, municipalities and counties are then set projects based on the provincial plan, and township officials focus on the day-to-day tasks to meet project goals—each level of government is charged with a role to match their scale of governance. Coordination bodies operating at larger scales issue "responsibility work contracts" to their counterparts operating at smaller scales with a specific list of regulatory obligations for each year.

Gaps in management emerged as food safety directives were developed into plans and then into targets, and, finally, into tasks. When looking at the evaluation criteria set by coordination bodies, it was clear that food safety disasters were to be avoided (-20 points), but no criteria was put in place for how this was actually supposed to be achieved, and no clear rationale was provided as to how the day-to-day food safety tasks contributed to this broader goal. In one county in Sichuan, food safety officials, including the head of the county food safety committee himself, indicated that while targets from municipal coordinating bodies, such as "0% clenbuterol" and "ensure 100% vaccination" appeared straightforward, they often entailed complex and challenging enforcement schemes that the county struggled to develop (ZZ FSC). Some officials confessed that they were at their wit's end trying to manage and diminish food safety risk, and all they could do was hope that a major incident did not happen on their watch. "The guys after me will have to figure this out," one county director said (ZZ FSC). In addition, officials operating at smaller scales commented that as targets and tasks were assigned by higher levels, these planning committees ignored their objections and suggestions. One researcher noted: "committees at the provincial level are not competent and too far removed from the ground" to develop sensible work plans (ZJ 40).

Further fueling tensions was an evaluation system biased in favor of "large-scale" managerial goals rather than "small-scale" tasks. For example, while there are large penalties for failing to achieve a provincial-level target, such as preventing a major food safety scandal, there are few benefits for officials who perform well on their regulatory tasks, for example, operate on a smaller managerial scale, performing tasks such as visiting pig farms, auditing production records, and conducting market surveillance. Broad targets are emphasized, and day-to-day tasks are discounted. As one academic notes, "It's an unfair system, if a food safety event happens [larger scale managerial goal] they get all the blame, but if nothing happens they get no reward for doing their job [smaller scale managerial task]. No one is getting promoted on the basis of food safety, but people are getting reprimanded" (HK 1). Under this system, it is no surprise that despite the increase in punitive evaluation measures, local officials are still more likely to focus on economic development, which offers a clearer path to promotion, rather than food safety, where officials are incentivized to disregard tasks and instead develop strategies to avoid blame in the instance of a food safety disaster.

More broadly, tensions on the managerial dimension of scale were fueled by the nebulous nature of what "coordination" really meant in practice. For example, Ningxia SFDA officials asserted that one of the major challenges in facilitating coordination across governing scales is that it is a "soft target" (NX 3). While inspections, penalties, and food safety campaigns can be counted and recorded in food safety reports, coordination in practical terms is more difficult to assess. Officials explained how it was challenging to evaluate whether they are facilitating "clear lines of communication," "inter-ministerial contact," or "inter-level planning" (NX 3). Aside from the physical establishment of committees, and instituting new reporting requirements, most regulatory officials were unclear as to how to coordinate their activities with other ministries and scales of governance.

This problem was exacerbated by the lack of procedures for coordinated activities. None of the preexisting agencies have written mission statements or bylaws governing how to plan coordinated food safety regulation, interact with other agencies on a routine basis, or adjudicate conflicts between ministries and different levels of government (Balzano 2012). For example, when the new SFDA was developed, individuals did not understand how to interact and redirect their workflows in the new system. A former director of the central-level SFDA described the scenario as follows: "it was frustrating because, of course, we have 'food' in our agency name, so people expect us to be in control, but no one listened to us. We took all the blame from the public, but were never empowered to do our job" (CC 1).

Ignoring Local Emerging Conditions

Coordinating bodies were also ill-equipped to identify and address scale externalities at the local scale (i.e., the spillover effect of noncompliance from the local to the national). First, an issue that was raised by many food safety officers of various agencies was the lack of technical capacity on the part of coordinating bodies to identify local food safety problems. Husbandry officials in one county complained that few of the Food Safety Committees (FSCs)—the coordinating bodies that took over after 2010—understood the major risks involved in pork farming and had little experience in monitoring local distribution networks. Second, given the FSC's limited staff, monitoring is still directed by local agencies, which keeps the FSCs in the dark with respect to new food safety developments. One official asserted, "These guys have no idea what they are doing. They don't do any of the real regulatory work. They have to depend on the 20 other agencies involved in developing food safety. When the clenbuterol campaign started they didn't do anything" (ZZ FSC). Agriculture and Aquaculture Bureau officials reflected the same concerns, describing the FSC as a mere "reporting body" (ZZ 55; ZZ 56). As a physical indicator of the irrelevance of FSCs, officials highlighted that laboratories and technical equipment remain embedded within their individual agencies rather than at the FSC. In one county, the husbandry bureau purchased an RMB 3 million laboratory, which is staffed by its own technical personnel: "the county has a 3 million RMB food safety laboratory, and it's in the husbandry bureau, not the FSC. What does that tell you about the FSC's use?" (ZZ FSC)

Many FSCs are "empty conference rooms" for most of the year, aside from planning and reporting periods. One food safety director likened it to the "Japanese Emperor" on account of its high visibility, but limited legal authority (ZZ FSC). As local problems emerged, most regulators turned to their local agencies rather than reporting to the new coordinating bodies. As a result, information on emerging problems at the local scale failed to be transmitted to higher levels.

A telling story of how failing to identify emerging conditions at the local scale can lead to major food safety scandals that extend far beyond a locality is the "Fuyang Milk Incident" of 2004. As Tam and Yang (2005) highlight in their thorough analysis of the event, as early as 2003, there were reports of children dying at local hospitals due to the consumption of substandard milk. The Ministry of Commerce had also received reports of the presence of "fake milk" in markets. However, due to its unclear position in the local food safety system and the fact that there were no pre-established plans for coordinated activity, the SFDA and its higher-level counterpart were not notified of these new developments. Local agencies failed to share information, discuss work plans, or set up monitoring networks. At a broader scale, the development of a widespread problem would have been easily identifiable had there been a channel by which local reports could be consolidated and analyzed. However, the loss of information, regulatory gaps, and bureaucratic turf wars—issues that the SFDA was specifically designed to address—ultimately led to a major scandal. By 2004, fake milk was being distributed in 10 provinces and thousands of infants were suffering from malnutrition.

In a multiscale context, coordinating bodies have only intensified scale politics regarding food safety management. Coordinating bodies serve as a partially centralizing reform to a regulatory system that requires a comprehensive restructuring. As a result, the institution of coordinating bodies has only contributed to the complexity and fragmentation of the regulatory system.

FOOD SAFETY CAMPAIGNS

The frequent state campaigns to address food safety problems have fared no better at ameliorating scale politics. Campaigns have been a common feature of Chinese-style governance as an inherited revolutionary tradition from the country's Maoist past (Heilmann & Perry 2011). Food safety campaigns, however, have had a negligible, if not negative, effect on governance outcomes.[3] In theory, campaigns can be used to establish centralized, hierarchical control, realigning actors operating at different scales through bursts of intense regulatory activity. But, the lack of institutionalization of these measures means that hierarchical control is established only in the short term. And, thus, food safety campaigns can only be considered a partially centralizing initiative.

Food safety campaigns can be broadly categorized into three types: (1) "strike-hard" campaigns (*yandaxingdong* 严打行动); (2) government

---

[3] For a discussion regarding the potentially negative effects of campaigns see Wedeman (2005); on campaign governance and its competitive role with institutionalization of a professionalized bureaucracy see Trevaskes (2002).

rectification campaigns (*zhengzhixingdong* 整治行动); and (3) holiday investigation campaigns (*jierixunchxingdong* 节日巡查行动). Strike-hard campaigns are typically initiated at the central and provincial levels and focus on recent food scandals of national scale. In 2011, for example, a nationwide campaign was launched following the discovery of gutter oil and clenbuterol in pig feed throughout China (Xinhua 2012a). These campaigns serve a dual purpose by restoring faith in government regulators and also instilling confidence among consumers (JS 1; Xinhua 2011). A typical strike-hard campaign involves the arrests of food safety perpetrators, food company executives, and unlicensed producers (Yao 2012). Targets feature prominently in the annual work plans and evaluations of local governments. For example, following the 2008 melamine scandal, inspections of all milk stations for melamine within Zhuguang County were highlighted as a key task in the annual food safety plan (FSDOC).

Government rectification campaigns may also coincide with strike-hard campaigns but with a specific focus on government officials. Officials found to be in collusion with food safety enterprises, or who fail to punish noncompliant companies, are disciplined. In 2012, the Central Disciplinary Inspection Commission investigated more than 300,000 cases related to food safety, and 40,000 officials were disciplined for negligence (Xinhua 2012b). During one recent campaign, evaluators were instructed to make certain that "officials follow all procedures, did not to simplify procedures, did not recognize certifications from other counties, and kept thorough records" (FSDOC87). Government officials found to be in error were to be disciplined.

Finally, holiday investigation campaigns focus on distribution points and dining establishments prior to significant holidays during the calendar year, when consumption of food is expected to dramatically increase. In September, one county's husbandry officials visited major points in their regulatory system, including township slaughterhouses, cold storage facilities, wholesale markets, and meat manufacturers. In addition to inspections, officers promoted food safety by passing out information pamphlets and making public food safety announcements (FSDOC82).

This section focuses particularly on how strike-hard and rectification campaigns have led to significant scale politics on the temporal dimension of scale. Ad hoc food safety campaigns have been launched with increasing frequency, but have further complicated the process of setting institutional procedures and converging on a unified view of food safety.

Temporal Challenges

In terms of scale politics, officials can be said to be engaging in contentious politics on the temporal dimension of scale. Governing processes at different scales operate according to different time frames that range from the short term to the long term. Campaigns have failed to reconcile the temporal processes of governing systems operating at different scales— the central government's need to quickly shore up consumer confidence and protect the "made-in-China brand" for its exports in the short-term, conflicts with local government's long-term task of institutionalizing regulatory norms and procedures.

Officials at the local scale have struggled to understand the purpose of campaigns, as campaigns have grown increasingly ineffective and work against the long-term institutionalization of regulatory procedures. Officials assert that producers know that campaigns intensify inspections only for a short period of time (YL 9; *Wall Street Journal* 2011). In many cases, noncompliant food processors simply move to another location and continue to produce substandard foods. Producers are well aware that they will once again fall out of government surveillance after a campaign. Officials contend that producers have now grown accustomed to this cycle. One producer confesses, "The government usually offers no real help . . . but [during a campaign] . . . they come around and inspect and make you do a lot of paper work" (ZZ 50). Many officials are at a loss as to why the provincial government still initiates food safety campaigns with such a high level of frequency.

Given the constant barrage of new food safety campaigns, on-the-ground personnel are finding it difficult to prioritize regulatory goals (ZZ FSC; YL 11). Many feel overworked and lack the manpower and sufficient funds to address daily food safety issues, let alone special campaigns (ZZ 1). An official in one county explained that for many campaigns, the local government does not have the necessary equipment and samples need to be sent up to the provincial level for examination, at local government expense (YL 11). Because new food safety implementation laws are still being written, food safety campaigns continue to take precedence over upholding the new Food Safety Law. One official complained, "We are at a loss as to how to handle food safety, there are standards, but with campaigns, these might change." (YL 11).

Food safety experts also highlight how the logic of food safety campaigns stands in contrast to that of building a risk-based food safety system that the Food Safety Law aspires to establish. A risk-based food safety system recognizes that food poisoning incidents are unavoidable, and that the key to developing an effective system is to assess weak points within a system and create procedures to ameliorate those risks (Balzano 2012). Campaigns, however, focus on arresting noncompliant individuals and blaming food safety incidents on "immoral" behavior, rather than instituting clear regulatory procedures for eliminating risks. A clear example of this logic at work is when Sudan red dye was banned by Chinese authorities in 1996: a series of arrests were made, but clear implementation measures were not established until 10 years later, after the dye resurfaced in 2005 (Hu 2005). Arrests may address a problem in the short term, but only long-term planning can guide and redirect uncertain producers with beneficial systemic results.

Rather than making the food safety system more understandable to officials, campaigns have led to regulatory confusion. Short-term targets conflict with long-term goals. Moreover, officials have increasingly come to question the purpose of campaigns as they have grown increasingly less effective over time.

Minimizing Scale Externalities

National campaigns are often ignorant of emerging problems at the local scale. Local government officials often cite the one-size-fits-all nature of campaigns often referred to as "one single cut" policies (*yidaoqie* 一刀切). Following a poisoning incident, the central government sends investigation teams to various localities in which a food safety problem has been identified. Food safety monitoring bodies in other localities are then instructed to carry out parallel investigations in their own jurisdictions. In recent years, food safety campaigns have targeted the use of clenbuterol in pig feed, melamine in dairy products, gutter oil, and counterfeit food products, among others. Local officials assert that they have a better understanding of the food safety risks in their communities and that targeted campaigns often miss emerging problems.

Higher-level regulators engage in a process of minimization with respect to the potential of nontargeted food safety problems at the local scale cascading into regional problems. Written off as "local problems," these issues rarely feature in campaigns until recognized by the center as a widespread problem. During the recent clenbuterol campaign, officials in one county were instructed to conduct urine tests of all farms with more than 50 pigs, which included several thousand farms (ZZ FSC). Local officials complained that because their farmers were too poor to purchase the additive, it was highly unlikely that clenbuterol had been used in production (YL 3). Instead, local regulators pointed to another health hazard that had been emerging in local markets. As one bureau chief in another county bitterly recalled, "We don't have a clenbuterol problem. We have a dead pig problem. Farmers keep selling diseased pork. Why does everyone have to have a 'clenbuterol' problem all of a sudden?" (ZJ 1) However, notifications about the prevalence of diseased pig meat circulating in local markets went unheeded. For many husbandry officials it came as no surprise when tens of thousands of dead pigs began appearing on the banks of the Huangpu River in 2013.

Local officials point to more systematic reforms in food safety management that can pre-empt small-scale problems from turning into regional scandals. In particular, officials in several counties assert that the current penalties for noncompliance are too low (ZJ 3). As a result, even when noncompliant activity is identified and the individual fined, these producers appear again later, and engage in similar noncompliant behavior. Other officials point to the need to invest in capacity building and increase the salaries of local regulators, rather than focus on campaigns (ZZ 1; ZJ 8).

Food safety campaigns feature prominently in China's state-led food safety strategy. Central and provincial officials use campaigns frequently to address emerging food safety crises, much to the chagrin of the local officials who are put in charge of implementing them. A failure to understand the temporal dimension of different scales of governance creates conflict within the system: while campaigns may address short-term goals, they often lead to negative consequences for the long-term institutionalization of food safety procedures. In addition, food safety campaigns have reinforced behaviors toward "minimization," in which small-scale problems are ignored to the detriment of the system.

MODEL PRODUCTION ZONES

The third prong of the state's food safety initiatives—the development of model food production zones—is a partially *decentralizing* measure. Borne out of the view that modernization of the agricultural sector is key to addressing China's food safety crisis (State Council 2007; Calvin et al. 2006), the establishment of model production bases has featured prominently in the State Council's Document Number 1 for several years. In addition, the 12th Five-Year Plan highlights the establishment of production bases as a top priority for the central government (MOA 2011).

The belief is that as farms become larger, adopt scientific procedures, and abide by global food safety standards, food safety problems will resolve themselves. In theory, the decentralized structure of the plan facilitates innovation by allowing governments to experiment with new production models that suit local conditions. In addition, local producers would be encouraged to participate in local base governance processes, addressing new challenges as they emerged.

But while agricultural production bases (APBs) (*nongyeshengchanjidi* 农业生产基地) are characterized as part of a decentralizing initiative, they are remarkably uniform, following a template of industrialized production developed by central-level planners. Governments have established APBs that serve as model production sites where farmers can learn new techniques and be easily monitored by government regulators (RMRB 2012). As of 2007, there were 24,600 hazard-free production bases, 593 central-level demonstration zones, 100 demonstration counties, and 3,500 provincial-level demonstration zones (State Council 2007). Bases are typically more than 25 acres in size and specialize in a select number of cash crops. According to a policy of "one village, one product," (*yipin, yicun* 一品一村) provincial and county governments select villages to produce a high-value crop, which is often a part of an agricultural branding effort (Han 2007).

Local government investment in APBs is significant. Many governments may work with corporate partners to secure much-needed capital to develop a base. In other cases, local governments may apply for financial transfers from higher levels of government to supplement limited budgetary outlays for agricultural upgrading (YL 1; ZZ 1). First, in order for modern production facilities to be built, farmers must be cleared from their land and rehoused. Second, new bases require the installation of modern facilities. In more isolated areas, governments must also invest in basic infrastructure such as roads, power transmission, and irrigation. Third, farmers that work on these bases are entitled to various subsidies to purchase higher quality inputs such as fertilizers, feed, and new breeds. In one county, for example, farmers receive an RMB 8,000 subsidy for using higher-quality pig breeds and feed (ZZ 21).

The Appropriate Scale of Production

In APB management, the primary conflict over "scale" relates to the appropriate scale of production and distribution. Provincial-level officials view APBs as an effective large-scale production model that could be seamlessly integrated into national distribution channels and could both address food safety problems and food security needs simultaneously (ZZ 42; ZZ 55). Provincial governments have had the strongest interest in developing APBs as part of a drive to create provincial agricultural brands (ZJ 4; ZJ 15; SD 1). For example, in Ningxia province, the provincial government has established 120 agricultural model bases (*xiandai nongye shifanjidi* 现代农业示范基地) to produce 13 "specialized" products designated by the provincial agricultural authorities (NX 2).

County and township officials' opinions of APBs are more mixed. APBs do offer increased national market access for local produce, and have substantially improved farmer incomes (ZZ 56). APBs have also made food safety monitoring much easier for regulators. Concentrating farmers in a single area enables regulators to enforce standards across a production base (ZZ 38). The specialization in particular crops also helps to focus training sessions (ZJ 15). When farmers follow uniform planting schedules, pesticide applications, and harvest at the same time, regulators can more easily identify problems while not overextending their resources.

However, local officials argue that central and provincial government planners fail to see the millions of farmers that cannot meet the standards of APB production and with whom local officials must interact on a daily basis. Local officials contend that provincial officials are often motivated by a vision of large-scale industrial agriculture that does not comport with local production realities of farmers (YL 10). They cite, for example, how the vast majority of farmers are too old or poorly educated to work on an APB (YL 17).

For those who do not operate on an APB, government surveillance is thin and food safety training minimal. Government regulators confess that because of their limited fiscal resources they are incapable of managing small farmers and household workshops. Small farmers often see government officials no more than three times a year during campaigns, or in the case of pig farmers, vaccination periods (ZZ 39; ZZ 40; ZZ 57; ZJ 21). As one farmer notes, "We rarely communicate with government officials . . . we are too small to matter" (YL 4). In terms of off-base food processors, QTSB officials assert that they are unable to close all noncompliant workshops. Even during more thorough government crackdowns, small processors will just wait and reopen their operations in another area until the next major campaign (ZJ 3). As a coping mechanism, officials try to concentrate problematic producers in certain areas in order to facilitate monitoring. While they cannot force them to stop production, they can at least try to limit their distribution channels (YL 11).

A fundamental conflict emerges concerning the appropriate scale of production: Should limited resources be disbursed to a select group of producers on APBs, or to the many small farmers in the country? In effect, the debate over the APB production model highlights two very different visions of agricultural development—one that sees China moving in the direction of conventional, industrialized agriculture, and another that envisions a more inclusive mode of production and distribution.

Knowledge-Related Problems

Another major challenge is transferring food safety knowledge developed by global scientific committees and standard-setting bodies, such as GlobalGAP, to local APBs. That is, how does one effectively scale down food safety practices on the knowledge dimension of scale? County and township officials hold that the APB production model is based on global understandings of food safety that work as a complete system of logistical support, which is not amenable to many localities. Government officials from a mountainous county in Yunnan, where there are few large tracts of land to build an APB, asserted that an APB would create more food safety problems than they would solve (YL 16; YL 17). First, the lack of infrastructure makes the movement of food products in a safe, efficient manner highly challenging. Lacking appropriate cold storage and express roadways to transport fresh produce increases the likelihood of microbial contamination after the farm gate. Second, certain areas do not have the organizational capacity to train farmers to produce for large production bases, and government regulators struggle to maintain producer discipline on APBs. One official comments, "most farmers do not know how to coordinate production and to operate as part of a team" (YL 10).

To expect farming households that consist of millions of poorly educated, elderly people to adopt GlobalGAP techniques is questionable, if not fanciful. Elderly farmers near one base assert that they are rarely invited to the training sessions on the base and that government officials largely leave them alone during the planting season. A rural NGO comments, "Large production bases tend to include only a select few farmers and at best can only address a small part of the overall agricultural production structure" (NX 5).

Further complicating the diffusion of global food safety knowledge is the fact that many local government officials themselves do not seem to understand the purpose of APBs. International food safety observers have noted that many localities have a different understanding of good agricultural practice that departs from global food safety understandings. They argue that officials often mistake an increase in production volumes as commensurate with the modernization of agricultural production. Modernization, however, entails more than the increased production of food, and requires investment in new, safer techniques and technology. One enterprising individual has been working hard to bring desert cultivation techniques, such as drip irrigation and other hydroponic systems, from Israel to China. She started as a young technician on a joint China-Israel experimental farm in Beijing and went on to found one of China's major agro-processor companies. Yet, when she observes these new APBs she laments, "It's not about industrialization. It is about modernization, and these are very different concepts. Only intelligent farming through modern technology and safer techniques will lead to food safety gains. Industrializing agriculture without modernizing will only lead to more serious problems" (NX 4).

When the APB model is forced on localities that do not understand its overall purpose in food safety development, APBs are often used to serve more political aims than they are to disseminate food safety knowledge. Some governments use APBs to develop "glamour products" to attract attention and funding from higher levels of government. Experts have reported that in Gansu, several townships have tried to cultivate lily bulbs, which take more than seven years for the first harvest (EX 1). In other areas, APBs are built around large agricultural exhibition centers to showcase local products. One agricultural expert comments, "They waste so much money . . . pouring money into useless demonstration farms or large bases . . . it's all for show. They build large exhibition halls and they try to plant a [fancy] vegetable in the wrong place" (NX 4).

Unintended Consequences of the APB Food Safety Development Model

Another problem with APBs is the lack of attention to scale externalities. Few individuals considered how a multitude of local experiments in food production could create problems at higher scales in terms of developing a national system of regulation. In many instances, different models compete with one another, creating impediments for integrating markets. Standards may conflict and testing procedures may be irreconcilable. For example, Shandong and Ningxia had different protocols for warm-house production, making it difficult for Shandong food producers to enter the

Ningxia market. Ningxia agronomists were unfamiliar with Shandong's warm-house prototype, and were hostile to outside experts interfering in Ningxia's agricultural development: "of course, the local agronomists didn't like the fact that I had entered into their territory. They had their own greenhouses, but they did not work" (NX 4).

Scholars note that interprovincial conflicts, such as the previous example, could pose a serious impediment to national integration.[4] Another notable example of interprovincial disputes occurred in 2006, following the discovery of excessive carcinogens in turbot fish from Shandong (Thompson & Hu 2007). Shanghai, Beijing, Guangzhou, and other provincial governments closed their markets to farm-raised fish from Shandong province. The Shanghai FDA sent an investigative team to the province to investigate fish farming practices in Weihai and Rongcheng. During the course of the investigation, the widespread use of nitrofuran and chormycelinin was discovered (Xinhua 2006). Significant disparities in how fishery bases were managed were exposed, and Shanghai refused to permit turbot fish from Shandong into local markets. In this particular case, a series of interprovincial agreements were brokered to "harmonize" standards and production base management that eventually led to the lifting of the ban. One can imagine how a host of these disputes could easily lead to the balkanization of the regulatory system.

Another significant problem may be that these varied local standards come into conflict with emerging standards of safety that are supported by international consensus, such as Good Agricultural Practice (GAP). Local standards may indeed improve compliance in some respects, but not if they lead to conflict with international best practices. Food safety experts hold that local variation is permissible, as long as they fall within the parameters of internationally established safety standards. For example, the China GAP II standard, which has fewer critical control points, was written to assist China's farmers to eventually transition to the more demanding GlobalGAP standard (EX10). Undirected local experimentation with no central guidance, however, could lead to substantial food safety coordination problems, and leave China worse off.

The implementation of the APB model has only contributed to regulatory incoherence due to scale politics. A partially decentralizing strategy does not provide local governments with enough leeway to design bases

---

[4] China watchers will recall that in the early 1980s when local protectionism balkanized China's internal market for certain resources (Montinola et al. 1995)

better suited to their production needs. As a result, these cookie-cutter projects based on a production template developed at the national (if not global) scale, fail to facilitate a broad based transition to sound food safety practices. Diffusion of best practices from the global to the local face serious impediments, and failure to develop a clear plan for integrating APBs has led to regulatory conflict across subnational units.

DISCUSSION

The domestic sector faces serious scale politics as it attempts to develop an integrated food safety system. Because policies are neither centralized and hierarchical, nor decentralized and collaborative, officials engage in intense scale politics, leading to significant contention regarding the primary scale of governance for coordinating bodies, food safety campaigns, and the creation of APBs. Although coordinating bodies are expected to streamline food safety management and realign interests across ministries, they have only contributed to more friction along the managerial dimension of scale. A lack of clarity regarding how regulatory tasks at the local level are to be coordinated with broader national food safety plans has led to regulatory confusion. Food safety campaigns pit national-level officials seeking short-term fixes to China's food safety problems against those who advocate long-term institutionalization of regulatory norms at the local level. Model APBs, which seek to disseminate best practices, have led to conflict between officials who believe APBs are the best model for training China's farmers and those who argue for a less advanced but more inclusive model of development. As APBs are established throughout the country, persistent disagreements emerge on the knowledge-related dimension of scale, as officials contest how local food production realities can comport with global food safety standards and methods.

The ineffectiveness of "partially deployed" policies in ameliorating scale politics points to the need for the implementation of comprehensive food safety reform. If coordinating bodies are to be used to impose centralized, hierarchical control of the food safety system, a complete restructuring of the regulatory system must occur to facilitate this transformation. Food safety campaigns should play a less prominent role in food safety management, and institutionalization of rules and procedures should be emphasized. If APBs are to be successful, decentralization must run its course so as to incorporate a multitude of food safety forms that can better serve a broader base of farmers. As it stands, the *schizophrenic*

TABLE 6.3 *State Initiatives and Scale Politics*

	Coordinating Bodies	Campaigns	Model Zones
Scale of Governance?	Central/Local Unclear	Central, but sporadic	Local, but according to central government template
Multidimensional Issues	Managerial	Temporal	Knowledge-related
Scale Externalities?	Local problems not addressed	Local problems not addressed	No template for integration at higher scales

nature of coordinating bodies, campaigns, and model production zones as a state-led initiative creates confusion rather than confidence in state interventions to regulate food safety.

The Fiscal Aspects of Scale

Another major problem in each of the state-led reforms is a failure to understand the critical relationship between scale and funding. The relationship between local fiscal health and food safety outcomes has been well-documented. The richest municipalities in Eastern China have higher rates of food safety policy implementation, system certification, and traceability, whereas Western China has the country's lowest (Yang et al. 2012). The same municipal survey reveals that out of 212 cities, 48.2% show that lack of funds was the biggest problem in food safety (Yang et al. 2012). Similarly, distinctions between rural and urban enforcement rates have been shown to be an observable function of fiscal constraints (Liu & McGuire 2015). These budget shortfalls and constraints affect the number of inspections, the ability to conduct testing on food products, and the establishment of monitoring stations.

Budget shortfalls also lead to an increase in corrupt behavior. Following further fiscal cuts at the local level, officials are increasingly dependent on the fees collected through licensing and auditing food enterprises for operating revenues (Tam & Yang 2005). Thus, it is often in the interest of the regulator to allow a noncompliant manufacturer to remain in business so as to preserve a steady stream of rents. Moreover, fiscal instability makes local governments vulnerable to regulatory capture. For example, Tam & Yang's (2005) exposition of the Fuyang Milk Incident showed many townships involved in the scandal emphasized the importance of employment as a reason for *not* cracking down on noncompliant firms.

The key here is to understand how scale often contributes to and exacerbates fiscal problems with regard to regulation at the local level. Regulators often fail to appreciate that costs of food safety governance are spread unevenly across different scales of governance. Central government policies often give little consideration to the cost of regulation as one moves down each level of scale. For example, as in the case of campaigns, higher-level officials who are driven by aggregate statistics—such as the ostensibly important goal of "0% melamine" in dairy products—ignore how this proscription translates to actual activity at lower scales. In a single county, for example, ensuring "0% melamine" requires the inspection of dozens of milk stations, and thousands of dairy producers—a costly undertaking for cash-strapped agencies. In other instances, provincial officials have requested the increase in organic or green food certification rates. Yet, at the local level, this often requires massive capital investments in land reclamation and agricultural upgrading. Another common scenario relates to disproportionate downstream fiscal consequences when central officials require new testing protocols. To meet these centrally mandated objectives at the local scale, counties sometimes have to direct scarce government revenues toward building entirely new laboratories. Or, as is more often the case, locally sourced samples must be sent to prefectural or provincial levels for testing, the costs of which again must typically be borne by local governments. More broadly, these examples of policy directives reflecting "unfunded mandates," could be seen as a basic failure to understand the cost structure of policies across scales.

A related scale-oriented fiscal problem is where policies are only cost-effective from the perspective of the central government's degree-of-zoom. Developing a new food safety coordinating body is far cheaper than reallocating food safety portfolios from other agencies to establish a well-funded ministry. But, the failure to comprehensively overhaul the bureaucracy has led to diminished rather than enhanced efficiencies and added significant coordination costs at all subnational levels. New task force meetings, increased reporting requirements, and the seconding of personnel impose additional costs throughout the bureaucracy. Campaigns are also often touted as a cost-effective measure for realigning incentives across highly heterogeneous contexts. Also, APBs are seen as a state-led initiative that allows the central government to devolve control of agricultural policy to localities while foregoing the need to develop and fund a national agricultural modernization plan. However, as was noted in previous sections related to these initiatives, local level entities, who are tasked with actually implementing these directives, do not think these centrally mandated policies are cost effective and, indeed, think that these initiatives are often counterproductive.

Given their scale of responsibility, actors at each level of government have widely different perspectives about how funding should be disbursed, leading to fierce conflicts. For example, township food safety officers at the agricultural technical bureaus explained that they needed to hire more inspectors. Their staff cited the large number of small farms, the geographic distances between production sites, and the inability to conduct thorough inspections due to time and fiscal constraints. Furthermore, due to low wages, it was difficult to recruit new employees, and, in field interviews, most staff members admitted to permanent wage decreases in the last few years despite the greater attention given to food safety in the overall system.

Most of these township-level fiscal concerns have been largely ignored by higher-level governments who are generally more focused on directing limited resources to model production bases. After establishing an APB, participating regulatory actors can capture large subsidies from both the provincial and central governments, who are less interested in the travails of local level inspectors. Local governments can receive funding for feed, agricultural inputs, and new equipment provided they are used on base. As previously mentioned, grants can be sizable—in the tens of millions of RMB. Working level regulators often can do little but watch to their chagrin as funding is directed toward projects that only include a fraction of the county's producers. In summary, though often overlooked, the fiscal aspects of scale and ensuing politics are critical to effective governance: budgets must scale in line with capabilities, if policies are to succeed.

CONCLUSION

China's 2009 Food Safety Law took more than six years of deliberation before being enacted by the National People's Congress (Thompson & Hu 2007). And, in 2013, the law was challenged by producer groups, government officials, and consumers, leading to an amended Food Safety Law in 2015. Many are highly skeptical that the FSL will serve as the template for coherent food safety governance. A comprehensive food safety reform package must be developed with appreciation for the intense scale politics involved in any policy solution.

Important variations in the effectiveness of certain policies should be noted. Coordinating bodies have operated successfully in Shanghai and Ningxia. APBs have performed strongly in counties in Sichuan and Zhejiang, where governments have been able to invest in their development. In Yunnan, however, geographical constraints make it difficult to establish large-scale APBs. Campaigns that have been focused on clear targets have been successful in ferreting out certain illegal additives. Increasingly, food safety experts have observed that certain illegal pesticides are difficult to purchase on the market because of campaign efforts. To be sure, the effective implementation of China's coordination bodies, food safety campaigns, and model production bases can vary from place to place. But when these policies do fail, a predictable pattern of trade-offs and bureaucratic tensions emerges due to scale politics.

As we conclude this chapter's discussion of the state-led initiatives in food safety and their shortcomings in the large-scale domestic sector, further questions emerge: Are there other approaches to manage China's scale problem? Can new frameworks of governance be developed to attenuate the politics of scale and to make the adoption of comprehensive policy more feasible? Where state policies fail, can private sector initiatives be more effective? These, and similar, questions will be addressed in the next chapter with specific regard to notable successes and limitations in food safety governance among the millions of China's small farmers.

7

Coregulatory Initiatives

China's Big, Small Farmer Problem

Food supply chains in China's domestic sector are notoriously complex. Producers are linked to a host of local, regional, and national wholesale markets through numerous food trader networks with varying capacities to ensure the safety of food. Complicating matters are the inclusion of millions of "small farmers" (*xiaononghu* 小农户) whom food safety officials deride as "backward (*luohou* 落后)," guided by "a peasant consciousness (*nongminyishi* 农民意识)," with a "quality problem (*suzhiwenti* 素质问题)."[1] Because of these small farmers, officials claim, traceability is nearly impossible and accountability and monitoring measures extraordinarily challenging. Government officials, quick to deflect criticism of their own initiatives, emphatically assert that to solve the food safety crisis, China's food producers, particularly its small farmers, must be reorganized to fit into "scientific (*kexue* 科学)," "modern (*xiandai* 现代)," and "standardized (*guifan* 规范)" supply chains. Needless to say, given these attitudes and objectives, the ambitious state-led plans to modernize the agricultural production system have thus far failed. The frustration on both sides of the regulatory equation, between both the regulators and the regulated, is palpable. Given this challenging context, this chapter will consider in more specific detail the issues at hand in addressing the daunting task of reorganizing the small farmer.

"Dragonhead" enterprises (*longtouqiye* 龙头企业) and farmers' cooperatives (*nongminzhuanyehezuoshe* 农民专业合作社) have been tasked with rationalizing food production by vertically integrating suppliers, and

---

[1] For a more in-depth discussion of "suzhi" as it relates to social and political hierarchies in China see Kipnis (2006).

transmitting food safety knowledge to China's producers. In addition to monitoring their own supply chains, dragonheads and cooperatives are also responsible for "leading" (*daidong* 带动) other nearby producers by providing training courses, technical assistance, and quality inputs.

China's enlistment of dragonheads and cooperatives in food safety regulation can be viewed as a coregulatory approach to food safety.[2] Coregulation refers to collaborative regulatory efforts between the state and industry in which the state sets broad standards for production quality and enlists industry to develop its own specific standards (Martinez et al. 2007). By including state authorities, businesses, and civic groups, coregulation better aligns incentives and lowers the surveillance costs of the state (Martinez et al. 2007; Loader & Hobbs 1999). In theory, coregulation combines the strengths of self-regulation with the benefits of state oversight. Direct participation of stakeholders in the regulatory process helps to create responsive rules that reflect producer concerns (Eijlander 2005). Also, state backing for these codes of practice provides predictability and the threat of sanction for noncompliance (Martinez et al. 2007).

Studies from other developing countries have shown that vertical integration and the development of intermediary organizations, such as farmers' cooperatives, have led to improved outcomes in food quality and safety (Okello & Swinton 2007; Reardon et al. 2004; Moustier et al. 2010; Hobbs et al. 2000). But these studies have largely been conducted in countries with different scale conditions than China's, where supply chains are far more complex. The coregulatory initiatives in China must integrate various scales of production and distribution, including small farming networks, regional wholesalers, and large-scale agro-processors with national reach.

As is the case for the country's state-led food safety policies, China's coregulatory efforts have failed because of unattended scale politics. First, neither dragonheads nor cooperatives have complete control over their respective supply chains. The dragonheads, which operate according to a hierarchical, centralized governance framework, cannot control suppliers in regional and local networks. Cooperatives, which operate according to a model of decentralized, collaborative governance, face opposition from production networks operating at larger scales. Second,

---

[2] In China, however, these new arrangements do not have a statutory basis, and can thus only be considered a quasi-coregulatory policy.

the practical challenges of integrating production systems of different scale have not been thoroughly considered.

DRAGONHEADS

Dragonhead enterprises—large-scale agro-processors—have been employed to vertically integrate China's producers into advanced supply chains from the top-down. These corporations are referred to as "dragonhead enterprises" because the headquarters of the company operating at the largest scale, the "dragon's head," vertically integrates supplier networks operating at smaller scales along its "tail." Dragonhead enterprises emerged in the mid-1990s as part of a government effort to industrialize the agricultural sector (Zhang 2012). In 1996, there were only 5,381 firms, but this number had grown to more than 61,286 by 2006 (Huang 2011). These firms seek to rescale Chinese food production from networks of small household farms to supply chains operating on a national, if not global, scale, employing knowledge and network-related managerial practices aimed at larger scales of production and distribution.

As the beneficiary of state subsidies, preferential loans, and tax breaks, the dragonhead is expected to facilitate economic development and implement food safety policies as regional and local producer networks are incorporated into its supply chain. The dragonheads follow a model of centralized, hierarchical control. Strict quality control regimes are imposed through production contracts and periodic on-site inspections of processors who are responsible for their own producers (ZZ 35). Agricultural products are graded and priced by dragonhead agents, helping farmers to better understand the relationship between price and food safety (YL 23). Dragonhead firms also provide suppliers with high-quality inputs at subsidized prices, which help to eliminate risks arising from the use of substandard or counterfeit products. If discovered, farmers who run afoul of their production contracts are severely penalized: they are liable for the cost of all inputs provided by the company and must sell their products at half their value (YL 21).

Centralized, hierarchical control begins to breakdown as smaller production networks are integrated into the dragonhead's large-scale production and distribution system. Studies have highlighted shortfalls in the ability of dragonheads to vertically integrate household producers that are further upstream (Jia et al. 2010; Huang et al. 2007). Dragonheads are not in direct control of local production networks, but often must partner with local officials and production networks. In addition, direct on-site monitoring is often unfeasible, and firms must instead resort to sporadic spot checks or delegate this authority to agents.

Local Production Networks vs. National Dragonhead Corporations

Two scalar visions regarding production come into conflict as national dragonheads face off against local production networks. Head offices seek to attain GlobalGAP certification, focus on national and international markets, and seek to develop standard operating procedures that can be imposed uniformly throughout the supply chain. But, because of their status as outsiders, dragonhead quality control technicians complain that their suppliers, particularly small farmers, are highly uncooperative in adopting new production standards (NX 3, NX 4; EX 11; ZZ 35; ZZ 36). One government official who works closely with dragonhead producers comments, "Small farmers are difficult to handle. We can't control them and we can't get them to listen. Since our capital is incredibly tight, we simply cannot invest in managing [them]." (ZZ 56). A fundamental question arises as to what scale is best positioned to govern the system: Should local production networks determine food safety practices and production protocols, or, should they be subsumed within a larger scale framework of governance that enforces standardization and global food safety norms?

From the perspective of local production networks, many believe dragonhead enterprises are trying to extract high-quality product at below-market prices, and refuse to cooperate with procurement officers. A majority of the farmers view their produce as being safe enough for their families to consume and, thus, do not understand why dragonhead agents provide a lower price point: "I don't like working through [dragonheads] because they always purchase at a lower price. We are at a loss how prices are worked out because the processing center is a mystery" (ZZ 18). Farmers complain that even though they abide by their contracts and provide safe products, the enterprise safety grading system is highly arbitrary (YL 21). Accordingly, local producers view company representatives as predatory agents. Many believe that when dragonheads enforce food safety, they do so only in the interests of their downstream clients in the global marketplace, with little interest in the local community (ZZ 35). On both sides of the scale boundary, pervasive mistrust leads to failed regulatory coordination.

Dragonheads have attempted to assert hierarchical control by circumventing local production networks by organizing their own producers on a base. On-base production avoids most of the regulatory conflict arising from scale politics. Similar to state-run agricultural production bases, dragonhead bases have on-site management and producers are hand picked. A production base can range in size from 10 to 1,000 hectares. The base may also have an on-site or readily available testing laboratory and basic processing facilities. Farmers who work on base are subject to extensive training. Under these conditions, food safety processes are well understood by employees, and on-site management can address problems that emerge in real time.

Due to restrictions on land use, however, most dragonhead firms are unable to source exclusively from production bases and must also procure crops through unregulated production networks. Therefore, scale politics within the supply chain between dragonheads and local production networks is unavoidable. And, when dragonheads are unable to assert their authority throughout the supply chain, regulatory coordination suffers.

Knowledge-Related and Managerial Issues across Scales

Linking networks of various scale also requires addressing potential mismatches on the knowledge-related and managerial dimensions of scale. A lack of hierarchical control, however, leads to conflicts between producers and the dragonhead regarding food safety standards given their different scale orientations. On the knowledge-related dimension of scale, farmers frame food safety issues in local terms, whereas dragonheads emphasize global and national food safety demands. In terms of management, dragonhead standard operating procedures that are designed to be uniformly imposed throughout the entire supply chain do not comport with local food safety realities.

Food safety technicians from the head company struggle to teach farmers who resist the adoption of new food safety knowledge developed at the global scale. Exasperated, control staff claim that resistance is largely a result of farmers having a "peasant consciousness" and being unwilling to change (ZZ 30). Dragonhead technicians complain that local officials and producers insist that their products meet company standards, but that most of these actors have little understanding about the real science behind food safety rules: "the major problem is lack of agricultural knowledge. Forty- to sixty-year-olds have no idea about agricultural best practices, and are trying to lead the way, yet they themselves know nothing about safe techniques" (NX 4). One executive believes this is a result of the underdeveloped food market at the county level and below: "the [lack of understanding] is due to the lack of exposure to high-quality products" (ZZ 30). Farmers have a weak conception of food safety and are less likely to accept new standards (NX 4). More sympathetic auditors admit that certification schemes imposed by dragonheads such as GlobalGAP are ill-suited to Chinese farming conditions; requirements concerning "energy-saving" and "environmentally friendly" agricultural techniques seem irrelevant to Chinese farmers who face harsh production environments (EX 1).

Dragonheads have tried to overcome this conflict over food safety know-how by establishing local development projects to upgrade agricultural production. Programs have included the building of schools and training centers for peasants, poverty relief efforts, and infrastructural investments. One dragonhead enterprise, for example, has established a school and model farming areas that work in tandem with the local government's agricultural training network: HM Horticulture in Shandong province trains 300 agronomists a year, and provides technical assistance to thousands of farmers (EX 11).

Dragonheads must also address scale politics on the managerial dimension of scale, as standard operating procedures (largest scale) are broken down into actionable tasks (smallest scale). Dragonheads seek to impose standard operating procedures across the breadth of their supply chain. But, because these large-scale enterprises are not in unilateral control of the production process, they must also negotiate with numerous officials who seek to protect local practices often diametrically in opposition to standardized operating procedures. One food safety expert explained that China's production conditions are extraordinarily diverse, and producing a uniform production protocol is a foolhardy enterprise. He recalls how he was taught about desert cultivation when he was a young QA inspector in Gansu:

The head office had sent us off to work with farmers on a new type of seedling, we spent all day teaching them how to plant them properly. At the end of the session, a group of farmers starts pouring two to three inches of sand on top of them. In frustration, I ran over the field and berated the farmers. That evening a huge gust came and blew all the sand off the seedlings...except for the field with my foot prints...that field had been completely destroyed. We had no idea what we were dealing with (EX4).

Local producers argue that integrating with dragonheads has been challenging because head offices implement policies without understanding local growing conditions. One farmer comments: "We don't like the dragonhead model because the company isn't close to the ground . . . they don't understand the real situation and that can cause significant problems" (JS 1). Dragonhead executives, however, comment that because they manage large supply networks, they cannot possibly integrate all local practices into their standard operating procedures, nor should they be expected to (ZJ 19).

Tensions on the managerial dimension of scale are evident when assessing dragonhead contract relations. In an ideal system, companywide food safety guidelines are scaled down to specific tasks that are mandated in contracts. However, many farmers admit that they do not understand the terms of their contracts and are unclear about how contract conditions relate to "food safety" more generally. And, for many, rather than viewing food safety specifications as binding, these farmers prefer to understand them as optional, which frustrates dragonhead quality control personnel. They view contract commitments as "production" matters, which are unrelated to food safety: "We don't know what we are doing in terms of food safety . . . we just follow what is specified in the contract. We don't 'get' food safety in that we don't understand the laws or anything of that sort . . . it's a production matter, not a question of safety" (YL 21). In effect, as a matter of food safety, farmers remain uncertain as to how their day-to-day tasks cohere into a broad strategy to ensure safe food.

Scalar Ignorance and Agronomists Who Don't Wear Boots

In terms of sensitivity to developments at the local scale, dragonhead enterprises are relatively detached from on-the-ground production conditions. Many head offices are not located within the provinces in which production takes place. One dragonhead, for example, operates all of its eel farms in Guangdong province but is headquartered in Zhejiang province (ZJ 19). An anecdote from a foreign auditor in China highlights the disconnect between many agro-processor head offices and their production sites. He recalls when technicians from the head office were sent down to monitor his progress when he was managing a farm in Shandong. Conflicts arose concerning production volumes, storage, and water usage. But, the most frustrating problem was that none of the inspectors were wearing boots. Exasperated, he told me, "How can you inspect a farm without walking the land? Many of these young agronomists from the head office have never even been out on the land before. So, we trudged along – them in their patent leather shoes and me in my boots. It's crazy, really" (EX 1). The farm eventually failed.

As a result of this distance, farmers enumerate how dragonhead offices are unaware of the scale externalities that flow from their production decisions. First, dragonheads do not understand how costs translate across different scales of production. For example, decisions to cut costs or increase the price of inputs at headquarters disproportionately hurt local farmers who already face thin profit margins. Individuals find that inputs purchased from the dragonhead firm are prohibitively expensive, and while farmers may fetch higher prices by selling to dragonheads, the costs of inputs quickly erode profits (Calvin et al. 2006). Second, strict production rules imposed from above make it difficult to respond to changing conditions on the ground. Some auditors note that given the widespread pest conditions that farmers face, dragonhead stipulations specifying a certain amount of pesticide usage may prove inadequate, leading to widespread infestations (EX 4).

The lack of feedback about the effect of dragonhead decisions on their local-level producers is exacerbated by asymmetries in economic power. Farmers have little ability to negotiate the terms of their contracts, or to participate in decision-making concerning food production. Decisions are made unilaterally by head offices that specify the volume and quality grade of production based on the demands of a national market. When dragonheads lower purchasing prices, producers have no choice but to cut costs by using inferior inputs, which can lead to food safety problems. In addition, a lack of open dialogue fosters significant mistrust between contract farmers and the dragonhead: "if you join a dragonhead enterprise, you lose your voice and are kept out of the decision-making process" (ZZ 58). Farmers cannot communicate their concerns to dragonhead agents, impeding information flows, and promoting widespread noncompliance.

In summary, disruptive scale politics emerge as dragonhead enterprises engage local production networks. Resistance from local production networks makes it difficult for dragonheads to assert control over producers, and food safety practices cannot be implemented at lower scales. As a result, dragonhead coregulatory policies have largely failed. Actors cannot agree on the appropriate scale of production and distribution, conflicts arise concerning knowledge-related and managerial dimensions of scale, and ignorance of scale externalities leads to coordination challenges.

Unaddressed scale politics pose real food safety risks. As interests are further misaligned, producers will be less inclined to follow food safety directives that they consider out of touch given their scale of operation. If producers fail to understand food safety rules, they may skirt rules they think are unreasonable. Moreover, head offices that ignore scale external-ities run the risk that local food safety problems spread throughout the supply chain.

COOPERATIVES ENSURING FOOD SAFETY FROM THE BOTTOM-UP

In the early 2000s, as a response to the challenges that dragonhead enter-prises faced when integrating farmers into their supply chains, the cen-tral government also advanced a bottom-up coregulatory effort involving farmers' cooperatives (Jia et al. 2010). While farmers' cooperatives had emerged as early as the 1980s, the national government only began sys-tematically promoting the cooperative model beginning in 2004 (World Bank 2006). Farmers' cooperatives exemplify a model of decentralized and collaborative control. Most operate as voluntary associations in which farmers collaborate to establish common standards, increase pro-duction volumes, and gain increased market share for their products (Zachernuk 2008). As of 2010, the State Administration for Industry and Commerce estimated that 311,700 cooperatives had been established, with nearly 10% of China's farmer population participating in them (Chen & Zhao 2010).

The cooperative's model of decentralized and collaborative control encounters scale politics as it links to supply chains operating at broader scales. Individuals accustomed to a bottom-up process of decision-making must engage with actors operating at scales that govern from the top-down. While cooperatives are favored by local actors, they face oppo-sition from buyers operating at larger scales because of their lack of organizational capacity and nonstandard practices. Moreover, coopera-tive members themselves often resist scaling up, that is, being subsumed into larger supply chains, because of the perceived loss of control over standard setting, production, and distribution. Cooperative producers are granted voting rights and are able to withdraw from the cooperative at any point in time, but these rights are quickly eroded as cooperatives are vertically integrated. In effect, the cooperative's struggles are an upended mirror image of the challenges that dragonheads face due to the conse-quences of scale.

Studies indicate that cooperatives in China primarily channel their goods to the wholesale market with some penetration into modern supply chains (Jia et al. 2010), but that few cooperatives have been able to adopt more advanced food safety practices (Zhou & Jin 2009). In general, a host of fiscal and coordination problems plague cooperatives, inhibiting the development of contract employment relations that could facilitate the scaling up of cooperative networks. Despite initial enthusiasm for the cooperative development model, one bureau director estimated in 2011 that nearly 40% of its county's cooperatives exited the market. The same official remarked that these now-defunct cooperatives constituted "the initial victims of the county's blind push for cooperative development" (ZZ 21).

Bureau officials explained that cooperatives are unable to operate in the context of larger scale production and distribution systems due to the weak management skills of cooperative leadership: "most of them have significant capital flow problems and don't understand how best to operate.... Cooperative management is weak. They lack the facilities and cannot coordinate production...only [large-scale] processing firms can expand production in the way to develop the county" (ZZ 21).

Conflict over the Scale of Governance

The cooperative is centered on dynamics at the village, township, and county scales of operation. In terms of knowledge, the cooperative provides basic guidelines for safe food production based on the experiences of producers in local townships. In most cases, the emphasis is on addressing local food safety issues, and not on seeking compliance with national food safety certifications. In terms of networks, cooperatives are locally based organizations composed of farmers from neighboring communities. Typically, the cooperative is led by wealthy producers or cadres who are considered local leaders. Some cooperatives also benefit from a shared history of collectivized agricultural production during the Maoist period. When cooperatives are successful, the organization can serve as the center of associational life. Much like CSA farms, it is the frequent face-to-face interactions lead to the creation of high levels of social trust among producers, which lends itself to better food safety outcomes.

When farmers' cooperatives remain locally oriented, interests regarding food safety and cooperative development are strongly aligned. At the local scale, frequent interaction and social ties among producers create strong pressures to comply with food safety rules. Participants are encouraged to abide by production standards in order to help the cooperative develop: "investing in food safety will help our cooperative develop faster and improve the livelihood of our village community" (YL 22). Members explain that they are willing to invest in food safety because this translates into higher selling prices and strengthens the cooperative's brand (ZZ 49; ZZ 50; ZZ 3; ZZ 45). Residents also view successful cooperatives as a vehicle for local growth more generally. As a result, cooperatives observe a higher level of commitment to baseline food safety and quality control.

Producers are also incentivized to join cooperatives and follow production standards because doing so offers tangible benefits to members in the form of small subsidies and information on market conditions. One cooperative, for example, offers discounted feed to co-op members, dispatches technical teams at regular intervals to assist farmers with production, and provides farmers with information on market prices (ZZ 10). As a result, farmers obtain higher prices in local food markets: "inputs were cheaper and we could spread our risk and control for price fluctuations . . . we learned techniques for fertilizer usage and got experience from the outside . . . our incomes increased by almost 30%." (ZZ 46).

However, as cooperatives link up with production networks operating at broader scales to distribute food on a wider basis, local cooperatives come into conflict over production practices. Cooperatives are generally more focused on local market development and do not foresee local markets demanding food safety standards beyond the basic provision of food that uses high-quality inputs. A crisis arises as to what "scale" should be emphasized in the cooperative system—the needs of local producers or the broader market.

The Multidimensional Challenges of Scaling Up

At a pork-producing cooperative, cooperative members understand and implement food safety measures that reflect local production concerns, such as pest infestations, water supplies, and agricultural inputs. Farmers attend classes on a monthly basis, and discuss concerns that have emerged in the past month. Director Wang, the head of the piggery, is constantly on his phone discussing the effects of veterinary drugs or record-keeping minutiae with his members (ZZ 3). However, he explains as his cooperative scales up to incorporate food safety best practices developed for the broader market, his producers struggle to understand the rationale for these rules (ZZ 3).

Unlike dragonheads, food safety practices employed by cooperatives are based on context-specific knowledge. Most cooperatives adopt a basic code of practice that requires members to purchase inputs from the cooperative, submit to cooperative management, follow a single food safety standard, and sell at the same time. This "unified management" (*tongyiguanli* 统一管理) model reflects baseline food safety concerns that local farmers face on a daily basis, rather than specifying technical food safety requirements (ZZ 3; ZZ 10). For example, the reason why cooperatives emphasize purchasing inputs from a single, approved distributor is because local markets cannot guarantee the quality of feed, pesticides, seeds, and veterinary drugs. In one county, middlemen had been discovered adding concrete, sand, and other cheap material to feed to increase its weight (ZZ 53).

However, as cooperatives seek to link to larger scale production networks and coordinate with agro-processors that impose stringent food safety demands, cooperatives struggle to comply. Problems emerge on the knowledge-related and network-related dimensions of scale. First, cooperative leadership points to difficulties in implementation of new food safety standards due to a general lack of education. One cooperative leader comments, "Too many people are illiterate and our knowledge base is weak . . . we can't implement complicated standards" (YL 9). Second, as cooperatives scale up, they face supply chain pressures that do not exist on the local scale. In particular, downstream buyers demand higher volumes, which complicates management of cooperative members (ZZ 35). Third, interviews reveal that cooperatives that have merged with larger production networks face a paradox—while their size and production volume makes them more amenable to adopting "green" or "organic" certification, they are less able to control their farmers to ensure that they understand these new rules (ZZ 3). As production networks expand, frequent interactions between members become more difficult, weakening social ties among farmers and compromising the ability of cooperatives to monitor and train producers.

A Victim of Higher-Scale Processes

Often, in appraising systems, one considers how well an organization responds to developments at lower scales. But, it is equally important to consider how well a system reacts to changing conditions at larger scales. Cooperatives are highly sensitive to changing conditions on the ground, but struggle to respond to developments occurring at higher scales.

Cooperatives hold bimonthly training sessions and visit farms a few times a month, which help to facilitate the transfer of knowledge among producers (ZZ 14). Farmers are invited to contact their representatives as new problems emerge and are encouraged to use a whistleblower (*jubao*

举报) system in which farmers can monitor and report on one another to the cooperative leadership. Farmers do not feel that they have the legal authority to impose restrictions on their neighbors, but many comment that if a neighbor's practices endangered their local community, they would immediately alert the authorities (ZZ 60). One farmer comments, "We need to look out for each other. Otherwise, it comes back and haunt us in the form of lower prices or hurts our reputation" (YL 22).

Cooperatives, however, are typically adversely affected by developments at higher scales. For example, as global markets demand firms to acquire food safety certifications, such as GlobalGAP, to enter into broader markets, cooperatives can do little but follow suit. Leaders assert that seeking certifications or adopting new best practices developed at larger scales creates significant problems for local producers because acquiring certification only increases costs without accruing enough benefits to producers (ZZ 3). Requirements imposed by downstream distributors involve significant investments in new machinery and food safety certifications, which most cooperative leaders believe will not be recouped (ZZ 17).

In summary, cooperatives face significant challenges from processes unfolding at higher scales of production and distribution. The strengths conferred upon cooperatives due to their local orientation also serve as weaknesses as these organizations interact with other downstream actors in a supply chain. Contracts replace face-to-face interactions. Collaborative meetings are no longer held. Instead, instructions are received through a buyer of an often faceless corporation. As different perspectives clash regarding the appropriate food safety approach, regulatory coordination suffers.

COMPETITIVE REGULATORY RELATIONSHIPS

Increasingly, both models of production have come into conflict with one another. It is notable that cooperatives emerged as a response to the failures of dragonhead enterprises, not as part of a comprehensive plan to supplement or assist dragonheads in integrating China's producers into modern supply chains. While the government began to advocate a model of integrated production known as the "Company + Cooperative + Household" (*qiye* + *hezuoshe* + *nonghu* 企业 + 合作社 + 农户) model, which could be understood as an attempt to integrate producers of different scale into a single system, procedures for coordinating production were left unspecified. And, because each scale of production represents a distinctive view of agricultural development, coordination has been difficult.

In some areas, a lack of coordination has escalated into open conflict between officials advocating cooperative development and those in support of dragonheads. Officials who oppose the expansion of cooperatives view cooperatives as only providing an intermediate step toward addressing food safety problems, and refuse to invest in what they view to be a failed coregulatory initiative. Their main objection to the further spread of cooperatives is that the model is ill-equipped to facilitate a transition to industrialized agriculture: "cooperatives are good for the initial development, but dragonhead enterprises are better at setting standards and moving toward a standardized (规范) development model." (ZZ 56). Provincial level officials, in particular, prefer dragonhead companies that can develop agricultural production bases focused on a single product (ZJ 3). By contrast, in their view, cooperatives "lack organizational capacity," "lack techniques," and are "incapable of meeting higher standards" (YL 3; NX 1; NX 2). Whether these assessments are accurate have yet to be empirically assessed, but the difference in views highlights the divergence of official views on the appropriate scale of agricultural production.

In many cases, government opposition toward cooperatives is displayed as much through a lack of support as it is through outright prohibitions. For example, some government officials have simply not promoted the cooperative model in their locality. Other times governments have provided only meager financial support and training to registered cooperatives. In one county in Sichuan, the vast majority of cooperatives were entirely funded by contributions from participating farmers. Lack of state support, in the form of subsidies, state-backed loans, or technical assistance, forced several cooperatives to exit the market. As one failed cooperative farmer explained, "The small subsidies the government provided were not enough to make up for the initial costs [of setting up the cooperative]. No one wanted to participate after a while" (ZZ 17).

Dragonhead enterprises can also face significant opposition from government officials, especially at the township level. First, some townships refuse to allow dragonheads to source from their farms because they view them as predatory, whereas cooperatives are viewed as promoting inclusive growth (ZZ 19; YL 16; YL 17). Second, other township officials block dragonhead entry into local markets because they are difficult to govern. One township official argued that dragonhead enterprises were difficult to regulate because of their economic clout and technical expertise, and implied that cooperatives were easier to manage: "everyone thinks that these dragonhead firms can improve food safety, but in the end I'd rather have several small cooperatives that do not comply with food safety due to ignorance than one large company that actively uses science to get around the food safety law" (YL 3). Especially in fiscally strapped localities, regulators suggest that dragonheads can have a disproportionate amount of control over how regulation is implemented. Third, high-quality products from the dragonhead are sometimes not permitted to circulate in the local market. One dragonhead corporation claimed that local officials believe that allowing dragonheads to sell products in townships would effectively drive out local products and would have a deleterious effect on local development (ZZ 30).

The lack of a comprehensive plan for integrated production has led to conflict between those advancing the dragonhead production model, and those preferring a more grassroots approach. Ad hoc policy making does not always lead to scale politics, but it does increase the likelihood of conflict, and can contribute to regulatory incoherence across scales.

A POTENTIAL SOLUTION?

Innovative approaches to address scale politics have emerged to better coordinate dragonheads and cooperatives in their coregulatory efforts. Increasingly, dragonhead enterprises have established their own cooperatives to manage upstream farmers (ZZ 30; NX 2; NX 3). Although this production model is designed specifically to lower transaction costs between enterprise and producers, this strategy has the added benefit of mitigating scale politics.[3]

Cooperatives established by dragonheads can serve as "scale-bridging organizations" (Cash et al. 2006). That is, an intermediary organization that can facilitate coordination across units operating at different scales. First, dragonhead enterprises provide high-level technical training to cooperative leadership, invest in cooperative production facilities, and link cooperatives to advanced consumer channels. Second, cooperatives then transmit and translate new food safety information into an understandable format for farmers to understand. Third, due to the cooperatives' local presence, they can more easily disseminate new production practices, and local networks can be employed to improve monitoring

---

[3] Investing in cooperatives also provides dragonheads with a number of advantages that are unavailable to them when contracting farmers directly—the most important being the acquisition of land through cooperatives.

and surveillance. Their elevated local status and position within the community also enables them to better communicate with the dragonhead's agents to facilitate improvements and highlight concerns.

Most significantly, the cooperative can facilitate communication between local producers and the dragonhead when conflicts emerge as how best to address food safety issues. Farmers can raise concerns with the cooperative and these can then be passed on to the company. Because the cooperative is accountable to its cooperative members and the company, it is viewed by all participants as a *credible mediator* acting in the interests of both parties.

This scale solution, however, does have its limitations in addressing scale politics. Studies regarding this production arrangement show that there is still a significant power asymmetry between company and farmer, even with the presence of an intermediary organization (Chen & Zhao 2010). Due to the sheer economic influence that dragonheads wield, cooperatives sometimes find themselves unable to effectively negotiate with their corporate sponsors. As a result cooperatives sometimes are captured by corporate elites who simply view cooperatives as corporate agents rather than as representatives of local production networks. Yet despite its limitations, the model does mitigate scale politics and provides a potential path to integrate cooperatives and dragonheads into a unified coregulatory strategy.

CONCLUSION

China's coregulatory policies to address food safety challenges face a significant scale problem. Despite the best intentions of upstream and downstream producers and government officials, coregulatory approaches

TABLE 7.1 *Scale Politics for Cooperatives and Dragonheads*

	Cooperatives	Dragonheads
Scale of Governance	Local production network vs. downstream distributors	National supply chain vs. local production network
Multidimensional Conflict	Knowledge- and network-related	Knowledge-, managerial-, and network-related
Scalar Externalities	Detached from food safety concerns in nonlocal markets	Detached from local producers; no feedback mechanisms

cannot avoid severe scale politics. Dragonheads cannot extend their model of centralized, hierarchical control to local production networks operating at smaller scales. And, decentralized, informal forms of governance used by cooperatives cannot engender the same degree of trust and collaboration with large-scale distributors. Government initiatives to use farmers' cooperatives and dragonhead enterprises to integrate agricultural production into "modern" and "scientific" supply chains to enforce food safety standards have fallen short.

This chapter reveals how the inability to reconcile the knowledge- and network-related dimensions of scale has led to poorly coordinated supply chains. The cooperative operates most effectively in local communities, and can be sensitive to emerging food safety risks and challenges at the local scale. A major concern, however, is the cooperative's inability to move beyond the implementation of basic food safety procedures and to comply with food safety demands that come from beyond the local market. To be sure, cooperatives do provide modest improvements in food safety, but the question remains as to how to transition from this intermediate level to advanced food safety compliance. Dragonheads face problems in the opposite direction. Dragonheads operate in large national production networks and follow scientific best practices for food safety. Yet their primary difficulty relates to enforcing their production standards on upstream producers who find dragonhead methods to be predatory.

China's coregulatory strategy is yet another example of how an uncoordinated, ad hoc approach has unintentionally fostered conflict between those who advocate cooperative development and those who support industrialization through dragonheads. In certain areas, government officials actively resist cooperative development, whereas in others officials undermine the activities of dragonhead firms. While a potential solution has emerged in which dragonheads establish local cooperatives, scale problems can still get in the way. Cooperatives do run the risk of becoming corporate tools of dragonhead management, which can generate resentment among local suppliers. The uneasy arrangements may point to a fundamental incongruence between organizations that depend on social trust to coordinate activities and those that are largely guided by price.

Focusing on the "problem of scale" in reorganizing China's multitude of small farmers offers an important vantage point regarding why some coregulatory schemes are effective and others are not. Even when producers possess a genuine commitment to sound regulatory objectives and have the technical capacity to improve food safety, it remains a challenge for them to overcome regulatory scale politics. This chapter suggests that coregulation advocates should consider the strengths and weaknesses of certain coregulators as they scale up and scale down on knowledge- and network-related scales. The Chinese experience of coregulation shows that policy makers must reassess the structure of supply chains, the types of coregulators available, and the nature of state-industry coordination in terms of scale and the resultant coordination failures (summarized in Table 7.1) before advancing coregulatory solutions.

8

Scaling Down

Moving from the Global to the Local

Is it possible for China's export sector to provide a viable solution to China's domestic food safety problem? Food safety policy studies often ask this very question, and then prematurely assert that the export sector can indeed serve as a model for the domestic food safety system (ADB 2005; UN 2008; Calvin et al. 2006). The assumptions are superficially appealing: (1) knowledge and best practices can be *gradually* diffused into the broader market; (2) export-oriented producers can *eventually* begin to supply the domestic market, driving out substandard producers; and (3) domestic consumers *will begin* to demand export quality goods for consumption that are comparably priced. However, these purported mechanisms for policy diffusion and market driven action are largely only asserted and not empirically demonstrated.

The question of whether the export regulatory food safety model—which emphasizes centralized, hierarchical control—can be extended to the domestic sector directly addresses the challenge of "scaling down" in a large, heterogeneous context. To reiterate, the notion of scaling down refers specifically to translating processes, procedures, and knowledge developed for large-scale production and distribution networks to smaller scale production networks. Can the model of a highly centralized export food safety regime be used to successfully integrate a multitude of decentralized policy communities at smaller scales that exist and operate in a more complex heterogeneous context? It is one thing to effectively convey global food safety practices, such as GAP, GMP, BRC, and ISO15000, to handpicked producers, and quite another to impose these standards on millions of small-scale farmers.

This chapter considers the challenges that exporting companies face as they expand operations into the domestic sector. In China, export producers are increasingly engaging in a dual production and distribution model, in which they supply exported foodstuffs to foreign partners and, concurrently, source and distribute food products locally. To accomplish their bifurcated objectives, these companies and their related distribution houses must actively ring-fence their export sector while they simultaneously extend their operations in the vastly more complex domestic sector. In effect, by observing the experience of these dual production exporting organizations, we can explore how a centralized, hierarchical mode of governance fares in the domestic sector. We will observe that as these exporters try to integrate the global and local aspects of food production and distribution activities in the domestic sector, they face severe scale politics on jurisdictional, knowledge-related, and network-related dimensions. We will then consider, relatedly, why policies effectively employed in a sector integrated with governance systems operating at a global scale have a different effect when they are applied to other scale contexts (i.e., right strategy, wrong scale).

MULTIDIMENSIONAL CHALLENGES

A centralized, hierarchical governance framework may operate effectively in small, homogenous contexts where policy communities are uniformly oriented toward the global scale, and global food safety participants are recognized as regulatory authorities. However, as exporters expand their operations into the domestic sector, they find that not all regulators and producers share a common view as to either the primary scale of governance (degree-of-zoom) or the multidimensional challenges (jurisdiction, knowledge, networks) that direct or guide their actions. Thus, these globalized firms encounter severe scale politics that impede centralized, hierarchical control.

Jurisdictional Issues

As an exporter of food extends its reach into the domestic sector, it faces numerous jurisdictional challenges. In the export sector, producers operate in a system of global scale and interact with a centralized regulatory bureaucracy (AQSIQ), which is enmeshed in the global network of food safety authorities and transnational organizations. Prior to the 2015 reforms, however, dual production companies had to work with domestic regulatory authorities that were relatively more fragmented and divided than those they dealt with in the export sector. Because this fragmentation of authority is replicated at multiple levels of government operating at different degrees-of-zoom, negotiating jurisdictional scale politics were particularly vexing.

Prior to the 2015 reforms, as an export producer moved from a system of global scale in the export sector to one that operated on the national scale in the domestic sector, it first had to contend with the Quality Technical Supervision Bureau (QTSB), which is the domestic arm of AQSIQ and manages the domestic food safety certification program known as QS. A common problem that enterprises who engage in dual production face is that standards used in the export sector, which are modeled on global best practices, are seen as failing to meet the standards employed in the domestic sector's system. Corporate quality control managers are often surprised when products certified as safe for export do not meet domestic standards for consumption. This bizarre outcome arises because export producers often supply food products that have not previously been circulated in the national market. Due to heightened food safety concerns, QTSB officials are highly suspect of new products, even from reputable producers. As one exporter comments, "They aren't that well trained and so they create unrealistic standards to protect themselves" (EX 6). Another company pointed out how the QTSB required a company to use high levels of irradiation technology to prevent microbial contamination of a product when using those levels of radiation were "out of line with global standards" (EX 6). Quality control managers were presented with an untenable dilemma where they had to knowingly violate global standards to comply with local ones, or be barred from the Chinese market altogether.

Several producers point to a broken and incoherent domestic certification process that is unnecessarily lengthy and costly. To acquire the QS certification necessary for the distribution of products in the domestic sector, companies must pass audits at the municipal and provincial levels, and each audit, which costs RMB 20,000, can only include 2 to 3 products (EX 6). Given that many producers may have as many as 50 or more different product types, the audit procedure can be prohibitively expensive and lengthy. And, because standards differ from locality to locality, companies may have to have their products approved in other jurisdictions. This seems particularly burdensome to producers who had already attained global certifications and passed far more stringent audits. These problems have become less acute following the 2015 reforms, but exporters still highlight the challenge of navigating the domestic regulatory environment.

But perhaps most frustrating to these QC managers is the perception that QTSB officials are usually less educated than their AQSIQ counterparts and are unfamiliar with best practices developed at the global scale. Quality assurance managers at three major corporations held that the QTSB is far less professionalized compared to AQSIQ in the export sector (EX 1; EX 3; EX 6). Feelings of mistrust and suspicion that fuel scale politics are compounded by rumors that QTSB's heavy-handed approach is especially targeted toward foreign food producers and distributors. Walmart, for example, was forced to close all 13 stores in Chongqing for food safety violations, whereas local retailers were not punished (Bradsher 2011).

Knowledge-Related Problems

Jurisdictional concerns, however, are relatively less complicated than facilitating the transfer of knowledge from producers and regulators from the global to the local. The export sector's producers have long operated in a regulatory environment in which scientific processes and risk assessment represent standard practice. In the export sector, producers spend significant time performing tests on soil content, water quality, and pesticide residues. Even smaller exporters regularly submit reports to independent labs, third-party certifiers, and government regulators. Producers, auditors, and AQSIQ government regulators are well-integrated into the global food safety knowledge production regime and attend global conferences on food safety and quality. The Global Food Safety Initiative, for example, has played an important role in influencing food safety practices in China's export sector.[1]

Government authorities within the domestic sector, however, must balance a commitment to scientific, risk-based analysis in food production with other political realities. Provincial, municipal, and county officials do not operate regulatory systems in a vacuum, but must consider how scientific information disclosures could lead to public panic or weaken a supervising agency's bargaining position. Food safety experts assert that the state is still somewhat uncomfortable with relinquishing complete control to technocratic experts. Specifically, exporters have complained that local government officials in the domestic sector do not respect the impartiality of scientists. One food safety auditor complained: "more must be

[1] For conference details please visit: www.chinafoodsafety.com/

done to ensure that standard setting is based on scientific risk analysis, and the integrity of testing procedures is protected" (EX 4). While food safety risk assessments may reveal weaknesses in a food production system, this type of information should be welcomed by administrative officials rather than regarded as subversive (Balzano 2012). The Shanghai SFDA has now developed a reputation for being a highly specialized agency that has given greater autonomy to its technical staff (Asian Development Bank 2005; Brewer 2012). However, many local agencies have yet to set up procedures and a culture toward science that are similarly committed to independent scientific analysis. It is important to note that export food safety regulators are operating at a global degree-of-zoom; they meet in the rarefied conference rooms of the Codex Committee, and do not face the same political pressures as local governmental authorities who must also contend with potential social unrest and other local economic realities.

An exporter provided a telling anecdote about a cucumber poisoning incident in Qingdao, which illustrates the government's conflicted views regarding scientific assessments of risk. In 2006, several hundred people in Qingdao were hospitalized after consuming cucumbers laced with a poisonous insecticide (QDZB 2006). The government immediately sent a text message to the city, warning that cucumbers should not be consumed. Government officials provided samples to an independent lab for testing. Upon discovering that cucumbers had residues of aldicarb that were at near lethal levels, all cucumbers were pulled from several wholesale markets. The less-publicized reality, however, is that the official who brought the sample to the lab was likely summarily disciplined for going outside of the government structure (EX 10). The reality of local circumstance, and the bitter lesson learned, are that one may use science to adjudicate food safety risks, but one must also be prepared to face the social and political consequences of being a whistle-blower.

Another problem is that local government authorities have a weak understanding of the risk regulation discourse and evolving food safety standards being developed at the global scale. Despite the prominent risk management and risk assessment provisions in the 2009 Food Safety Law, Balzano (2012), who writes on socialist jurisprudence, contends that risk management as a concept is not well understood in socialist governance. Whereas in Europe and North America, risk regulation acknowledges that a certain amount of risk is acceptable, in China the acceptance of risk constitutes an acceptance of noncompliant behavior, which Chinese officials have difficulty understanding. One county official in charge of aquatic production explained the confusion regarding risk management: "for us, either a producer has broken the law and needs to be punished, or he is compliant. If a producer is 30%, 50%, or 60% likely to have an incident, it doesn't matter...the question is whether he actually breaks the law (ZZ 56)."

This incoherent attitude toward risk management and science is also compounded by a lack of technical capacity among a large swath of regulators. Given the expense of testing, some officials do not subject all samples to testing. Sometimes labs will test for a limited selection of pesticides (EX 1). To be sure, some contend that this is because officials purposefully do not test for pesticides most commonly found on produce to inflate inspection pass rates (EX 4). Yet other food safety experts suggest that this is less a result of overt political manipulation, and more the simple result of a lack of knowledge regarding testing techniques: "major issues have to do with testing, you can use different tests to test for moisture. Results can be very different and the interpretation is just as difficult" (EX 10). Moreover, despite significant investment in recent years, China's network of laboratories still remains thin. Few townships have express testing labs that farmers can use. While most county offices are now equipped with sufficient laboratory capacity to test food, more complicated cases are still sent to the prefectural and provincial levels (Han 2007).

Network-Related Scale Politics

As exporters extend their mode of hierarchical, centralized control in the domestic sector they also face significant opposition from local production networks. Local producers resent what they perceive to be the overbearing, ill-informed, and costly monitoring and surveillance programs of these large multinationals, and resort to their own food safety fixes. As such, export managers say export practices are difficult to replicate in the uncontrolled setting of the domestic sector. One exporter comments, "The domestic market is not really capable of meeting such standards...pursuing standards would bankrupt the vast majority of farmers...so the real bleed over into the domestic sector is not possible" (EX 9).

Exporters themselves are hesitant to work with local production networks. The practices that enable export-approved companies to maintain high levels of food safety in the export sector also penalize the same companies for linking to production networks operating at smaller scales. Corporations express reservations about extending their supply chains to off-base production sites and domestic local networks due to heavy resistance regarding food safety practices (EX 3; EX 6; EX 16). Executives cite low levels of education, lack of exposure to global food safety knowledge, and the lack of experience with supply chain management among domestic producers (EX 9). Given the short shelf life of certain food products, and the high risk of microbial contamination, farmers need to operate according to strict schedules and standardized procedures.

The experience of the "AR" company is a typical example of an export-oriented firm that is hesitant to scale down its operations to local production networks (EX 16). AR employs more than 6,000 individuals and exports more than 100,000 tons of fish a year. Due to food safety concerns, the company imports all of its raw materials. Each employee is trained through an established series of lectures, classroom activities, and on-the-job training, which occurs over a three-month period. Given the grueling nature of the work, individuals are typically employed for three to four years, after which workers are recycled.

The processing center functions as part of an integrated production process operating on the global scale, which they call a "sea to fork" protocol. Trawlers bring in fish from the North Pacific. Each crate has a certificate specifying the area in which the fish were farmed, which boats they were handled by, and information regarding the overall fish population. Fish are then processed in China in accordance with global certifications such as BRC, GAP, and GMP. Management is also compliant with the ISO 9001, 14001, and 22000 standards. These fish products are then distributed to global buyers in Asia, Europe, and North America.

Company officials and agents have chosen not to integrate themselves with local fisheries due to the significant risks they pose. Raw materials come from outside of China to ensure food safety, and processed foodstuffs are then promptly shipped out to foreign buyers. One executive mentioned that, at least for now, many firms in the export sector simply view China as a major labor resource for processing export foods, and will reconsider integrating with the Chinese market only in the future (EX 16). An executive asserted that because their company is listed in international markets, any malfeasance or supply chain mismanagement would have significant ramifications on their public valuation (EX 16).

These large export facilities may offer a model for China's future, but, thus far, these standard-setting prototypes are closed off from the domestic market. Ironically, those firms that are in the best position to modernize China's food production sector are the firms least motivated to do so given the potential risks of food contamination.

TABLE 8.1 *Challenges to Scaling Down Direct, Adaptable Control*

Scale Challenges	Export Sector
Jurisdictional	Conflicts with QTSB and fragmented bureaucratic structure
	Local governments emphasize production volume and investment.
Knowledge-Related	Independence of "scientific analysis" is questionable
	Unfamiliar with risk analysis
Network-Related	Off-base production difficult to monitor
	Supply chain management incongruent with local conditions

Significant contestation on jurisdictional, knowledge-, and network-related dimensions across scales leads to regulatory coordination problems. As export producers try to scale down food safety management systems in the vastly more complicated domestic sector, they find it difficult to address these mismatches. As a result, exporters find it challenging to establish a centralized, hierarchical mode of governance.

RIGHT STRATEGY, WRONG SCALE

Another major operational challenge dual production organizations face concerns the effectiveness of export sector strategies when applied to systems that are of a different scale than those for which they were originally designed. In the domestic sector, the Chinese state has promoted two aspects of food safety control first pioneered in the export sector: (1) an emphasis on on-site monitoring and surveillance techniques (i.e., direct control); and (2) third-party certification. These policies succumb to significant policy sinkhole effects in which strategies fail to alter preexisting incentive structures, and instead are absorbed into the overall dysfunctionality of local systems, as described in the following section.

The Uneven Cost of Monitoring and Surveillance

In China, the development of stringent monitoring and surveillance systems is, at present, only practically and financially tenable when producers are operating within a market of global scale. Typically, producers are willing to invest in expensive monitoring and surveillance when they are able to recoup costs. Exporters receive higher payments for their food because consumers in foreign countries are willing to import food so long as food is cheaper than a good of the same quality in the home market. Given that a significant portion of this consumer base is from developed countries, the demand and, consequently, the willingness to pay for food safety is also higher. Export producers make a substantial premium from sales made to foreign consumers (ZJ 19; EX 3; EX 9). Similarly, because importers commit to purchasing higher volumes of food, exporters find it in their interests to comply with food quality and safety demands. In many cases, an exporter will serve as the primary supplier to an importer, and is integrated with the internal quality assurance program of an importer (EX 3). As a result, exporters are incentivized to invest in new equipment, food safety protocols, and constant inspections.

Moreover, the scale of production of export producers is amenable to these practices. Even within the export sector, while the premium on safe food is higher than food slated for the domestic market, smaller producers already face razor-thin margins due to increasing labor costs. Maintaining on-site personnel, developing sensitive surveillance systems, conducting tests for microbial contamination, and certification are expensive.[2] If export producers are already experiencing cost pressures, adopting such practices for domestic producers whose revenue streams are much smaller is unfeasible.

Markets operating at a national scale, thus far, cannot support these intensive monitoring and surveillance practices. In the domestic market, frequent food safety scandals have led to a complete collapse of the price mechanism as an indicator for quality and safety. In properly functioning markets, consumers are willing to pay more for guarantees that a product is of higher quality. However, in the domestic sector, where some of the worst scandals have involved China's most reputable producers, there has been a collapse of consumer confidence (Inocencio & Ke 2013). Domestic producers explain that few of them seek to employ export-grade monitoring and surveillance techniques because prices rarely reflect the actual investment in food safety (ZZ 17; EX 9). Despite the increase in the importance of food safety for the general populace, this has not translated into the willingness of most consumers to pay for it. According to one survey, key determinants for purchasing were product freshness, convenience,

---

[2] The minimum cost for the ChinaGAP certification is RMB 12,500, but larger farms may pay upward of several RMB 100,000.

and competitive pricing, with only 30% of respondents citing product quality as an important factor in their purchasing behavior (Revell 2008). Mckinsey's 2008 consumer behavior study showed that, while 91% of consumers surveyed were concerned by food and beverage safety, 44% of respondents would pay no premium, 30% would pay a premium of less than 5%, and 26% would pay a premium of no more than 20% (Dixit et al. 2008). Such modest price premiums for food quality are unlikely to induce a change in producer behavior.

Given the small premiums for extensive monitoring and surveillance in domestic markets, many rely on a cost-effective mix of traditional food safety monitoring practices and science-based monitoring and surveillance procedures. Many farmers use a series of organoleptic, visual inspections to assess the safety of food, in addition to the occasional lab test. Pig farmers, for example, will observe a pig's gait, skin color, and eye pigmentation to determine whether a pig is healthy. Following slaughter, butchers will look at the amount of water in the meat and the color of the flesh to determine if a farmer has used illegal additives. During campaigns, farmers may conduct lab tests on pig urine samples. For vegetable produce, processors may use an express residue test, or will depend on visual aids. At best, this mixing and matching of monitoring and surveillance techniques is highly ineffective. Perhaps, more problematically, even if consumers begin to demand expensive food safety measures of producers, producers are only likely to nominally comply, creating a false sense of confidence in faulty food safety measures.

Food safety scandals continue to erode consumer confidence even in cases where China's best producers claim to employ globally accepted monitoring and surveillance techniques. Because domestic consumers are unwilling to pay higher prices for safe food, producers are even less incentivized to invest in monitoring and surveillance systems. Some argue that this is a market timing matter and simply a case of getting the prices right. However, getting the prices right is, of course, contingent on getting regulations right, which in turn is a direct function of getting the scale of governance right.

The Failure of Third-Party Certification

The failure of third-party certification is also a consequence of a nominally correct policy at one scale (the global export market) operating at the wrong scale. The increased expansion of third-party certification schemes has only provided lackluster results in the broad domestic food production and distribution sector.[3] Experts who assert that a combination of independent labs and private auditing used in the export sector will assuredly help to address domestic food safety problems must also consider issues related to scale applicability.

In the domestic sector, the scaling down of third-party certification quickly encounters a structural barrier: most small- and medium-scale producers lack the technical capacity and the capital to invest in global certification systems. Third-party certification schemes are only cost efficient at a certain scale of production and distribution. For example, at the time of research (2009–2016), the minimum cost of GlobalGAP certification was approximately RMB 12,500, which included application costs, on-site inspection, licensing and registration, monitoring and examination costs, and an annual fee. Larger farms and production sites located further in the interior incurred even higher costs. Some experts estimated that the average audit may cost as much as RMB 18,000, which is extraordinarily high considering that in Europe similar audits cost approximately RMB 3,000 (EX 1). Given that the average Chinese farmer's annual net income in 2010 was RMB 5,919, the use of such certification schemes is not tenable for small-scale production networks (China Statistics 2010).

Beyond issues of financial feasibility is the actual subject matter of the certification schemes themselves. Most certification schemes, such as GAP, were created in western countries with well-developed food markets and for a small, professional class of farmers with high levels of education and large production yields. European farming conditions are more benign with more cultivable land per person, moderate climates, greater access to water, and far fewer pest pressures. For many Chinese farmers, discussions regarding energy conservation, environmental protection, and the appropriate use of mechanized agriculture are not relevant (EX 1; EX 4). In the domestic sector, even those farmers who manage to acquire certification are often ill-equipped to consistently maintain the food production standards following the audit. Indeed, nominal compliance with certification has been the norm, which is why China is regularly placed on a watch

---

[3] Academic studies on consumer confidence (as measured by a consumer's "willingness to pay") are mixed, with some asserting that consumers are increasingly willing to pay for government-certified products (see Ortega et al. 2011), and others, such as Wu et al. (2011), that consumer confidence in certified products is low due to low public awareness and questions of affordability.

list of countries with well-known problems with third-party certification (EX 8).[4]

Moreover, in contrast to the domestic sector, in the export sector, third-party certifiers operate as part of a *global* system of accountability. In theory and observed practice, independent auditing companies are responsible to importers who are themselves liable to end users of their products. Importers require exporters to acquire third-party certification verifying that product, production grounds, and protocols are compliant with global standards. Third-party certification is valued because they are viewed to be an independent authority of food safety and are entirely accountable to the importer (Meidinger 2009). Where a third-party certifier is found to have been deficient and unsafe food is found, that certifier is likely to lose credibility among importers and be forced to exit the market.

This system of independent, market-driven accountability is seen to operate differently in actual practice in China for the following reason: local governments are often the financial sponsors of third-party certification because farmers lack the funds to pay for an audit. This clearly complicates oversight of the certification process as independent auditors become enmeshed in local politics (EX 8; EX 1; Fan et al. 2009). Auditors will sometimes visit a locality once, and then delegate future monitoring to local authorities, who may or may not have the capacity to ensure food safety (Bottemiller 2010). Certification can become especially problematic when local governments hold a commercial stake in the state farms being audited. For example, in 2010, the USDA had to ban an American third-party certifier when the agency discovered that the company had delegated auditing authority to local government officials monitoring state-owned farms (Neuman & Barboza, 2010).

The fundamental scale mismatch between third-party certification and monitoring and surveillance programs, and the market realities under which most Chinese farms operate has led to the regulatory incoherence of the market. Significant sinkhole effects result when both certification and ongoing monitoring policies fail to alter the incentive structures to address the appropriate scale of markets and production. This is not to

---

4 Increasingly, food safety experts are championing a more scaled-down certification regime for smaller producers, using basic food safety trainings on pesticide usage and soil management techniques that can yield immediate food safety results. Experts are more favorably inclined to endorse the ChinaGAP II standard, which has fewer critical control points and was written to assist China's farmers in transitioning to modernized agricultural production (EX 10).

say that these policies will never work in the domestic sector, but rather that large "scale" transformations—in terms of market development and production technique—must precede their adoption.

CONCLUSION

Scaling down the export sector has proved to be challenging. First, as new actors and policy communities at different scales are added to a system, contestation over governance is more pronounced. Globally oriented actors struggle with local production networks and cannot cooperate with government officials with a different agenda and assessment of the relative costs and benefits of certain food safety strategies. Centralized, hierarchical control quickly devolves in the face of a fragmented system. Second, as export sector practices are applied to systems of different scale than that for which they were designed, they fail to overcome significant sinkhole effects. Third-party certifiers and global best practices in monitoring and surveillance are designed to operate in specialized systems, but are less effective when applied more broadly.

It is relevant to observe that the successful diffusion of best practices of an export sector to the domestic market in developing countries is not common. China's experience is not dissimilar to those of Brazil, India, or Kenya, among others. In Brazil, export-oriented fisheries were required to acquire HACCP certification from the government. Fisheries were managed by a specialized office in the Ministry of Agriculture and training was provided to producers in the export sector. Studies indicate that HACCP certification in Brazil has not diffused to the broader domestic-oriented fisheries (Donovan et al. 2001). Producers commented that they could not recoup costs by selling export-grade products in the domestic market, which is largely consonant with comments made by Chinese food exporters. In India, a strict bifurcation of the domestic and export sectors is still in place (Umali-Deininger & Sur 2007). The Kenyan Nile perch export trade has not led to major changes in food safety for the domestic market (Henson & Mittulah 2004).

Assertions that the so-far successful export sector can serve as a "cookie-cutter model for food safety" practices to be implemented throughout the Chinese behemoth, particularly among the countless small farmers, unidentifiable food processors and multitude of distributors, ring hollow. The applicability of export sector best practices across varying scales of food production in the domestic sector is neither obvious nor practicable: global best practices cannot be easily diffused; export producers struggle to survive in the domestic sector; and domestic consumer demand for export-grade food safety does not coincide with an equal willingness to pay.

The export sector may, for some food safety goal-setting regulators, serve as an ideal hypothetical model for the broader domestic market. But, I conclude that, for now, the notion of scaling down proven standards of excellence from that sector only provides a politically expedient image of a distant regulatory future. If *scaling down* the exacting protocols of the export system is not practicable, I next consider whether *scaling up* successful practices from a grassroots system will prove helpful.

9

Scaling Up

From Local Experiments to National Solutions?

If scaling down successful export sector practices has proven difficult, what of scaling up effective local food safety projects? The CSA's decentralized, collaborative governance framework was observed to be highly effective, but what happens when these self-contained systems scale up in large, heterogeneous circumstances? The strong performance of community governance has led many to emphasize the spread of local governance models to address national policy problems. Can the CSA market, or at least aspects of it, serve as a model for national food safety?

The existing literature offers little guidance as to whether the social trust—which is the glue of collaborative governance, embedded in local, self-regulatory communities—is scalable (Ansell & Torfing 2015). Scholars contend that social trust is intrinsically tied to local communities (Bowles & Gintis 2002; Ostrom 2010). Dietz et al. (2003) highlight local, informal institutional arrangements that effectively govern the commons, but remain uncertain as to whether these arrangements can operate at a larger scale and involve nonlocal influences. Some contend that in larger scale settings, local governance is unlikely to be as effective because resources are not closed-access (Pretty 2003). Despite strongly held norms of behavior in discrete governance settings, individuals are likely to behave differently as groups incorporate an increasingly diverse base of participants (de Oliveira et al. 2009). Dietz et al. (2003) offer general principles to guide scaling up, such as multilevel analytic deliberation, nested institutional arrangements, and a commitment to institutional variety. However, these only serve as general guides to scaling up, and do not consider the political challenges of establishing large-scale multilevel information channels and power-sharing arrangements.

At first glance, the notion of effective policy diffusion based on small-scale experimentation can be deceptively compelling. For example, China, in particular, has often used small-scale policy experiments as a basis for developing broad national models with great success (Teets & Hurst 2014; Heilmann & Perry 2011). But, Schulman (1975) observes that policy makers should be careful when trying to expand limited scope trials. First, such trials occur in relatively controlled environments with significant amounts of investment and attention, which do not mimic broader realities. Second, as more individuals participate in such experimental schemes, power structures are altered and incentives are transformed. Third, information asymmetries develop and individuals may seek to take advantage of such information flow problems to enhance personal rather than shared objectives. And, finally, global economic forces, which may have been irrelevant to smaller communities, may create significant problems for scaled-up markets that are more exposed to them.

More broadly, an increasing number of scholars have begun to question the benefits of local governance in a multiscale world (Berkes 2007; Dressler et al. 2010). These scholars suggest that policy makers have failed to heed Ostrom's (2007b) warning toward the end of her career that local solutions should not be viewed as a panacea. Ostrom makes a strong case that local communities cannot be shielded from broader dynamics in a rapidly globalizing economy (Ostrom 2005). These local communities must be connected and learn to coordinate with larger political economic subunits (Andersson & Ostrom 2008).

This chapter examines what happens to a successful, decentralized, collaborative governance system when it is scaled up. Specifically, it shows that the manner in which a system scales up can lead to different types of scale politics that have important trade-offs for regulatory coordination.

Scaling up is a nonlinear, multidimensional process that confounds even the most adept policy makers. Scaling up a local food production system involves linking to large-scale supply chains (network scale) and joining the national certification system (jurisdictional scale) in order to reach a broader population. Local systems based on informal, collaborative governance must somehow codify and routinize procedures that can be understood by consumers and producers that are separated by great distances (spatial scale). Local commitments to food safety standards must interface with global food safety best practices to gain broader market access (knowledge scale). To operate on the national scale, the CSA system must scale up jurisdictionally, spatially, and in terms of knowledge and networks.

Scaling up the CSA model requires the injection of expertise, capital, and labor. Experts who understand how to manage large production bases must be recruited. Distribution managers who understand how to deliver food safely and efficiently must be consulted. Increases in production require capital investments for land reclamation and the purchase of inputs, such as organic fertilizer and seed.

The actor that initiates the scaling up process in many ways determines the politics of scale that emerge. Within the CSA movement in China, government officials, corporations, and NGOs have attempted to scale up CSA projects with different trade-offs. The first prototype is the corporate CSA model, which involves financial backing from entrepreneurs who view the CSA sector as a potentially profitable market in China. The second prototype is the government CSA model, which seeks to promote CSA in the broader context of China's agricultural development, and to develop a new national standard for ecological farming. The third is the NGO-sponsored CSA farm, which emphasizes the development of local, sustainable farming. Each faces its own brand of scale politics that presents problems for scaling up the successful system.

THE CORPORATE CSA

Corporate CSA farms can be distinguished by their emphasis on large production volumes and substantial capital investments. Investors in the CSA concept believe that the recent food safety scandals in China provide a unique opportunity to develop a new market for organic, safe food (CSA 3; CSA 16; CSA 8). In order to expand the market, producers have increased production volumes and invested in distribution centers to reach consumers beyond the local scale. One CSA has distribution centers within Beijing to provide customers with the convenience of picking up produce directly within the city (CSA 3). Production bases are large, with some bigger than 66.7 hectares, roughly 10 times the size of a typical CSA producer. Capital investments have been sizable, with some farms spending hundreds of thousands of dollars on integrated pest management facilities, water treatment plants, and research and development labs. One farm is in the process of preparing an orchard for cultivation, which will take 10 years to ensure that the soil has been purged of chemical contaminants and the correct level organic material has been restored (CSA 3). As larger producers, they do view themselves as distinct from their smaller counterparts, and consider themselves market leaders paving the way for other organic producers: "we understand that we are a big movement with many participants. But, given the advanced nature of our production techniques and the significant investments we have made, we consider ourselves as walking in front of everyone (CSA 3)."

In their efforts to link to broader supply chains, corporate CSAs begin to delink themselves from smaller scale CSA production networks. Large corporate CSA farms produce their own organic fertilizer, construct their own nurseries, and maintain private seed banks and do not join local CSA input supply systems (CSA 14). The largest farms have eschewed models of open surveillance and collaborative producer-consumer councils in favor of a permanent staff to manage production. One farm has organized producers in teams, with each team taking responsibility for a particular parcel of land and then being made accountable for any food safety incidents (CSA 4). Increasingly, they rely less on traditional, low-yield organic methods and reach out to purveyors of best practice, hiring international consultants to advise them on how best to maintain food quality. Taiwanese and Japanese agronomists are particularly in high demand.

One of the largest corporate-sponsored CSA farms is located in Pudong (a district of Shanghai) and has more than 86.7 hectares of land under cultivation, with plans to expand to 116.7 hectares. Total investment in the project was more than RMB 300 million, with RMB 200 million from private investors and RMB 100 million from the government (CSA 16). The farm distributes to more than 8,000 households in Shanghai, 40% of which are expatriates. The farm also operates as part of the "special supply system," providing guaranteed safe food to more than 40 government SOEs and agencies throughout the Shanghai municipality and the broader region.[1] They operate their own packaging center on site and deliver approximately 1,600 3 kg boxes of vegetables per day.

The farm employs 300 individuals—100 are involved in management, distribution, and quality assurance and 200 individuals are involved in production (CSA 16). On site, they employ four agronomists from Taiwan to monitor production. They also have an inspection center with 6 to 8 individuals who collect 160 water, soil, and vegetable samples from around the farm every day. There are 16 growing fields, and 2 fields are equipped with real-time monitoring technology to assess soil temperature, humidity levels, and water quality. While testing is an important part of food safety assurance, the farm holds that food safety is best protected by investments in the method of production and the quality of inputs.

---

[1] The large farm operates as part of the "special supply" (tegong) system, which delivers high-quality, safe food to Chinese government offices and SOEs. See Demick (2011).

Farmers are trained on a weekly basis in new techniques and are organized in production teams to create an internal accountability system. All inputs are carefully processed on the farm. The farm spent RMB 66 million on a water processing center (CSA 16). While they attempted to purchase some inputs from the surrounding community, the management felt that doing so might place the farm at risk of contamination, and instead opted for 100% self-sustainability.

As the corporate CSA goes in search of capital, spatially dispersed shareholders exert more influence on production than locally based networks of producers (CSA 4; CSA 9; CSA 10). This move toward increasing shareholder value has fundamentally altered local governance practices. In order to appease investors, these farms must increase production and capture market share. Production teams are viewed as laborers rather than integral parts of the farm system. One consultant commented that corporate CSAs alienate many of the farmers, which affects their level of commitment: "We need to develop a new model for peasant relations. They really need people to come in and be invested in producing quality food. We should create an employee and employer stockholding agreement" (CSA 14). Rather than develop social trust through community-building efforts, corporate CSA farms invest significant amounts of cash to attain certification and then expand production. For example, one farm acquired organic certification from Demeter, which cost them approximately RMB 2 million (CSA 3). Given the primitive stage of market development for organic food, it is nearly impossible to recoup investment. As such, corporate CSA farms have engaged in alternative profitable activities unrelated to farming. One farm has had to develop a resort in order to help buffer the losses from farm sales: "currently, we are operating at a loss. We need to make far more money. You can't make money from simply selling vegetables. Consider the level of investment? We can't recover it" (CSA 14).

Collaborative governance is eroded as corporate CSA farms turn to shareholders for guidance. There is little emphasis on building personal relationships between consumers and farmers (CSA 10). Moreover, producers under contract with corporate CSAs participate in production, but do not have rights to the land or engage in decision-making (CSA 3; CSA 10). These large farms do not partner with local CSA networks, CSA producer associations, or traditional distribution channels.

The corporate CSA has also registered for the national government's organic certification, which generates significant tensions with other local CSA producers (CSA 8; CSA 9; CSA 16). While corporate CSA internal safety procedures are more stringent than those of the government, they assert that participation in the organic certification program serves as an important signal to both the government and producers that they are committed to producing safe food and that they are open to being inspected by an outside agency. They also recognize that their participation helps to redeem the reputation of the organic label, which they believe is necessary to expand the market. Other local CSA members view the acceptance of the government label as a sign that corporate CSA members have compromised the values of the CSA network. In fact, the Shanghai Farmer's Market agreement specifically forbids participants from acquiring the state's organic certification.[2] Corporate CSA directors argue that despite these concerns, national certification for organic production is necessary for the distribution of their products on a national scale.

Although corporate CSA farms lack social trust, this is not to say that these farms produce unsafe food. As corporate CSA farms expand, their emphasis on collaborative governance lessens as their focus on financial capital intensifies. In order to maintain food safety, corporate CSA farms must then compensate for the diminished level of social trust by paying for enhanced surveillance, monitoring, and quality inputs. Needless to say, this approach is highly expensive. Up-front costs are prohibitive, few farms can acquire large portions of land to build these bases, and the overall market demand for such products at the prices they are currently being marketed at is small. As a result, the corporate CSA model of scaling up cannot be considered a viable model for the vast majority of farmers in China.

THE GOVERNMENT-SPONSORED CSA

The government has also sought to scale up the CSA farming model. China's State Research and Technical Development Plan (2006–2020) emphasizes the increased experimentation of different types of "ecological zones" and provides infrastructure and capital support to projects (Art II, 1). Local governments have directly partnered with CSA farms as investors. In Pudong, for example, officials invested several million dollars to start a special organic farm and were active in management and operations. In other instances, the government provides land to CSA farmers

---

[2] In addition to prohibiting participants from joining the government organic certification program, the agreement also forbids farmers who are affiliated with corporations and government agencies and ministries.

as part of broader agricultural development plans. On Chongming Island near Shanghai, CSA farms were granted land-use rights as part of the district's "Good Agricultural Standard" development zone (CSA 8). In Anlong village, Sichuan, CSA farms were subsumed under the "Model Agricultural District" program in 2007 (CSA 5). The government might also serve in a more auxiliary role, offering subsidized inputs, guaranteeing loans, or investing in agricultural infrastructure projects.

The relationship between the CSA movement and the government, however, remains tense due to different perspectives on how the organic market should develop. Jurisdictional scale politics emerge, as local, decentralized CSA networks focused on small-scale, sustainable agriculture come into conflict with a national food regime emphasizing certified organic production, high production volumes, and industrialized agriculture. As the CSA sector attempts to scale up via government support, each level of government presents certain jurisdictional challenges based on their scale of governance. Irreconcilable tensions arise concerning who is allowed to certify producers, what production methods can be considered organic, and how markets should develop. CSA farms gradually see their independence and social networks eroded as they are subsumed within the government's food production regime.

The national government supports the CSA market's broader goal to provide safe, organic food to China's consumers, but does not agree with its delimiting methods and objectives. The central government is still primarily concerned with increasing food yields and moving toward large-scale agriculture that is integrated with global supply chains. Ultimately, the government seeks to transition the CSA movement to its own national organic certification scheme. Pressures for certification are high as provincial leaders are increasingly evaluated on the percentage of land that meets the "green-food" or "organic" criteria.

When assessing the organic and green food certification, it becomes clear why CSA farmers resist being co-opted by the national food safety regime. CSA farmers critically note that the green food and organic policies favor large-scale, capital-rich, export-oriented production. A survey of 40 certified organic producers shows that on average a producer yields 500 tons of food annually, a volume that is uncommon among traditional CSA farms (EUCTP 2008:15). Approximately 30% of producers surveyed export to Japan, which has one of the strictest food safety standards in the world; 80% supply local supermarkets and nearly 70% supply government agencies. These are typically marketing channels that most CSA farms cannot enter into due to their own limited production volumes. Prior to 1999, more than 95% of state certified organic producers exported their products to Japan, the EU, and the United States (EUCTP 2008:4). Certification can cost up to RMB 18,000 and must be renewed annually, creating a significant barrier to entry for the vast majority of small-to-medium producers operating in local producer networks (US Department of Agriculture 2010). The 2005 Organic Standard sets strict rules for production, which are prohibitively expensive. Also, the green food standard actually specifies a minimum farm size that well exceeds traditional CSA limits. Naturally, when an organic farmer's market began to promote its own "certification," CNAS officials openly criticized the movement and warned that only accredited bodies could issue certificates (CSA 18).

Agricultural departments at the provincial scale view CSA projects as a potential development model and are eager to set up "ecological farming" zones in order to stake their claim as leaders in agricultural development. But, these ecological zones rarely reflect the needs of CSA projects. Farmers note that provincial governments do not actively support the CSA market in terms of building networks among farms, finding new customers, or promoting sustainable farming practices (CSA 2). One farmer reports: "the [provincial] government really offers no support. I mean, they came and painted our house, and helped to rebuild our pig pen, but they really haven't done anything substantial.... No one from the government cares about what we do" (CSA 6).

At the township level, the relationship between township cadres and CSA leaders grows more complex. CSA farms can provide a boost in agro-tourism and serve as showcase centers for local agriculture. The CSA movement does bring media attention to the village, which also helps the local party leader's reputation. Particularly, when innovation can lead to promotion up the party-state hierarchy, local government support of these new ecological projects can advance the careers of local cadres. But, CSA farms are less than ideal for township cadres: production volumes are low and land that could be otherwise used for lucrative development projects remains under cultivation. Moreover, CSA farms do not purchase inputs from the local governments' agricultural extension service centers, which sell seeds, fertilizers, and pesticides.

Ultimately, local CSA projects have an ambivalent relationship with township government officials, and are highly susceptible to the vicissitudes of politics at the local level. When government coffers ring empty, CSA farmers note how the local government seeks to push them toward large-scale agricultural projects, reemphasizing the need for green-food or pollution-free certification. When that fails, township officials push CSA farmers off the land in favor of real estate developers. As one farmer notes, "The only thing the local government is focused on is about constructing houses. They can't make money from agriculture" (CSA 5).

The pressures for government-supported CSAs to expand are strong. CSA leaders explained how even accepting funding from the government often leads CSA farmers to move toward large-scale, standardized production, creating conditions that can lead to serious food safety problems. CSA farms are generally strapped for capital, and with such high start-up costs, securing loans is important. Despite the demand for funding, farms prefer to receive financing from other CSA farms or from entrepreneurs who are committed to sustainable levels of production, as opposed to government-funding bodies that are aimed toward promoting industrialized agriculture: "we don't want loans from the government, though. The lending system has the perverse effect of forcing farmers to produce more than they need and to expand at rates that are at odds with ecological farming. All of a sudden, you find that the loan system has farmers locked in to a vicious cycle in which they have to produce more in order to pay off a loan" (CSA 2). Farmers must then move into industrialized agriculture using large volumes of pesticides and other chemical inputs to increase production volumes, which have been the cause of food poisonings in the broader market.

As the government facilitates the scaling up of CSA projects, the locally governed, decentralized producer networks gradually see their independence eroded. Independence is desired because CSA farms can then dictate who is allowed to participate. The Beijing Farmer's Market committee notes: "we enjoy our independence. We are very selective who we get to work with. These are all people we have come to trust on a personal level. Once the government or larger companies become involved the market will become more subject to nepotistic behavior. We pride ourselves on impartiality" (CSA 11). Organizers shared how government officials sometimes allow noncompliant producers to join supply networks, which threatens the farmer's markets ability to enforce quality control standards. A favored local company, or a firm with connections in government are permitted to join government-sponsored ecological zones, much to the chagrin of CSA leaders.

The social trust engendered by the collaborative governance framework is also weakened. Government policies favoring large producers sow division between small and large producers within the movement. Small and medium producers grow increasingly less inclined to participate with larger producers. Farmers fear that as the government co-opts the CSA program that it will be largely dominated by large actors: "We are just nervous that [the increase in the number of industrial players] will squeeze out peasants" (CSA 2). The government's promotion of an organic standard directly conflicts with the more informal practices developed by local groups of CSA farmers, which leads to a breakdown in common understanding of what constitutes fair, sustainable, and safe agricultural practice among CSA members.

The fear is that the government program will force the CSA sector to adopt the same industrialized agricultural practices that have led to widespread food poisonings. Higher production volumes require larger amounts of pesticides. If pesticides are too expensive, farmers will have to purchase substandard inputs in order to make a profit. As soil quality deteriorates due to intensive agricultural practices, even more chemical inputs will need to be purchased. Moreover, a move toward high-volume production requires substantial investment in cold storage and logistics infrastructure. Failing to make these changes will increase the risk of microbial contamination. Higher volumes imply higher risks. The CSA market would then simply adopt the very unsafe practices that they sought to avoid when the sector was first organized.

THE NGO-SUPPORTED CSA

NGOs are aware of the risks associated with partnering with corporations and government-related actors, and have actively resisted pressures to scale up. Instead, NGOs seek to extend their influence through a model of replication by increasing the number of local CSA networks of the same scale rather than linking farms to large-scale supply chains and wider networks. Since the mid-2000s, NGOs have planted small, local networks of CSA farmers around major municipalities throughout the country (Jiang 2011; Luo, email communication, 2011). NGOs concede that this model is spatially limited; it cannot expand to rural areas distant from municipalities because only urban consumers have the required income to support CSA farms. Leaders, however, claim that despite the limits of the physical reach of their products, they do seek to scale up "ideologically" by engaging and transforming the narrative about agricultural production at the national scale.

The NGO-supported CSA serves as the ideal typical example of a CSA food safety system. In addition to a commitment to provide safe food, NGOs address the growing rural-urban divide by providing farmers a means to earn higher incomes from agriculture, stemming urban migration, and reinvigorating the local economy. NGO-sponsored CSAs work to transform the common mindset of viewing the countryside as a source of extraction to one that emphasizes mutually collaborative growth (Shi et al. 2011). Thus, NGOs emphasize investments in social capital, rebuilding social relations among farmers and between farmers and their urban consumers.

The model example of an NGO-supported CSA project is Anlong village in Sichuan, which was sponsored by the Chengdu Urban River Association (CURA). In 1994, CURA was tasked by the Chengdu municipal government to clean up the heavily polluted Dujiang River that runs through the city. Following a major river renewal project that lasted for more than a decade, CURA officials still found high levels of pollution in the water. An investigation revealed that the water pollution was a result of agricultural runoff from rural areas located 100 km upstream in Ande township. Following consultations with farmers, government officials, and academic experts, CURA moved forward with an ecological farming project in Anlong village in 2005 based on CSA principles.

The project set up a 33.3-hectare river protection zone in the village, which prohibited the use of chemical fertilizers and pesticides. Initially, two families, the Wangs and the Gaos, were recruited, and the movement spread slowly in the village to include 22 farms. CURA sought to develop "ecological households," which would emphasize sustainable farming as part of an ecological lifestyle. Human waste would be recycled and animal waste would be composted for fertilizer. Farmers would use methane tanks for energy. Grey water filtration units would be installed to conserve water usage. Food safety would naturally rise as the result of a commitment to ecological principles.

CURA played a crucial role in facilitating relationships among farmers themselves and also with their urban consumers. Farmers would be brought together for training sessions and to help one another with transitioning to organic farming. CURA's attempts to foster solidarity among producers led to the emergence of a certain esprit de corps among farmers. In addition, because many of the peasants did not have connections to individuals in the city, CURA helped to identify families who would be willing to purchase organic produce and supplied farmers with credit to purchase cars and vans to distribute their product. The NGO would also host town hall meetings between farmers and their consumers to foster mutual understanding. Publicizing the project through the media created increased interest among urbanites looking for a source of locally sourced, safe food. These outreach activities helped foster social trust, creating a dense social network.

CURA would actively manage various social pressures in the village. NGO leaders believed that in order preserve high levels of social trust and local harmony, producers would have to be relatively similar in size. They feared that larger producers would distort the CSA market by driving out smaller producers, and would lead to hypercompetitive behavior among participants. CURA would also act as a buffer between farmers and local government, and serve as mediators during disputes.

NGOs seek to replicate the model in villages around the country, creating local networks of CSA farms. Suitable locations for CSA farm networks, however, are limited. CSA programs are geographically constrained, doing best in areas near major urban centers. Consumers and farmers must be in close proximity in order to facilitate frequent exchanges between consumers. Given the high prices of produce, CSA farms also require large, upper-middle-class populations (Shi et al. 2011; Gale 2011). As such, the majority of CSA farms are located near major metropolises such as Beijing, Shanghai, Guangzhou, Chengdu, and Chongqing. Thus, expanding to less cosmopolitan areas is not practicable given these constraints. Geographic limitations make it difficult to establish CSA farm networks in all areas of the country. Poorer, less developed areas would likely be excluded from expansion plans. As one NGO director states: "the main issue is that the model can only be extended around cities . . . of course, we know that we can't take over the market" (CSA 2).

Instead, the NGO CSA movement has focused on serving as an ideological counterpoint to the conventional food production system. By producing safe food through ecological farming techniques, NGOs hope to facilitate a shift in consumer preferences for organic food across the country. While a few CSA farms believe that organic farming yields can match those of conventional farming yields (CSA 10; CSA 3), the vast majority of individuals believe that the CSA organic food production will constitute a relatively small part of the overall food market in China. The symbolic impact, they believe, will be more important than the number of people it serves.

TABLE 9.1 *Comparing Scaling Up Models*

	Corporate	Government	NGO
Primary Scale Problem	Network-Related	Jurisdictional	Spatial
Scalable?	Yes, but expensive	Yes, but problems in food safety likely to arise	Confined to urban areas, symbolically "scalable"
Regulatory Adjustments	Adopt direct control methods	Adopt government organic standards	Social trust

CONCLUSION

The process of scaling up is an intensely political process. The dynamics of a localized, collaborative system emphasizing social trust are fundamentally altered as a system scales up. As a system scales up to include different actors—each with their own conceptions of food safety, different obligations to their supply chain network, and to their respective governance systems—scale politics emerge. Contrary to seeing policy diffusion as a relatively apolitical process, this chapter has shown that scaling up governance of a sector becomes highly contested, with each actor seeking to address food safety that best reflects their own scale interests across a range of dimensions.

Moreover, who scales up the system has important consequences for regulatory development. Corporate actors with less interest in maximizing social capital and a far greater stake in increasing their financial capital will quickly erode local systems of social trust to gain access to broader distribution channels. Government sponsorship requires compliance with national certification and expanding production, which can lead to jurisdictional contestation between CSA leaders and local, provincial, and national officials. NGOs may seek to expand their system but only by replication and not by scaling up.

The scaling up of CSA production encounters unique trade-offs in terms of regulatory coordination. The scaling up of systems need not lead to regulatory failure. However, altering the scale of a system may preclude the use of certain strategies to be employed for effective governance. Social trust, for example, may be a less tenable strategy when local communities play a less central role in production and distribution. Instead, strategies of direct control may be employed at significant cost that will preclude participation of the vast majority of China's producers.

Governments may seek to impose standardized requirements rather than operate on the basis of an informal system of mutual obligation. To preserve social trust, some systems can replicate themselves in different areas around the country, but finding potential sites can be challenging.

The CSA movement, while remarkable in its ability to provide food safety, does not offer a viable solution for a national food safety strategy. Sometimes local solutions cannot become national solutions. Ostrom was right: *local governance is not a panacea.* And, scaling up is hard to do.

The Scale Politics of Regulatory Giants, Compared

A key question to consider is why scale politics in China's food safety system are particularly acute when compared to other regulatory giants. The "politics of scale" framework introduced in this book identified three major sources of conflict in large-scale polities: (1) because scale is a social construct, regulators find it challenging to define the scale—national, provincial, municipal, county, or township—at which a problem is likely to emerge and be effectively resolved; (2) each scale of government operates according to multidimensional logics (temporal frames, types of knowledge, institutional preferences, and managerial styles) that make it difficult to coordinate governance across scales; and (3) scale externalities—decisions at one scale of governance can affect other scales in a nested system in unexpected and costly ways. Previous chapters have tried to establish the theoretical and empirical ground to explain why China's food safety policies have been unable to address their scale politics. This chapter now explores the deeper issue of how China's fragmented, unitary framework has undermined its ability to manage scale politics by comparing it to the multilevel and federal frameworks of the EU, India, and the United States.

Previous and recent history shows that food safety crises inevitably arise in all large, heterogeneous polities. The EU, India, and the United States encountered major food safety problems following the rapid expansion of their food markets. In the EU, the dioxin scandals and BSE crises in the 1990s led to a collapse in trust in governments across the continent. In India, mass beverage contaminations in the 2000s resulted in major pressures for food safety reforms. In the United States, severe microbial contaminations involving E. coli led to the strengthening of the FDA, and spawned several food-related social movements. In the course of their regulatory evolution, China, India, the EU, and the United States developed food safety regimes with remarkably similar elements: (1) the establishment of a national food safety bureaucracy, (2) the enactment of a comprehensive food safety law, and (3) the creation of new monitoring and information sharing systems. However, notwithstanding similar regulatory measures, the EU, the United States, and India have proved to be more adept at systematically correcting their food safety problems, while China's governmental food safety apparatus remains paralyzed by scale politics.

The EU sits at the top of most global food safety rankings; and India, with similar demographic and economic constraints as its neighbor to the east, still outperforms China, which occupies an unenviable bottom position across a number of transnational food safety rankings.[1] Why then have similar food safety reform programs in all four countries resulted in such varied food safety outcomes?

Most observers would point to significant differences in economic development, state capacity, regime type, and corruption as explanations for this variation, all of which will be tested. But, the focus of this chapter is on the broader macrogovernance framework in which food safety institutions (i.e., bureaucracies, regulations, and networks) are embedded. Whether they are unitary, federal, or multilevel systems, macrogoverning frameworks define how governance systems at different scales operate and relate to one another. First, a macrogoverning framework determines which scale dominates policy decision-making: in unitary systems, the national government dictates policy, whereas federal and multilevel systems share policy making responsibilities across governments operating at different scales. Second, a macrogoverning framework establishes how decisions made at different scales of governance relate to one another across multiple dimensions, horizontally and vertically, as teased out by considering the following questions: *Horizontal*—Are regulations developed in one subnational unit considered equally effective, and thus deserving of comity, by other subnational units of the same scale? *Vertical*—Can rules developed at the state or provincial scales of governance contravene national regulations?

Macrogoverning frameworks set a template for scale politics with wide-ranging implications for regulatory governance throughout a polity.

---

[1] The 2013 EIU ranking ranks China no. 48; The RASSF 2013 worst-offender ranking places China as no. 1; Food Sentry 2013 Food Risk ranking places China as no. 1.

This chapter conducts a structured comparison of how the prevailing macrogoverning frameworks of the EU, India, and China affect the scaling down and scaling up of food safety systems. In the EU, food safety actors operate in a *multilevel framework* and share regulatory authority across scales. Various EU commissions collaborate with regional authorities and member states in multilevel fora, and a system of mutual recognition and comity facilitates productive collaboration among member states. India's food safety system has evolved in a *decentralized federal framework* in which the subnational scale dominates food safety policy making. As such, India's federal government has been unsuccessful in integrating governance systems at the state scale in its ongoing effort to create a new national food safety system. China's *fragmented unitary system* presents significant problems in the scaling up and scaling down of food safety. A fragmented central authority and the constant flux of regulatory authority between central and local scales promote severe scale politics. Following the structured comparison, I examine the United State's *centralized federal framework* in which state food safety systems have conformed to a national regulatory template.

NESTED DESIGNS AND STRUCTURED COMPARISONS

This chapter employs what Lieberman (2005) refers to as a "nested analysis" to conduct a structured comparison of the EU, India, and China. Most would conclude that, due to significant differences among the countries, it would be difficult to justify a comparison, but a nested analysis that "nests" a small-N study within a large-N statistical analysis can overcome these limitations. The large-N analysis establishes general relationships between variables and an outcome of interest. Intensive case studies are then performed to assess the validity of the model, and to tease out causal mechanisms.

The justification for a structured comparison in a nested design is as follows. Provided that factors that would typically render comparisons impracticable are shown to have less explanatory weight in the Large-N model, a researcher can proceed with a comparative analysis. For example, let us suppose that a food safety model highlights how scale is strongly related to food safety performance, whereas other factors such as, economic development, state capacity, and democracy are not statistically significant. Based on the model, we can make the argument that because these variables (development, state capacity, democracy) are shown to have less explanatory weight, a comparative analysis of the EU,

China, and India, which have different values on these variables, is still justifiable. Moreover, if the cases are of similar scale—the only variable found to be statistically significant—but still vary in terms of the dependent variable, food safety provision, this would compel a focused analysis of these countries to explain why scale is problematic for some countries and not others.

The first step in the nested analysis then is to specify a regression with the relevant dependent variable (food safety) regressed on the explanatory variable (size and heterogeneity, as a proxy for scale politics) and other controls to assess the strength of the relationship. Food safety is measured by the Safety Index, which identifies the level of food safety risk that a country poses to the global trading system (Convertino & Liang 2014). Using recall and food safety incident data from the EU's Rapid Access System for Food and Feed, investigators determine a country's food safety score by taking the ratio of how frequently a country issues food alerts against food products from other countries, over the frequency of alerts issued against the same country by its trading partners.[2,3] A higher Safety Index ratio implies a higher level of food safety. This study uses a logged four-year average (2005–2008) of the Safety Index for 165 countries. Due to data limitations, the United States has been dropped in the analysis.[4]

---

[2] The transgressor and detector indexes are determined through a network approach, which takes into account the number of countries that issue an alert against a country, and the frequency of food alerts between two countries (Nepusz et al. 2009). The indexes are also dynamic: more recent food alerts are weighted higher than those that occurred in the past.

[3] Convertino & Liang (2014) contend that the ratio of DI/TI better captures a country's level of food safety; the food safety of a country should not be determined only by the number of times other trading partners raise food safety alerts against it, but also by the number of times a country alerts other countries about unsafe food. While there are limitations to this index, the Safety Index is the only cross-national food safety measure that exists, which utilizes actual recall alert data to assess a country's risk to the global trading system. Moreover, the Safety Index of a country is highly correlated with actual food contaminations in countries, which suggests the strong validity of the food safety measure.

[4] Due to the limitations of the RASSF data that is used in the model, the United States has been dropped from the large-N analysis. The RASSF data adopts a Eurocentric view of food safety. Consequently, food safety warnings issued against the United States often reflect qualitative differences between the United States and EU regarding what constitutes "safe" food (e.g., GMO rules, hormones in beef), rather than an objective measure of food safety in the United States. This suggests that the RASSF ranking could be unfairly biased against the United States, which is why the United States' food safety performance is far lower than expected (on par with Nigeria).

TABLE 10.1 *Summary Statistics*

Statistics	N	Mean	Std. Dev	Min	Max
Food Safety Index	114	−1.38	0.71	−3.98	1.183
Scale Index	124	10.33	2.9	5	19
Revenue	109	22.19	10.87	2.349	61.87
FDI	152	7.05	13.2	0.005	154.2
GDP per Capita	164	9748	18427.31	163.5	157200
Corruption	175	−0.22	0.868	−1.83	2.32
Food Exports	114	27.93	27.30	0.027	98.33
Polity	131	12.29	6.32	0	20

Note: For data sources please see Appendix.

To measure the size and heterogeneity of a country, I construct a "Scale Index" which includes population, surface area, tiers of administration, level of biodiversity, and agricultural production.[5] As shown in the previous chapters, countries that are large and heterogeneous are expected to have high levels of scale politics. A country is scored from 1 to 4 points for each element of the index, where a "1" identifies the country as below the 25th percentile and a "4" above the 75th percentile. Countries with high scores on its Size Index (above 15) include China, India, Russia, and Brazil, and countries with low scores (below 5) include Cyprus, Iceland, Jamaica, and Singapore.

An OLS regression of a country's Safety Index regressed on its Scale Index shows that scale indeed has a robust negative association with food safety across a variety of specifications (see Table 10.2).[6]

---

[5] Each of these measures is negatively correlated with a country's food safety. Please see the Appendix for a rationale of the index.

[6] Model I provides our primary independent variable of interest without controls, and size and heterogeneity is indeed significant. Model II includes GDPPC squared, which is statistically significant, but has no effect on the estimated coefficient of interest. GDPPC has a curvilinear relationship with food safety higher at lower and higher levels of GDP per capita. This would suggest that as citizens become wealthier and begin to transition from basic grains to more processed foods, food safety becomes worse at moderate levels of GDP per capita, and then resolves at higher levels of economic development. In Model III, with a series of governance controls the coefficient for scale remains robust. The positive coefficient on the polity score, which is statistically significant, suggests that countries with open government, strong civil society, and rule of law are more likely to provide higher levels of food safety. Although not statistically significant, the positive coefficient on budget revenue suggests that countries with greater resources are more able to implement food safety regulations, and also incur the fixed costs of establishing agencies, testing centers, and inspection facilities. Corruption is not found to be statistically significant.

TABLE 10.2 *OLS Models for Nested Design*

OLS	Model I		Model II		Model III		Model IV	
Scale Index	−0.12	***	−0.13	***	−0.15	***	−0.15	***
	(0.02)		0.02		(0.03)		(0.03)	
GDPpc (log)			−0.98		−0.40		−0.42	
			(0.62)		(1.3)		(1.48)	
GDPpc (log)^2			1.75	**	2.46	**	2.52	**
			(0.62)		(0.85)		(0.94)	
Corruption					−0.20		−0.22	
					(0.19)		(0.22)	
Budget revenue (log)					0.66		1.07	
					(0.81)		(0.8)	
Budge revenue (log)^2					0.63		0.93	
					(0.75)		(0.74)	
Polity score					0.04	*	0.03	
					(0.02)		(0.02)	
Food exports (log)							−0.04	
							(0.09)	
FDI (log)							−0.014	
							(0.14)	
Intercept	0.07		0.001		−0.86	.	−0.54	
	(0.24)		(0.24)		(0.49)		(0.73)	
Adjusted R-squared	0.24		0.31		0.32		0.29	
$n =$	94		90		59		47	

. = .1; * = .05; ** = .01; *** = .001.

Even when controlling for economic development, governance quality, trade openness, and FDI, it is the Scale Index that carries the most explanatory weight for a country's food safety outcomes.

At first glance, some researchers may question the weak relationship between political regime type and food safety outcomes. After all, in both the EU and in India it was electoral pressures that precipitated fundamental food safety reforms. Moreover, given the limits of press freedom in China, some could argue that noncompliant producers are subject to less scrutiny from the media. But, as discussed in Chapter 2, authoritarian regimes can become highly responsive when issues are politically salient.

Model IV considers the robustness of scale, controlling for market openness (FDI and % food exports). Surprisingly, neither level of FDI nor the relative of importance of food exports in trade have an effect on food safety. The coefficient on the Scale Index remains robust.

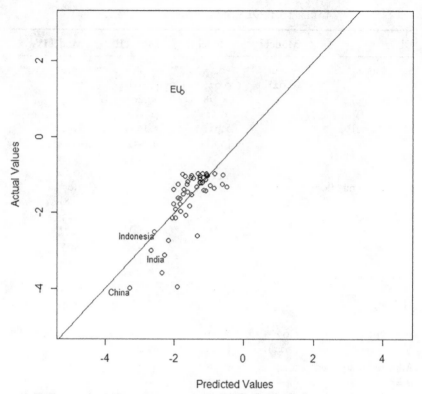

FIGURE 10.1 Structured Comparison Case Selection Plot
Source: Adapted from Lieberman (2005), p. 445.

In the case of food safety, the regime has invested time, capital, and labor to address the crisis. Also, party officials, all the way to the top, have openly acknowledged how the mishandling of food safety has impacted regime legitimacy. As far as media freedom is concerned, journalists have had substantial leeway to openly report on food safety issues. It should be noted that a country's polity score is significant in the bivariate model, showing an inverse relationship to food safety, but has less explanatory weight in the full model.

After specifying a food safety model, we can then use this regression to guide our case selection for a structured comparison. Using the output from this regression, we can plot a country's *predicted level* of food safety based on the regression model against its *actual level* of food safety. As seen in the Plot at Figure 10.1, the EU performs far better than its predicted value, whereas India and China are better predicted. In other words, why does a scale-based model poorly predict the EU's food safety performance, but more closely predict China and India? Or, put another way, why is scale highly problematic for some countries (China), moderately problematic for some (India), and not at all problematic for others (EU)?

Typically, countries such as the EU, India, and China cannot be meaningfully compared due to vast differences on key explanatory variables. But, in the context of a nested analysis, the OLS regression has shown that even when controlling for economic development, corruption, regime type, and other covariates, the Scale Index remains a robust predictor of food safety. And because these countries have similar scores on the Scale Index (~19), the cases can be meaningfully compared in the context of a nested analysis.[7]

A reasonable first step in theory building is then to examine the macrogoverning frameworks of China, India, and the EU, which are directly related to how these countries manage scale. I do not claim that the designated model serves as the definitive cross-national study on food safety. Moreover, it should be noted that the presentation of the nested analysis is not to say that other potential explanations—such as the history of state building, bureaucratic culture, and the particularities of each country's civil society, among a host of other factors—may well have important implications for food safety outcomes in general. Indeed, Lieberman (2005) notes that nested analysis is an iterative process between model testing and model building. But, for a model that emphasizes the importance of scale relative to a number of other predictors, a closer look at the macrogoverning frameworks for each of these countries is a logical starting point to better understand why scale negatively impacts some countries and not others.

THE EU MULTILEVEL SYSTEM

The EU's food safety system operates according to a multilevel governing logic. The system is credited with being one of the strongest regulatory

---

7 Undoubtedly, GDP per capita is an important explanatory factor to consider in food safety performance, which is statistically significant across a variety of specifications. But, GDP per capita alone cannot explain this variation. First, looking at the added-variable plots of GDP per capita, the EU is still a significant outlier with respect to its provision of food safety (Appendix III). Second, India still outperforms China in terms of food safety, despite its lower GDP per capita. Finally, when using a measure of relative importance developed by Silber et al. (1995), scale is found to contribute more to the variation in the dependent variable than GDP per capita in Model 4 (Appendix IV).

systems in the world in terms of responsiveness, regulatory stringency, and the low incidence of mass food contaminations (Vogel 2012). Experts claim that the EU has "solved the problem of scale" by employing a regulatory framework of multilevel governance (Alemanno 2009). One would expect that scale politics in the EU food safety system would be severe because of the size and complexity of its EUR 1.1 trillion food market (FoodDrink 2016). As a regulatory union, the EU must govern 28 member states, each with their own unique food safety systems and regulatory standards. In addition, these systems are highly heterogeneous in terms of different food production traditions (Echols 1998). Moreover, the EU has become even more heterogeneous in terms of regulatory capacity since 2004, as countries from eastern and central Europe have become member states (Jacoby 2006).

The genesis and framework of the EU's multilevel governing system could be understood to be an institutional response to the fundamental problem of scale in governance, as described in this book: How does one in fact integrate European, regional, national, and local scales of governance across multiple dimensions within a common framework? To find an answer to this question, a 50-year journey of conflict and compromise provides some clues.

Initially, the lack of a clear template for regulatory integration in the 1960s led to substantial conflict between member states and the evolving European system. The key question that policy makers have had to address was what the primary scale of governance should be in the EU food safety system: Is food safety a European problem or a member state issue? European commissions were primarily focused on adopting food safety policies that would facilitate integration of the food market on a European scale. Member states, however, were more concerned with protecting their own standards regardless of the consequences for European market integration. In some instances, member states would deny regulatory equivalence to other member states. And, because European Community harmonization of food safety laws required a unanimous vote, attempts at building a fully integrated food safety system at the European scale were stymied. By the 1970s, food safety standards across member states had developed into serious barriers to intra-European trade, and were often used as a pretext for protectionist behavior. Governing systems operating at the European and member state scales were at a fundamental impasse regarding food safety.

The establishment of a key guiding principle of the EU's integrated, multilevel regulatory system, "mutual recognition," provided the basis for a macrogoverning scale solution. In 1979, the European Court of Justice ruled on the now-famous *Cassis de Dijon* case concerning the use of food safety as a non–tariff-based barrier to trade. Germany had prohibited the importation of crème de cassis, a type of liquor, from France, due to its failure to meet German alcoholic content requirements for liquor. The European Court of Justice ruled in France's favor, citing that member states can only insist on different standards if they can demonstrate that the divergence satisfies an "urgent need."

Following the ruling, member states were required to adopt a policy of "mutual recognition" of their food safety regulations. The resulting system created a clear template for how the regulatory systems of member states relate to one another—that is, a product deemed to be safe for circulation by one member state should be considered safe by all (Ansell & Vogel 2006). This basic principle of mutuality enabled the creation of a European market for food products while preserving the national regulatory traditions of each member state. Thus, the mutual recognition mechanism preserved the primacy of the member-state scale, while also creating a loose framework by which authorities could adjudicate food safety conflicts as they emerged on the European scale.

The emphasis on mutual recognition, however, limited the range of regulatory action the EU authorities could take as food safety problems began to emerge at the European-wide scale, as was the case in the Bovine Spongiform Encephalitis (BSE) outbreak in the 1990s. And, because of the primacy of the national scale, from 1986 to 2000, the EU was not able to introduce legislation to manage the risk of BSE because member states blocked reforms (Krapohl 2007). British interests had dominated the Scientific Veterinary Committee at the European scale, and played down risks of BSE for human health (Krapohl 2007). By the time the UK government announced the presence of BSE in its livestock in 1996, the European public experienced a collapse in trust in regulatory authorities (Ansell & Vogel 2006). A new committee was then established in the form of the Scientific Steering Committee, but regulations were still blocked by member states. BSE's Europeanization highlighted the need for a new solution to Europe's scale problem to prevent the system from being captured by member states' interests, and the EU consequently reorganized its food safety regime.

The resultant food safety framework was a multilevel system that optimized governance based on the strengths of each level's scale of governance. This, however, required a careful renegotiation of governance processes across multiple dimensions of scale. As a matter of jurisdiction, the

EU recognized the fundamental importance of various traditions in food safety and provided substantial leeway for member states to develop their own systems, and to participate in decision-making at the European-wide scale. Member states still retained the right to manage food safety, but also had to comply with a more comprehensive bill on general food regulations. The newly established Directorate General for Health and Food Safety (DG SANCO) was placed in charge of implementing EU food safety laws across Europe, and would ensure the enforcement of the new European food safety regime by auditing member states and examining whether their national statutes were in compliance with EU food safety laws. In emergency situations, DG SANCO was given the authority to intervene in member state systems and force recalls. However, this authority is only invoked in highly specific instances against a particular product or geographical area.

To address potential mismatches on the knowledge-related dimension of scale, multiscale information systems were established linking Europe from top to bottom. The EU's Rapid Alert System for Food and Feed (RASFF) system was created so that member states and other third countries could notify RASFF of serious food safety problems emerging at lower scales within their jurisdictions, and RASSF would then transmit European-wide trends back to localities. The European Food Safety Agency (EFSA) was established in 2002 and is responsible for conducting risk assessments of member states and the common market, and transmitting scientific advice to member states. The food safety authorities of member states are represented in the EFSA and scientific authorities of member states also have direct channels to the EFSA to inform EU risk assessment bodies of emerging food safety problems. The strengths of governments operating at different scales were harnessed to facilitate information sharing and regulatory coordination across various dimensions of scale.

Together the various institutions of the EU promote feedback between different scales of governance, support member state regulatory initiatives, and provide a clear template for regulatory action between European, regional, and national authorities based on their individual degrees-of-zoom. These systems prevented the more typically observed responses of *ignorance* and *minimization* to scale externalities in multiscale systems. Alemanno's (2009) recounting of the EU's reaction to the Chinese melamine infant formula scandal highlights how effectively the system works in response to crisis at multiple scales. At the European scale, following reports of melamine-tainted products entering into the EU,

DG SANCO moved forward to ban all dairy composite products for infants and young children. On the basis of scientific advice from the EFSA, DG SANCO also required member states to check products containing at least 15% of dairy product. Member states then reported test results via the RASSF. The system was also sensitive to developments at the member state scale. A year later, based upon recommendations from member states through the RASSF, the commission then amended inspection requirements. Member states through the RASSF highlighted high levels of melamine in soya products from China. As a result, DG SANCO amended its inspection protocol to include complete testing of all soya-based products from China. The EU system responded flexibly and reactively to the Chinese food threat by harnessing multiple actors at multiple scales, ultimately leading to negligible negative food outcomes for the EU.

Europe watchers assert that the EU is still in the beginning stages of multilevel governance. Institutional compromises have led only to partial solutions that address food safety differences between authorities at different scales (Ansell & Vogel 2006). The balance of power between European and member states is still in search of jurisdictional resolution. Some observers speculate that as the authorities at the European scale gain power at the expense of member states, member states may begin to challenge the legitimacy of the European food safety system. But, thus far, Europe's multilevel framework has successfully mitigated scale politics in food safety. Even as the EU has admitted new member states with weaker regulatory regimes, the system has managed to provide a high degree of food safety for the European market.

INDIA AND DECENTRALIZED, FEDERALISM IN FOOD SAFETY

India's food safety system is embedded in a decentralized, federal framework in which the state governments play the dominant role in determining the scale of food safety management. As the central government in New Delhi has sought to reassert itself in food safety, state resistance has led to severe scale politics. In practical terms, defining the "scale" of the food safety problem is severely contested, multiscale conflicts have emerged across several dimensions, and feedback mechanisms between scales are compromised. However, India's decentralized, federal framework still outperforms China in terms of food safety outcomes.

India's federal system was originally established as a highly centralized system of governance. Prior to the 1990s, Indian states exercised far less power relative to the center: India's governmental revenue collection system was managed entirely by the central government; state boundaries could be redrawn by simple majority of parliament; and "Presidential Rule" gave New Delhi the right to dissolve state governments in perceived crisis (Parikh & Weingast 1997). It has been broadly observed that the guiding logic of the system was that a strong central government was needed to prevent destructive interstate disputes and to address regional inequalities (Parikh & Weingast 1997). Especially when India gained independence, the government's primary concerns were of national scale: there was a felt need to increase national food availability, control rationing, and develop national, uniform standards for training (Dasgupta 2001).

Beginning in the 1990s, central-local relations changed as states began to exercise primary authority over industrial and economic policies (Sinha 2005). That is, the state scale of governance increasingly took precedence, leading to a more decentralized type of federalism. In 1994, the Indian Supreme Court set limits for "President's Rule," which has effectively prevented unilateral action from New Delhi (Manor 2001). Local governance was also strengthened with the establishment of panchayats and other municipal bodies, which created new political resources at the local scale (Mitra 2001). This new framework has led to the "creative management" between the center and localities dependent on carrots and sticks (Manor 2001). The bargaining system is not equal for all states, with some receiving extensive privileges from Delhi and others less so (Sinha 2003). This new macrogovernance framework thus should be viewed as a "joint production" of central rules, state choice, and subnational institutional variation (Sinha 2003).

Food safety governance in India's decentralized federalism has proven lacking in terms of managing scale politics. A tradition of center-state bargaining has encouraged states to bargain for exemptions to food safety laws developed at the national scale, thwarting attempts at standardization to govern food safety for the country as a whole. Under such conditions it has been difficult to define the scale of governance—should the national or state scale prevail? Moreover, the federal structure lacks clear linkages to state regulatory machinery, creating problems for the system as it attempts to scale down food safety practices across the jurisdictional, knowledge-, and network-related dimensions of scale.

India's food safety system in the 1990s was highly fragmented at the national scale. During this period, food safety regulations were scattered over eight different acts of parliament and involved four different ministries (Jha 2013). These enactments and operating procedures were meant to complement and supplement each other to achieve total food safety and quality standards, but, instead, led to an overly complex regulatory system (Palthur et al. 2009). In 1998, a new food safety bill was proposed that repealed conflicting acts and orders, defined standards, accredited laboratories, and established a licensing system for food businesses (Umali-Deninger & Sur 2007). However, with small-scale markets dominated by small farmers, a poor extension system, and a lack of political will to force the agricultural sector to comply with national regulations, food safety improvements were limited.

A complex web of controls existed below the federal level, which impeded the jurisdictional integration of state systems into a common framework of governance. All agricultural commodities were required to be sold through wholesale markets controlled by state governments. In 2005, there were 800 regulated markets in the country (Umali-Deninger & Sur 2007). Once products entered these markets, produce would be combined with products from other suppliers across a state, creating significant problems for quality and traceability. In addition, laws restricted the processing of certain commodities to small-scale workshops. The unintended consequence of these regulations created significant legal barriers to developing a coherent regulatory system that could operate at the national scale.

Pressures for new food safety reforms erupted in the early 2000s, following a major soft drink scandal involving Pepsi and other distributors who had used contaminated water in their products. In 2006, the Indian government moved forward with a fundamental restructuring of the system. At its helm, the federal government developed the Food Safety Standards Authority of India (FSSAI), which was to serve as the single point of contact for all regulators in the system, rescaling food safety governance to the national scale. The FSSAI was to provide scientific advice and technical support for central and state governments, create an information network, and establish standards for the country (Palthar et al. 2009). The agency would also represent India in global technical standards meetings (Shukla et al. 2014). The agency ambitiously declared that "the act aims to establish a single reference point for all matters relating to food safety and standards, by moving from multilevel, multi-departmental control to a single line of command" (FSSAI ACT).

As the new food safety system was implemented in 2011, significant contestation over regulatory authority emerged between the national government and state governments. And qualitative evidence suggests that the new system has resulted in negligible gains in food safety (Jairath & Purohit 2013; Biswas & Hartley 2015). Neither state nor federal governments could decide on the appropriate scale of governance. Despite the move toward a "single line" command system, India's decentralized, federal framework presented several difficulties because it was highly dependent on subnational acquiescence. The new food safety act requires state governments to establish food safety systems at the state level. A state food safety commissioner then would designate officers at the district level and food safety officers at the subdistrict level (Dhar 2012).

As the federal government attempted to rescale food safety governance, scale politics arose across multiple dimensions. In terms of jurisdiction, state governments in India have challenged the authority of the FSSAI in terms of standard setting, licensing policies, and monitoring. Although the FSSAI did create a forum at the national scale—in the form of a central advisory committee with state representation to monitor implementation of the law—many states felt disenfranchised by this new system. As a result, through 2012, several states were still not in compliance with the law. Kashmir had not appointed a commissioner or implemented new food safety regulations (GK News 2012). Maharashtra challenged the new FSSAI in a Bombay high court, arguing that it was the prerogative of states to legislate on alcohol, and that there were already state laws governing the manufacture and sale of liquor (Ghosh 2012). In Kerala, the state government asserted that a resource crunch, staff shortages, and lack of infrastructure made it impossible to implement the new food safety provisions (Nair & Antony 2012).

Federal attempts to reassert control over states failed. In a letter to the states, K. Chandramouli, the FSSAI Director, implored governments to move quickly with implementing the new laws (Dhar 2012). State governments rejected federal authority in food safety across the board. For example, in 2012, state governments spoke out against an FSSAI audit report on milk adulteration, denying the severity of the problem in their own regions. By 2014, states still had not established food safety tribunals as required by the law. The FSSAI chastised state food safety officials for being disinterested and insisted that states should learn from other states in compliance with the law (Singh 2014).

Producer associations and traders have argued that the rescaling of the food safety system benefitted large-scale multinationals over local food producer networks, and unfairly favored food safety knowledge developed at the global scale. New laws requiring the licensing of all food vendors and small businesses have been criticized as "impractical, undemocratic, and dictatorial" and as a "mere copy of food safety laws prevalent in developed countries" (Sharma 2012). Merchants' associations rallied at protests across 19 states, asserting that new food quality standards were based on American and European laws, which did not account for local climactic differences and the significant soil pollution that has occurred since the 1950s (More 2012). In Tamil Nadu, the Madras High Court also sided with the Tamil Nadu Hotels Association, arguing that the commissioner of Tamil Nadu did not have the right to enforce provisions of the new law, which failed to take into consideration local conditions (Parekh 2012).

These allegations were not necessarily unfounded concerning the new law's lack of sensitivity toward the local degree-of-zoom. The basic laws for the new food safety system were initially proposed by major players in the food processing sector who sought to reform India's overly complex system as a way to make the sector more competitive on the global scale. In 2002, the prime minister's taskforce suggested that a major goal was to align Indian food safety with new international standards. The first draft of what was to become the Food Safety Standards Act of India was prepared by the Ministry of Food Processing, rather than health or food safety officials, suggesting a bias in favor of large-scale producers (Palthur et al. 2009).

Indeed, the Indian federal government has focused primarily on new food safety standards developed by international scientific bodies, which create tensions with traditional practices of food storage, hygiene, and distribution. Some argue that most food-borne illnesses occur at the household level, suggesting that strict regulation and compliance for manufacturing will not be sufficient to address food risks. There is a clear need to integrate traditional knowledge with science to facilitate a shift in safety practices (Gavaravarapu & Nair 2015).

India's decentralized federalism poses significant problems for scale politics. Rescaling the food safety system to the federal level has led to significant contention. State resistance has prevented the successful scaling up and scaling down of the food safety system. Each policy community continues to operate at its own governing scale, and cannot align interests across multiple dimensions (particularly in terms of knowledge, networks, and jurisdiction).

The federal system in India, however, institutionalizes state representation in multiple fora, which helps to structure the bargaining process. In India, states are engaging in obstructionist activity, but at least they are using their power as a bargaining tactic to effect real change in national laws. As we shall see, this is not the case in China's fragmented, unitary system.

CHINA'S FRAGMENTED, UNITARY SYSTEM

China's fragmented, unitary framework of governance has engendered fierce scale politics throughout its food safety system. Unlike Europe or India, China lacks a template for governing across scales. China is neither federal nor multilevel, but is a de jure unitary state in which state authority is vested in the central government and then delegated to local governments. In China's "line-and-block" system, the "lines" (条 *tiao*) refer to central ministries that are represented at each level of government, and the "blocks" (块 *kuai*) refer to local governments. Theoretically, central directives are to be transferred down the *tiao* and implemented in accordance with the needs of the *kuai*.

In other words, in terms of the primary scale of governance, the national scale should dominate policy making, and local scales should be taken into consideration during implementation. In reality, the system is fragmented across various ministries, across different scales of government, with scale politics emerging across multiple dimensions (knowledge, networks, jurisdictions, managerial, and spatial). Moreover, frequent cycles of centralizing and decentralizing regulatory authority have exacerbated regulatory coordination by constantly shifting the primary scale of governance between national, provincial, and local scales.

The lack of a clear, stable framework for central-local relations has led to tensions among governing communities at different scales across multiple dimensions. As governance is constantly rescaled, it shifts power relations, inhibits institution building, and complicates coordinated regulatory action. Scale externalities are typically ignored as policies developed based on one scale of governance are sometimes forced on systems at other scales, which operate according to different time frames, managerial practices, and knowledge-generation processes given their different degrees-of-zoom. There is no clear mechanism by which the interests of governing systems at smaller scales are communicated to governing systems at larger scales. Unlike India, for example, which grants states guaranteed policy making powers and a clear legal basis to influence the national system, provinces bargain, evade, or fight with central authorities without regard to national coherence.

This complex background of central-local relations has had a profound effect on China's food safety system. Beginning in the 1990s, central ministries, including the MOA, MOH, AQSIQ, and MOC, were in charge of various aspects of food safety. As new standards and rules were developed at the center, the implementation of these policies was delegated to local governments. However, owing to massive food safety scandals in the early 2000s, food safety authorities were then reconfigured in 2004, with the new SFDA piloting a largely top-down food safety apparatus. Since then, the food safety apparatus has gone through several restructurings involving a mix of partially centralizing and decentralizing initiatives. The most recent reform involves the creation of a single super-ministry, the China Food and Drug Administration, which has been given the mandate to "control food safety from the center." However, each new sequence of reforms has failed to clarify in practical terms how central and local governments are to function as part of a multilevel regulatory system.

Preceding chapters have shown how central and local degrees-of-zoom conflict and confound one another in China's food safety system. In the domestic sector, regulators and producers could not develop a unified view about how to address food safety on a comprehensive, country-wide basis. Rescaling the system to the national scale through coordination bodies, such as the SFDA, streamlined regulatory authority, but the approach alienated local officials. In addition, authorities at different scales faced significant difficulties as they attempted to integrate their managerial processes with a national food safety strategy. Local-scale solutions through model agricultural production bases produced a better fit between regulatory rules and food production contexts, but lacked a mechanism to integrate this patchwork of local solutions into a national food safety system. The launching of national campaigns sought to realign incentives through mass mobilization across scales. But the increasing frequency of campaigns reduced their effectiveness and impeded institution building for day-to-day food safety management and collaboration of policy communities at different levels of the system.

The failure of China's food safety system to address scale politics implies the need for a new division of labor between the center and locality regarding regulatory control. The fragmented, unitary framework lacks effective institutional fora and bridging mechanisms to integrate policy communities at different scales.

ANOTHER NOTE ON FEDERALISM: THE UNITED STATES

Although it was excluded from my nested analysis due to data limitations (as previously explained), I will also consider how the US variant of federalism affects its food safety system. The United States is, of course, another large and heterogeneous polity that may lend comparative insight in the development of a more effective food safety regulatory regime in China. The United States suffered from major food safety disasters in the early 20th century, and even in recent years scandalous microbial contaminations, such as the deadly 2008 salmonella-tainted peanut butter misadventure,[8] continue to be uncovered in its food supply system. However, despite these unpalatable scandals, Food Sentry, the EIU, and OECD studies rank the United States higher than India and China, but lower than the EU (Newsdesk 2014; EIU 2017; La Vallee & Charlebois 2014).

The United States' food safety system has developed under a *centralized, federal framework* in which the national scale dominates policy making to ensure safe food for its citizens. Federal governing bodies are involved in setting policy, coordinating regulatory inspections across jurisdictions, and monitoring food producers. States have largely acquiesced to federal control.

Under a centralized, federal framework, food safety is defined in national terms. The preponderance of US federal agencies involved in food safety is derived from the government's role in regulating interstate commerce. In addition to its own inspections, the federal government also contracts with state governments to conduct inspections on its behalf according to the federal food safety standard. States play a limited role in the management of food safety for retail distribution and in eating establishments within their jurisdictional scale, and are permitted to devise state protocols, provided they are in line with federal regulations. Some states' rights advocates contend that the federal government should not exercise primary control in their food safety systems. Utah, for example, proposed legislation that would exempt food grown and consumed entirely within the state from federal regulation (Strauss 2011). However, even in this instance, the state still recognized the federal government's role in managing food produced for interstate consumption.

In the United States, food safety scale politics is less a struggle between the governing authorities at the national and state scale, and more about the consequences of severe national-level fragmentation on the entire system. The federal food safety system has long been criticized for being a highly fragmented system. In evaluating the institutional arrangements regarding site-based inspection and certification for the United States, it is important to recognize that the United States actually has (at least) two systems of food safety governance—one for meat, poultry, and eggs regulated by the US Department of Agriculture (USDA) and another for

---

[8] The widespread US 2008 salmonella outbreak resulting from tainted peanut butter paste killed 9 people and sickened 714 others in 46 states and, according to national news outlets covering the scandal, "resulted in one of the largest food recalls in American history"—see www.cnn.com/2015/09/21/us/salmonella-peanut-exec-sentenced/

other food products regulated by the US Food and Drug Administration (FDA). Today, the FDA manages more than 150,000 food facilities, a million restaurants, 2 million farms, and millions of tons of food imports (Strauss 2011). The USDA is in charge of more than 6,000 large-scale slaughtering facilities (FSIS). Food safety monitoring is also conducted by the Environmental Protection Agency and the Centers for Disease Control and Prevention. Smaller roles are delegated to various agencies scattered throughout different governmental departments.

Overlapping authority, scarce resources, and unclear regulations due to haphazard policy making have led to severe infighting at the national scale. Like other regulatory systems, the US food safety system emerged as a response to crisis rather than as part of a comprehensive program. In the 1860s, the USDA was primarily focused on expanding production for the country's growing population. Following the publication of Upton Sinclair's *The Jungle*, the federal government moved swiftly to implement the Pure Food Act of 1906 and the Meat Inspection Act of 1906 (Endres & Johnson 2011). All food safety inspection was conducted primarily under the jurisdiction of the USDA, until 1940, when the FDA was transferred to the Federal Security Agency. The split FDA-USDA system then continued to develop, with the USDA acquiring primary jurisdiction over meat, poultry, and egg production, and the FDA focusing on seafood and processed foods. As other issues emerged in the national food market regarding pesticide usage, environmental protection, and land usage, food safety portfolios were parceled out to other new agencies. The result of proliferating regulations and regulators was a highly complex regime operating at the federal scale.

Since the 1960s, no national legislative committee or executive oversight body has been able to unify the US food safety system. In 1977, a study led by Senator Ribicoff represented a federal effort to consolidate food safety in the FDA, but this initiative failed to produce concrete regulatory reform. An attempt to unify the system again in 1998 also proved unsuccessful, despite evidence showing that the US system would be better served under a single central authority at the national scale. The effort to develop a unified food safety system in the federal government was constantly stymied by other interested parties who advocated for a multiagency coordinated system, citing the difficulties of implementing a single-agency model. Proponents of the multiagency model argued that because both the USDA and FDA had developed independently of each other for 100 years, it would require a multiyear implementation period to eliminate duplication, resolve turf battles, and harmonize differences in organizational culture (Pape et al. 2004). As a result, the United States' multiagency model has remained largely unchanged, with serious consequences for food safety in the United States.

The fragmentation of food safety management at the federal scale has important implications for the politics of scale. Due to a lack of a single implementing agency "at the top," it is difficult for governing bodies operating at smaller scales to effectively interface with the federal government structure. Particularly in terms of the managerial dimension of scale, a lack of uniform testing and reporting requirements at the federal scale leads to substantial confusion. State and local officials complain that they must perform multiple tests on a single food sample to report issues to different federal agencies (Merril & Francer 2000). In addition, producers and distributors operating at different scales assert that this complex and conflicting web of regulations and testing is burdensome and unclear. In some cases, the confusion has resulted in slow food safety recalls, poor information collection, and weak monitoring.

The potentially debilitating effects of this fragmented system at the federal level, however, is ameliorated by a number of institutional practices. The federal-state contracting arrangement, for example, helps to coordinate food safety activities across multiple scales of governance, leveraging the resources of governing systems given their scale. Each year, the FDA specifies a certain number of inspections that state inspectors will conduct on behalf of the federal government. The federal government then audits state systems and certifies that they are capable of carrying out the federal inspection regimen. In this way, the federal government can standardize implementation of policy, conserve its own resources, and better utilize state inspectors with better knowledge regarding local circumstances. The federal government also provides expert guidance on technical issues and standards through broad food codes for certain products (Taylor 1997).

Because of the historical predominance of the federal food safety system, states have developed their systems to better integrate with federal standards, enabling seamless integration on the knowledge dimension of scale. When states seek to develop their own protocols for food safety, they model their own inspection and monitoring systems on federal food safety policies. For example, 25 states operate USDA-approved meat and poultry inspection programs (Merril & Francel 2000). Safety standards are relatively similar from state to state, enabling interstate collaborative ventures such as the Interstate Milk Shippers Conference. In this instance, centralized, federal framework has provided a clear framework against which governing systems at lower levels can coordinate with higher level authorities on food safety best practices to facilitate the formation of an integrated regulatory union at the national scale.

Recently, persistent and well-publicized food safety problems have again resulted in a push for a massive overhaul of the US regulatory system, which has remained unchanged for almost 30 years. Concerns about the substantial influx of foreign food imports, the increasing frequency of widespread microbial contaminations, and the weak monitoring standards of an ever-growing food production sector led to the enactment of the Food Safety Modernization Act of 2010. The new law now strengthens the FDA's control over food safety and preserves the primacy of the national scale in food safety regulation in the United States. The new law substantially increases the power of the FDA in manpower, regulatory reach, and information collection. In addition, the new law recognizes the potentially debilitating effect of scale externalities in which small-scale problems can disrupt the entire system. Specific provisions of the new law include a new FDA mandate to regulate all food safety measures from the farm level, to establish hazard analysis critical control points in all food processing facilities, to develop regulations for safe transport of food, and to have immediate recall authority (Strauss 2011; Endres & Johnson 2011).

During the negotiations of the new Food Safety Modernization Act, several states were concerned that the federal government was overreaching by enforcing new and unnecessary regulations on small family farms with a different risk profile than large producers that operate on a regional or national scale. In response to state concerns for local production networks, several amendments were made to the bill that limited the scope of applicable federal food safety regulation. Small farms and medium-sized processing centers were instead put under the sole regulatory authority of state and local governments. Scholars contend that this exemption was a "scale-sensitive" solution to accommodate highly divergent interests related to food safety (Hassanein 2011).

Despite the 2010 food safety overhaul, potential scale-derived coordination problems remain unresolved. Critics of the US food safety system still argue that the new law does not address the fundamental question of coordination at the federal level. Also, debates about the merits of developing a unified agency still persist (McKenna 2015).

COMPARATIVE ANALYSIS OF FOUR REGULATORY GIANTS

The macrogoverning frameworks of the EU, India, the United States, and China have important consequences for each country's scale politics. The EU's multilevel model appears to be the most successful in addressing scale politics. Multiple forums facilitate negotiations about safety

TABLE 10.3 *Macrogovernance Frameworks across Countries*

	China	US	EU	India
Macro Framework Scale Fix	Fragmented Unitary Decentralization/ Centralization	Centralized Federal Centralization (Federalization)	Multilevel Multilevel Forum/Mutual Recognition	Decentralized Federal Centralization
Defining the Scale of Governance	Constant flux between central and local scales	Federal government template	Multilevel governance facilitates governance across scales	Weak federal food safety agency cannot scale down; States resist federal "view" of food safety
Multilevel Multidimensional Coordination	Multidimensional problems	Multidimensional tensions addressed	Multidimensional tensions addressed	Multidimensional Problems
Scalar Feedback Mechanisms	A lack of scalar feedback mechanisms	Federal-state cooperation	RASSF EFSA	Legal challenges

standards between member states and European authorities. In addition, jurisdictional clarity encourages the coordinated participation of governing communities operating at different scales. The United States' centralized, federal approach to food safety provides a clear scale orientation for the entire system, with state governments converging on the federal view of food safety. India's decentralized, federal system is nominally centralized, but in practice highly dependent on state governments for the implementation of food safety policies. Food safety policies developed for larger scales are unsuccessfully translated and implemented in governing systems operating at the subnational degrees-of-zoom. However, resistance is still more constructive than obstructive, as states seek to actively amend the system in ways that are more amenable to their more parochial degree-of-zoom. China's fragmented, unitary system provides a weak template for managing the process of scaling up and scaling down governance, leading to poor food safety outcomes.

Addressing the macrogoverning frameworks brings into focus broader historical trends that affect scale politics beyond individual policies. In the case of federal systems, federal legacies in food safety management matter. The United States was a first mover in securing the federal government's role in managing food safety at an early stage. State systems were co-opted into the federal regulatory system and the federal field offices that were established began conducting many of the inspections. This early set up led to the accumulation of substantial local knowledge of food safety conditions and prevented significant antifederal food safety politics from developing. This system contrasts with India's decentralized, federal system, where state regulators had previously managed their own food markets independent of proscriptions from New Delhi. The imposition of the new top-down regime met with stiff resistance from governing systems operating at smaller scales due to a lack of familiarity with or capability to operate within the new regime. States insisted on securing individual concessions from the new federal food safety agency, which only led to further fragmentation.

The sequencing of market and regulatory development also has important implications for scale politics. In the EU, the creation of a supranational food safety regime occurred only after the development of the common market. Because member states had developed their own food safety systems, the EU had to actively incorporate views from member states and formally acknowledge the role of national regulatory systems. This form of multilevel scale accommodation is distinct from India's unsuccessful attempt to rescale food safety to the federal level without adequate state support.

In many ways, China's fragmented, unitary framework is most akin to India's decentralized, federal approach to food safety governance. The development of food safety policies occurred following a long period of directives emphasizing increased agricultural production. While central policies had long guided food safety, in practice, local governments were in charge of managing food safety and hygiene. In China, as in the case of India, the central government's attempts to rescale the system and its failure to actively incorporate local governments also led to severe scale politics.

Top-down approaches, however, are not necessarily more prone to regulatory failure than bottom-up approaches. As in all cases, context matters. In the United States, a centralized, federal framework facilitated a top-down approach. In India and China, top-down approaches failed due to a fundamental unwillingness by local officials to adopt national food safety practices. Given these underlying conditions, perhaps a more EU-style mediative process, which grants substantial flexibility for governing systems at different scales, while maintaining a clear standard for the common market, would result in more effective regulation.

Scale politics are less severe in federal and multilevel systems because these systems have a host of supportive institutions to address conflicts and inconsistencies between scales. Contestation can be quite severe even in the US and European contexts, but the presence of institutionalized fora creates predictability and stability within the system for regulatory governance. Specifically, these federal and multilevel systems are more adept at defining the scales of governance, addressing the multidimensionality of scale, and dealing with inevitable scale externalities.

LESSONS FOR CHINA AND CAUTIONARY TALES

We have seen that macrogoverning frameworks have important consequences for scale politics and regulatory coordination. China's fragmented, unitary framework poses significant challenges for its regulatory development. Can China follow the lead of other polities to ameliorate, if not "solve," its scale problem, which lies at the heart of its food safety failures?

Chinese policy makers may find the EU's multilevel approach to food safety to be an effective regulatory template to follow. Despite the obvious differences between the EU and China in terms of market and regulatory development, both polities do face similar scale challenges. First, both the EU and China must coordinate actors at multiple scales in highly complex systems with their own regulatory traditions. Second, both entities govern subunits with varying levels of regulatory capacity, different supply chain management styles, and highly diverse geographical conditions. Finally, both the EU and the Chinese central government must ensure uniformity of standards across the vast "common markets" they govern. Consumers must not only be protected from unsafe food in local markets, but also food from other jurisdictions.

The EU's multilevel approach to food safety governance applied in China would delimit the authority of the central government, which would only govern the "Chinese common market" and actively facilitate integration of provincial food safety systems. Provinces would be empowered to develop their own food safety systems, but would have to abide by a minimum national food standard to engage in commerce in other provincial markets. In addition, provinces would be guaranteed representation in central-level decision-making bodies concerning the development of common market standards, risk assessments, and enforcement policies.

The primary problem that policy makers must address to fix China's continuing food safety problems is that the multilevel solution would require a reconfiguration of China's fragmented, unitary governance framework. Simply copying the successful institutions of Europe will do little to ease the long-embedded politics of scale in the Chinese context. It is notable, however, that the model of the 2002 EU Food Safety Law significantly influenced Chinese policy makers in the drafting of their own 2009 Food Safety Law (EU Interview). Moreover, with specific reference to another multilevel (federal) system for guidance, Chinese reformers were positively influenced by the United States FDA when establishing the China Food and Drug Administration in 2013. But, when looking beneath the surface of each attempt at institutional mimicry, one sees again and again the central government has not rethought its overarching macro-governing framework.

Although the EU model offers the clearest design solution to China's scale problem in food safety, it is also the most politically challenging to replicate—given China's prevailing "line-and-block" (*tiao-kuai*) system, controlled by the center. Scholars will quickly point out that there are numerous reasons why the center is unlikely to adopt a centralized, federal framework or a multilevel system.

First, a province in China is a fundamentally different subnational unit than an autonomous European member state. And, perhaps most notably in China, the center has been loath to cede powers formally to its provinces because of a persistent fear of centrifugal proclivities that the state has carefully reined in through a host of institutional reforms

(Naughton & Yang 2004). That is, regulatory autonomy might ostensibly be construed as political autonomy, and with the secessionist threat of Xinjiang and Tibet ever looming, any initiative toward the development of a federal structure would be problematic. In fact, most of China's reconfiguration of subnational distinctions have been undertaken precisely to enhance central control and to prevent subnational units from becoming too powerful. In this regard, one needs only to remember how Chongqing was separated from Sichuan province due to concerns that the province would become politically unwieldy. Second, the delegation of regulatory autonomy would require ceding fiscal control, which is unlikely to be repeated. China watchers will note that previous experiments with fiscal decentralization nearly resulted in bankrupting the center. Also, the redesign of the fiscal system in 1994, though ultimately successful, was politically taxing. Consequently, the center is unlikely to cede its hard-won fiscal authority back to the provinces. Third, federalism has long been considered a signature characteristic of an often-gridlocked, Western-style, bourgeois democracy. The democratic bent to the federal design thus makes it highly incongruent with China's current leadership's focus and intent on preventing a "peaceful evolution" of the Chinese polity.

The political challenge of reconfiguring its unitary system does not mean China will not modify some of its regulatory policies to mirror certain aspects of multilevel governance. While the development of a formal federal, multilevel system is not likely, the Chinese food safety system could develop a de facto federal system—if it were limited in scope—to resolve its ongoing food safety problems. China scholars, for example, have observed how the Chinese government did establish a form of market-preserving federalism in the past to enable markets to develop (Montinola et al. 1995). To deal with changing market realities, the central government "devolved" significant economic powers to local governments and "loosely committed" to noninterference in local economic activity or enforcing hard budget constraints on local governments. In these flexible systems, the central government would only police the common market, and allow local governments to create their own pragmatic solutions to deal with local economic realities. As local economies developed, the center was shown to be disinclined in practice to interfere in local markets, which would harm growth. Moreover, local governments themselves independently generated or gained access to increased financial capital, fiscally empowering them to resist central government intervention. As a result, a durable central-local relationship emerged.

Of course, this system was not without its costs. The de facto federal system also created notable cases of local protectionism where local fiefdoms often became hotbeds of corrupt activity (Qian & Weingast 1997). This later led to high levels of policy obstruction which in turn forced the central government to pursue a policy of soft centralization in the late 1990s and 2000s (Mertha 2005). These trade-offs will have to be assessed by Chinese policy makers. What is important to note, however, is that no part of this federal arrangement requires a shift toward the promotion of individual rights and political freedom (Qian & Weingast 1997). While the system lacked a constitutional basis, a series of institutional arrangements served as the foundation for an effective de facto federal system.

In fact, policy makers in China have been studying the United States and European experience in food safety quite closely. Former EU representatives to China indicated that the State Council was highly interested in the design of the EU food safety system, and that state councilors had gone on numerous study trips to Europe. Moreover, Chinese policy makers have not hesitated to observe that they have modeled the recent China Food and Drug Administration on the American FDA. In addition, the state has been actively engaged in redrawing jurisdictional boundaries in other regulatory sectors as well, such as in the field of environmental protection, to better calibrate policies within regions.

In the next chapter, I take up the important issue of China's continuing adherence to its inherited tradition of unitary governance from the center, the fluid reality of central-local relations, the conditions under which China has been willing to deviate from its inherited tradition, and future prospects for food safety reform. The overriding and critical question then remains: In order to address food safety in China, can new frameworks of governance be developed to attenuate the politics of scale and to make the adoption of *any* comprehensive, nationwide food safety policy more feasible?

Parting Thoughts on Scale

China's food safety crisis presents a formidable policy challenge for food safety experts. Egregious scandals—as varied as the sale of liquor laced with Viagra and the distribution of fake eggs—reveal how regulatory best practices have been stretched to their limit in a system that must govern more than 1.3 billion people across provinces that are as large as entire countries. In this context, the crux of the policy design challenge lies in how to effectively manage the regulatory politics brought on by·China's scale.

The preceding chapters have shown that the country's existing approaches to food safety regulation have failed to integrate systems of decisively different scale. We have observed that policy makers cannot determine the appropriate scale of governance, nor is there a consensus at what scale food safety problems are likely to emerge. Policy approaches developed at different scales conflict across a range of dimensions that extend beyond the jurisdictional and spatial, but have knowledge-related, temporal, managerial, network-related, and institutional implications. Local community governance systems conflict with national certification authorities; global, national, and local scientific communities jockey for influence over food safety standard setting; and producer organizations throughout an extended supply chain seek to set industry best practices. Even as producers, regulators, and consumers seek to work with one another to create an integrated, coherent regulatory system, the lack of a clear solution to address China's embedded "scale problem" poses a serious impediment to effective governance.

Faced with the daunting task of reforming China's food safety system, an exasperated SFDA director asked me directly during my research, by way of general inquiry and personal challenge, "How would *you* design a system with over 240 million producers that sell their goods in thousands of unregulated markets throughout this country? Show me how it is done!" (CC 1) This book is in many ways my response to that fair question and urgent imperative. It has shown that any solution failing to attend to scale politics will face severe challenges as policies are transmitted, translated, and implemented throughout a regulatory system. The chapters have documented the significant coordination problems that have emerged in three different food markets stemming from an inability to define the scale of the problem, address scalar externalities, and translate policies across scales.

Neither centralized, hierarchical approaches, nor decentralized, collaborative systems of governance have been able to effectively address scale politics in a large, heterogeneous context. In the CSA sectors, producers developing a decentralized, collaborative system based on social trust in localized markets could not scale up their food production model beyond suburban areas. The elite export sector's centralized, hierarchical governance framework that emphasized a strategy of direct, adaptable control succumbed to policy sinkhole effects in the broader market. Expanding the reach of either a decentralized, collaborative system or a centralized, hierarchical system to other scales without a clear road map led to severe regulatory dislocations, rendering a once-successful system ineffective.

In the domestic sector, I considered how the mix of centralized and decentralized state initiatives in the form of frequent campaign-style crackdowns, the haphazard development of policy experiments, and constant restructuring of coordinating agencies have complicated institutional goal setting and fueled interagency rivalries across multiple scales. China's coregulatory approaches to addressing food safety through farmers' cooperatives and large, vertically integrated "dragonhead" enterprises have fared no better in addressing scale politics. These specialized producers were employed to streamline and modernize agricultural production to improve food safety. The hierarchical governance model espoused by dragonhead enterprises faced challenges scaling down food safety practices because local production communities did not trust quality assurance specialists whose understanding of food safety was focused on the global scale. Also, farmers' cooperatives encountered challenges scaling up, finding it challenging to enter broader distribution channels.

In previous chapters, I focused on China's food safety failures as regulators, producers, and third-party certifiers transition from a fragmented to an integrated approach of governance. This chapter seeks to finish on a more hopeful note by presenting design principles to aid China in the ongoing reconstruction of its food safety system. I will explore the broader implications of China's regulatory style, consider regulatory lessons from recent food safety reforms, and appraise proposed solutions. In addition, sectoral comparisons will be made to outline how my analysis of scale politics in food safety might guide similar studies of regulatory governance deficits in other sectors. I then conclude with some thoughts on the political consequences of failing to address food safety as China's population becomes more concerned about risk, safety, and prevention, and the distribution of risk in society at large.

ON REGULATORY STYLE

China's struggle for food safety reveals the limits of the country's "regulatory style" to effectively manage complex markets. The literature on regulatory styles argues that nations develop specific "styles" of regulation that reflect culturally, politically, or institutionally embedded practices to achieve regulatory goals. Regulatory styles can be persistent and powerful because they reflect institutionalized traditions of domestic-market regulation, well-ensconced political constituencies, and resilient patterns of national consumption. While "regulatory style" may sometimes be an overly generic label for effects that might be better disaggregated, the coevolution of industries, politics, and regulatory regimes often makes it difficult to disentangle these distinctive aspects of governance. Some scholars have argued that China's authoritarian politics affect how regulators define problems and craft solutions (Van Rooij et al. 2016), while others have pointed to the country's socialist legacy on regulatory development (Pearson 2005; Liu 2010). I would like to suggest that China's distinctive regulatory style has also developed in response to its scale problem, which has implications for how it establishes a comprehensive, coordinated system.

One could argue that the "scale problem" has been at the heart of China's governance challenge for centuries. The Chinese behemoth has long been concerned about how to integrate its distant localities, while maintaining at least the semblance of a unified polity (Fairbank 1973). As the imperial system fell into disarray at the turn of the 20th century, other approaches for organizing the state, such as federal arrangements, were fiercely debated by Chinese intellectuals such as Chen Duxiu, founder of the Chinese Communist Party, and Hu Shi, a Republican-era public intellectual (Waldron 1990). By the mid-1920s, a firm view began to take root regarding the need for a strong central state to prevent the disintegration of the polity. The Chinese Communist Party inherited this tradition of unitary governance from the center. While the designers of the new government did not explicitly address a "scale problem," they sought to develop a framework in which a highly heterogeneous system could converge on a single, unified vision of socialist reconstruction emphasizing the national scale, and defined as a unitary whole.

China's formal unitary constitution, however, belies a more fluid reality of central-local relations. During noncrisis periods, the local scale dominates the policy making process. National regulators forego a tortuous process of reconstituting national-level ministries and laws which are guarded by entrenched interests, and instead delegate regulatory authority to localities. Local officials understand that edicts from the center should be understood as broad guidelines, and that policies should be adjusted to suit local circumstances. Here, the scale of regulation focuses on local networks, local knowledge, and local managerial practices. During this period of relative stability, policy makers at different scales operate independently of one another, and each scale functions in accordance with its own parochial needs and perspectives.

A shift to the local scale also fosters innovation and intergovernmental learning. In China, policy experimentation is reflective of an enduring governance strategy called "proceeding from point to surface," which involves experimenting with policies prior to their implementation on a national scale (Heilmann 2009). The development of model production bases can be viewed in this light as test sites for potential large-scale models. Under a policy experimentation regime, China's size and heterogeneity actually work to the country's advantage by allowing for a broad range of test sites. Other examples of policy experimentation include the development of special economic zones in the 1980s, establishment of model environmental cities in the 2000s, and the more recent establishment of free trade zones.

During crisis periods, the national scale reasserts itself in terms of setting policy: local experiments are phased out; national bodies dictate rules; and funds are directed toward central government projects. As the scale of the problem is recast in national terms, the center responds by launching campaigns, restructuring agencies, and issuing binding directives. When faced with overwhelming jurisdictional complexity, local obstructionism, and numerous standards, the centralization of regulatory control gives priority to the need for national standardization over institutional diversity. In the case of food safety, the creation of a series of coordination bodies to address the food safety crisis fits well into this regulatory mold. The most notable examples in other sectors are the recentralization of fiscal control in 1992–1994, and the restructuring of state-owned enterprises in 1997, which took place in spite of significant resistance from provincial governors (Baum & Shevchenko 1999).

Another feature of China's regulatory style—"*segmentation*"—can also be understood as a response to its scale problem. Given the system's complexity, a common way to address regulatory failures is to reduce the scale of a system and create islands of regulatory excellence. Segmentation brings into focus how China often restricts its policy solutions to a specific sector, a limited number of actors, or a particular region. A system is ring-fenced because it is viewed as subject to different scale dynamics and processes that are different from the broader market. At times, this scale management technique reflects changing priorities in the state's industrial policy. China's "commanding heights"—its largest, and most sophisticated firms—are subject to a different regulatory regime than its broader economy. Enterprises that are part of the state's preferred policy program are granted subsidies, tax privileges, and preferential policies (Pearson 2005; Hsueh 2011). In other cases, segmentation may enable the gradual implementation of policies when reform of an entire sector might be impractical. In food safety, we observed how the government delimited its export sector to China's elite producers and subjected them to a distinct style of government. There are other examples of the segmented regulatory logic at work in domestic-sector food safety management. In Yunnan and Sichuan, for example, regulators limited the operation of uncertified workshops to certain geographical areas and controlled distribution channels, but did not actively impose penalties on these enterprises. In other sectors, such as the case of coal mine safety reforms, China first proceeded with formal government-supported large-scale mining facilities while ignoring township-level mining operations (Wright 2004).

China's scale problem features prominently in its regulatory style. And this factor of governance deserves equal attention to that given to the country's authoritarian and socialist legacies when considering defining elements in its regulatory style. Although the country's leaders have not framed its governance challenge as a "scale problem," China's leaders are constantly involved in a process of *rescaling* its large and heterogeneous system based on its particular policy needs.

Although this constantly evanescing central-local regulatory style has served China well in its past, the well-documented cases of regulatory failure in this book suggest that it serves as a weak template for policy standardization, predictability, and multiscale coordination, at least with specific reference to effective food safety governance, and likely with regard to regulatory shortfalls in other sectors. Standardization has never been the Chinese state's forte when implementing policy. Central laws are written in broad terms to permit local governments to implement laws in line with local conditions (*yindizhiyi* 因地制宜). Interprovincial relations remain unclear, the central-local balance of power ambiguous, and the bounds of policy experimentation remain undefined, all of which aggravates scale politics. As China transitions to a scientifically assessed, risk-based form of regulation, the state must work even harder to develop a common framework for standardization. As its trading partners place increasing emphasis on the adoption of global standards—such as GMP, GAP, and ISO certification—in their own domestic markets, China must follow suit. These evolving standards presuppose the existence of a clear legal framework for coherent regulatory integration from the global to the local.

The lack of standardization is not helped by the recurring cycles of "releasing" and "gathering" of regulatory control, which provides an uncertain foundation for a clear division of regulatory responsibilities. As a result, determining at what scale problems are emerging and the scale of government best equipped to address them proves highly challenging. Local governmental bodies are uncertain when a period of flexibility will end and austerity will begin. Some governments choose not to innovate because reforms at the center could render new local projects out of step with national objectives. In the past, the central government would centralize control in a crisis and severely punish officials who deviated from the central line. Strong regulatory practice, however, is predicated on predictability and the institutionalization of procedures for all stakeholders in a system.

Lack of standardization and predictability reflects a regulatory style that is thus poorly adapted to the needs of multiscale governance. Neither central nor local actors are equipped to address the food safety scale problem in isolation. A decentralized strategy of policy experimentation, without the strong coordinating hand of the center, fuels interprovincial disputes. Yet a unilaterally imposed centralized approach to food safety largely disregards problems and processes unfolding at smaller scales. However, as we have seen in previous chapters, problems in multilevel governance extend beyond the question of how central and local governments can work in concert toward a unified aim. The larger problem is that China's regulatory style lacks a strategy for how to nest systems within systems. Do local strategies cohere to a national plan for food safety? How do local rules relate to broader laws derived at different scales? Can information generated at the local, provincial, and national scales be integrated to provide a more comprehensive understanding of regulatory problems? How does a system actively address scale externalities? Failing to understand the relationship between processes generated at different scales has led to fundamental regulatory shortcomings that must be addressed.

The key for China to resolve its escalating failures in food safety regulation in the next decade is to transform its regulatory style to facilitate integration and overcome the disruptive effects of scale politics. Even if actors recognize that problems affecting the common market for food production and distribution require a united response, Chinese regulators seem to be trapped in a dynamic of unresolved scale politics despite their concerted efforts. In the ensuing period, regulators, the regulated, and the public must come together to rethink scale and integrated food safety governance.

REGULATORY LESSONS

What lessons from studying scale politics in food safety can China offer to other large, heterogeneous polities? A prima facie examination of the facts suggests that while China is an extreme case in terms of scale politics, the challenges it has faced are not dissimilar to other regulatory giants. In Chapter 10 I explored how the dramatic expansion of food production, lengthening of supply chains, and increased distributional coverage also created massive regulatory coordination problems in the United States, the EU, and India. In the development of food systems, the logic of regulatory constraint had to give way to the greater urgency of facilitating the rapid expansion of agricultural markets in these countries due to food supply concerns. Thus, food safety regulation was largely an afterthought as contaminated food entered the food production and distribution chain. As their food systems expanded, policy communities at different scales in these countries did come into conflict on a range of dimensions. A pattern of scale politics emerged, involving conflicting standards, poorly coordinated food safety agencies, and lapses in monitoring and surveillance.

This book has examined how China's food safety policy makers and academics have largely overlooked the varying nuances of scale in their proposed regulatory solutions. While officials often point to the country's substantial number of producers and geographic size as impediments to effective governance, they are hard pressed to identify solutions that adequately take into consideration scale's multiple dimensions. Many food safety experts have focused on the benefits of centralization and streamlining the bureaucracy on food safety outcomes, citing fragmentation as the primary problem in food safety management (Han 2007; Ni & Zeng 2009). That is, they largely address coordination problems along the jurisdictional dimension of scale. And little has been written about the challenges of the other important dimensions of scale amplified in this book. Policy papers on government food traceability systems, meat safety protocols, and penalties for noncompliers all highlight international best practices, but fail to acknowledge that food safety solutions that work on one scale context might be less effective on another (Li & Shen 2009; Xie et al. 2009). Others have emphasized the importance of industrial consolidation in addressing China's food safety problems, and transitioning to more advanced modes of production (State Council 2007; Zhou & Jin 2013). Yet, the transfer of knowledge is not problematized, and does not consider how food safety knowledge will encounter local resistance as it scales down. Government officials and academics have also discussed the need to address the deficit of social trust in the system by moral education (Xinhua 2011a; Wu & Zhu 2014). However, as my study of the CSA sector has shown, social trust does not scale up as a viable regulatory enforcement mechanism at the national scale.

Reformers can benefit from several lessons derived from China's battle to contend with scale. First, we have seen that gradualist patchwork solutions are less effective in facilitating systemic integration across scales. Marginal changes in policy at one scale may have unintended consequences at other scales. The urgency of response to crisis may lead to counterproductive, knee-jerk reactions by the state at the expense of the rational development of the system. Policies may come into conflict with one another as one regulatory failure cascades into another. To effect substantive change in regulatory practice, a reform program must target policy communities at all scales. Simply addressing issues at one scale is unlikely to affect good regulatory practice for the entire system.

China opted to take a gradualist response to its food safety problems rather than to develop a comprehensive reform program, and food safety management has suffered. Prior to major scandals in the 2000s, China did not have a food *safety* law, but rather a food *hygiene* law that lacked provisions for food recalls, risk surveillance, and testing. Since the 2000s, the central government has restructured the country's food safety system at least five times in major respects, and undertook many more minor reforms. Institutional artifacts from previous policies mix with new agencies and regulatory actors at different scales. The old SFDA offices, which were stripped of their coordinating role in 2008, still coexist with the new food safety committees. Local officials are confronted with conflicting pressures. Food safety authorities are encouraged to establish their own regulatory rules, only to have their institution building interrupted by intermittent national campaigns. Cross-cutting pressures have fragmented interests and have resulted in failed regulatory coordination across scales.

These chapters have also shown that governance solutions that focus solely on corruption, local obstruction, and deficient state capacity have limited effects and do not address the fundamental problem of scale politics. Treating these factors as the root causes of regulatory failure will lead to only short-term gains in the country's attempt to provide safe food for all of its citizens. Frequent drives against corruption will only provide a palliative effect on food safety outcomes if gaps persist throughout the system's complicated bureaucracy. Bolstering state capacity by the construction of labs, increasing personnel, and establishing monitoring networks will only be effective if a system for integrating information from different scales is built. If mechanisms for harmonizing standards and rules across different scales are not established, obstructionism is likely to persist. In short, the answer to the scale politics conundrum lies in *wholescale* systems design. To accomplish this, a new template must be created that accommodates the nesting of regulatory "systems within systems" to reflect the reality of the multiscale and multidimensional nature of a system.

FUTURE PROSPECTS FOR FOOD SAFETY IN CHINA

China's most recent reform proposals still have not taken into account the important scale dynamics at work in their food safety system. The creation of the China Food and Drug Administration (CFDA) seeks to consolidate and clarify food safety responsibilities under a single ministry. One commentator even suggested that the new ministry could apply "command-and-control" techniques to address "known" problems where the central state could "severely punish" those who broke the law (Xinhua Interview 2013). The CFDA is now the highest food safety authority in China. Implementing measures are still being written, but little has been specified regarding how to integrate local regulators into the reformatted central system. As such, based on what has been observed with previous coordinating bodies, the CFDA may well fall victim to similar obstacles to effective governance through regulatory integration. Another problem is the large, complex body of national standards that is being developed by the National Health and Family Planning Commission, to be monitored by the CFDA. These national standards have been described as "granular and rigid" and do not afford companies the flexibility of designing their own food safety programs that suit their needs based on their scale of operation (Balzano 2016). Perhaps, during this latest iteration of reform, the state will be able to deploy enough money and manpower to force food safety actors across the diverse polity to heed central commands. A respected food safety scholar in China, comments that because the head of the CFDA is also Deputy Secretary General of the State Council, the CFDA will have enough political clout to enforce its mandate (BJ 03). However, I suspect that scale politics will once again reemerge to confound, confuse, and prevent the establishment of a coherent system. Who will staff this ministry at the local scale? How will the new central ministry integrate local knowledge to discover emerging problems? Why should officials at other scales of government implement the plans of yet another coordinating body that is unfamiliar with local circumstances?

The revised Food Safety Law enacted in October 2015 is yet another comprehensive reform package. The new law regulates more stages across the supply chain, creates increased pre- and postmarket requirements for certain sensitive food products, such as infant formula, and also imposes more severe penalties for noncompliance (China Food Safety Law 2015). However, scholars note that even with these new changes, how the system will effectively coordinate food safety activities across different levels of government remains in question (Fu 2016; Balzano 2015).

In contrast to the CFDA initiative, others have called for a provincial solution to China's food safety problems. Thompson and Hu (2007) contend that rescaling the system to the provincial level could improve food safety management. Regulators would be closer to the ground and could develop strategies that are better suited to local production conditions. But the question of how to manage interprovincial disputes has been left unanswered. How to provide a common framework of governance that can integrate institutional diversity within a highly political context remains a key challenge.

Other scholars argue that China's food safety problems will attenuate following further industrialization of the agricultural sector. Fu (2016), for example, notes that changes to the Food Safety Law in 2015 that require increased inspections and traceability measures will increase costs for food producers and prompt industrial consolidation, which would make the food industry more manageable. However, advanced production and distribution methods will succeed only when strong supply chain management protocols are introduced that can effectively manage producers operating at different scales. Most experts opine that the melamine crisis of 2008 was a result of the inability of large-scale companies to manage China's small dairy producers that operate at smaller scales. The proposed solution to resolve food safety through industrialization of agriculture also appears lacking in light of evidence presented in the preceding chapters highlighting the challenges coregulators face. It is not a lack of industrialization that is failing in China, but the absence of a supply chain management plan that can link different scales of production while avoiding scale politics.

A more recent development emphasizes the introduction of third-party certifiers as a solution to China's food safety problems. Third-party auditors can serve as important bridge organizations linking the lowest levels of China's production systems to transnational governance systems. A senior executive of a food safety laboratory observed with skepticism that a real willingness by the government to have third-party certifiers participate in food safety regulation would represent "a springtime for independent auditing" (EX17). SGS and Moody's, for example, have significantly expanded operations since 2010. But auditors still face the challenge of "scaling down" the certification process. As was noted earlier, as international auditing practices began to spread out in the export sector, a number of problems arose: most major certification businesses used food safety standards that were out of touch with local production realities; international auditors, unfamiliar with local production practices, proved to be unable to detect noncompliance. One auditor recounted, "One company had specialized storage for pesticides... but I noticed that there were no trays or carts to move materials to the fields... this was for show" (EX18). Local state officials were not equipped with the know-how to ensure that, once producers were certified, they would continue to maintain an effective food safety certification scheme's exacting standards.

The Chinese government has dedicated considerable resources to solve its food safety problems. However, there is no quick institutional fix to resolve the problems of scale. In these last few pages, I believe it would be useful to reiterate that China's policy makers should re-examine the EU's multilevel approach to food safety, which provides the most effective template for managing scale. As in the EU, a similar approach to be undertaken would focus the authority of the central government on managing the "Chinese common market" while facilitating positive integration of provincial food safety systems. Provinces would be empowered to develop their own food safety systems, but would have to comply with minimum national food standards to engage in commerce in other provincial markets. Provinces would have representation in central-level decision-making bodies concerning the development of common market standards, risk assessments, and enforcement policies.

SECTORAL COMPARISONS, SCALE POLITICS, AND SOME CAVEATS

As China addresses notable regulatory shortcomings apart from food safety in areas as diverse as environmental protection, labor safety, ocean management, and product quality, it faces a similar problem in coping with scale integration. Across various sectors in China, the largest and smallest scales must be seamlessly integrated: local knowledge must conform to scientific research; local policy solutions must not disrupt long-term central goal setting; and local tasks must cohere to national plans.

I turn briefly to examine several other sectors with a similar, or distinctively different, combination of underlying characteristics to China's food sector to explore the generalizability of the concept of scale politics as an instructive way to view challenges to effective governance. While my examination is only illustrative (see Table 11.1), looking beyond the food sector, we should expect to see similar levels of scale politics at work in sectors that are decentralized, have low industrial concentration, and face high levels of interdependence among scales. As discussed in the introduction, decentralization in the context of this study refers to what extent a sector is embedded in local political economies. Industrial concentration refers to the number and type of actors being regulated. Thus, sectors with high industrial concentration are comprised of a few, large firms, while

TABLE 11.1 *Some Illustrative Sectoral Comparisons and Scale Politics*

	Food Safety	Environmental Protection	Fishery Management	Aviation Safety
Centralization	Low	Low	Low	High
Industrial Concentration	Low	Low	Low	High
Interdependence	High	Moderate	Moderate/High	Very High
Baseline Level of Scale Politics	Severe	Severe	Severe	Low/ Moderate

low industrial concentration involves numerous, small- to medium-sized enterprises.

The interdependence among scales of governance in a sector also has important implications for scale politics. Specifically, in my analysis, a sector is considered highly interdependent when collective activity engages systems operating at *multiple scales*, and failure in governance (be it regulatory oversight or managed activity) at any scale can directly lead to *system-wide* failure. For example, activities in a township marketplace that only trades in local products, and where participants strive to ensure that local products do not enter broader distribution channels, would be considered less interdependent on other scales. However, even when a system operates at multiple scales, interdependence also relates to how sensitive an overall system of multiple scales is to failure (noncompliance) at any single scale. Thus, in some systems, failure at one scale of governance leads directly to system-wide failure, while in other systems noncompliance at a single scale may be less consequential. For example, in aviation systems, failure of regulated activity of a municipal air traffic authority can lead to an aviation accident with multiscalar consequences, even if governance at other scales is "operating properly." By contrast, in other multiscalar systems, failure at one scale may exacerbate coordination problems within the overall system, but not lead to immediate system-wide failure.

Indeed, a high-level exploration of China's management of its fisheries sector and in the field of environmental protection regulation suggests that the adverse effects of scale politics in regulation extend well beyond the food sector, and might be usefully applied to other regulatory sectors with similar underlying characteristics. On the other hand, even where key underlying characteristics are dissimilar, such variances could also prove useful in aid of understanding the relationship between scale politics and effective governance. It should be noted at the start of this comparative examination that, to determine the baseline level of scale politics at work in each of these sectors (low, moderate, or severe), it is important to view the combination of the underlying factors at work in the sectors being regulated.

In China, the combination of underlying characteristics that are present in the governance of the fishery sector are substantially similar to underlying factors in China's food sector. Regulation of China's fisheries is *highly decentralized* and largely developed by local political economies. For example, in 2016, the vast majority of China's fishing zones were managed by a total of 2,969 fishery bureaus, tasked with managing local stocks (Mallory 2016). With regard to industrial concentration in the fisheries sector, as of 2010, China's coastal areas were the registered home of 11,351,254 fishermen, the sheer number of which (even apart from countless unregistered fishermen) makes the sector highly challenging to monitor (Ma et al. 2013). Against this context of the magnitude and decentralized nature of fishermen involved, attempts to reduce the registered number of fishing vessels to 160,000 to effect *industry concentration* have been largely unsuccessful (Shen & Heino 2014). Moreover, the number of China's registered and actual fishing fleet is not only uncertain, but most of the vessels are also considered to be "extraordinarily low tech" (Goldstein 2013).

Effective management of fishing stocks requires coordinated regulation due to moderate levels of *interdependence among scales*. Because fish stocks are migratory, management of this resource requires not only local, but region-wide coordinated action (i.e., multiple scales). Furthermore, the conservation of fishing resources is contingent upon the total ecological health of a system that includes local environmental factors, meso-level fishing trends and patterns, and regional oceanic dynamics. Failure of governance at one scale does create problems for other scales of governance, but does not necessarily lead to system-wide failure.

The sectoral characteristics of high decentralization, low industrial concentration, and moderate interdependence contribute to severe scale politics. Chinese authorities have struggled to address the appropriate scale of governance to address depleting fish stocks. Like other sectors, the system operates under an ambiguous partially centralizing, partially decentralizing framework referred to as a "unified leadership and decentralized administration." The Ministry of Agriculture's Fishery Bureau at the national scale sets broad targets and plans, but implementation is left to local fishery bureaus. The administration of fishing areas is divided into three major zones: a trawler restricted, an offshore, and a far-offshore zone. The offshore zones are directly managed by the central government, but the trawler zones are further subdivided into provincial and then county subzones. In addition to fisheries management, China has also initiated a related conservation program to establish special marine-protected areas (SMPAs) under the State Oceanic Administration. However, some SMPAs are directly controlled by the central government and others are established and controlled by local authorities (Ma et al. 2013).

The management of the fisheries sector has led to severe scale politics. First, it is difficult to address the problem of depleting fish stocks because local and central governments cannot align their degrees-of-zoom to address the problem of system-wide depletion. For example, summer fishing moratoriums mistakenly treat fish as a single stock rather than multiple smaller stocks, failing to account for the diverse species within local scales (Shen & Heino 2014). Second, this system does not create a clear template by which other systems can integrate their fishery management plans. Scholars have criticized the overall framework of this system as "lacking uniform management" (Goldstein 2013); having "no systematic planning" (Qiu et al. 2009); and possessing "inadequate coordination" (Lau 2005). Third, the national scale and local scales have developed irreconcilable perspectives. Authorities at the central level take the view that conservation is of primary importance, and are concerned by the negative diplomatic implications of overfishing in the region (Mallory 2016). Whereas at the local scale, the various actors involved largely focus on the management and exploitation of fisheries in relation to their parochial economic interests and employment pressures.

Multidimensional conflicts have also emerged across scales in the fishery sector. To manage fishing stocks, China has employed a broad set of regulatory tools and programs: a fishing license system; a midsummer fishing moratorium; a zero-growth policy; limitations on fishing boat size; a fishing boat scraping program; measures to combat illegal fishing; and establishment of conservation zones (Goldstein 2013). However, policy makers have rarely considered how these policies scale down. For example, in terms of the managerial dimension of scale, during the development of an integrated coastal management system, local governments struggle to understand how their conservation systems function as part of an overall national strategy. In fact, researchers have concluded that there were no clear strategic objectives (Qiu et al. 2009). Others have observed that the SMPAs lacked assessment systems for design and performance at the local scale (Ma et al. 2013). Studies reveal that temporal problems also emerged because national long-term plans extend far beyond the normally single term of administration of local governments, and there is no meaningful continuity of policies at the local level (Kong et al. 2015).

The failure to address scale externalities has also produced tensions across scales. First, the lack of a coherent regional plan has allowed local governments to compete to maximize fish production, threatening the collapse of regional fisheries in a classic "tragedy of the commons" scenario. Second, the failure to consider the migratory patterns of fish has fueled scalar tensions. For example, conflicts have emerged with regard to trans-boundary SMPAs, where adjacent SMPAs either bear the costs or suffer the consequences of poor protection in neighboring zones (Ma et al. 2013). Third, officials failed to consider how local conservation efforts could affect fishing patterns on the regional, and even global, scales. For example, local conservation policies have unintentionally led to an increase in distant water fishing, as local fishermen sail out of local waters, leading to the depletion of regional or distant fishing stocks, sometimes as far away as Africa (Mallory 2013).

The consequences of scale politics on regulatory outcomes in the fishery sector in China have been severe. Fish stocks remain severely depleted. For example, the Bohai Sea fish production levels in 2011 were only 20% of the levels seen in the 1980s (Goldstein 2013). Attempts to reduce the overall number of fishermen have not succeeded, with the number of fishermen tripling between 1980 and 2011 (Shen & Heino 2014). Also, attempts to reduce the number of fishing vessels by 30,000 from 2003 to 2010 have not been effective (Yu & Yu 2008).

In the field of environmental protection in China, similar levels of adverse scale politics have emerged, as participating actors, both regulators and polluters, fail to define or identify the appropriate scale of governance, ignore multidimensional aspects of scale, and manipulate scale externalities for their own benefit. Polluting industries are highly decentralized and embedded in numerous local political economies. Equally, in terms of industrial concentration, emitters may well range from small-scale processors to large-scale refineries. Moreover, the overarching task of protection of the environment must come to terms with moderate to high levels of interdependence between scales, calling for dedicated and concerted action. Air pollution is often a result of multiple scalar processes, including local emissions, regional weather patterns, and global climate change. Failure to manage these multiscalar dynamics can exacerbate the management of pollution at other scales of governance. Also, certain isolated events, such as major industrial accidents, have led to system-wide failure. For example, in 2005, an explosion at a petro-chemical plant in Jilin province created a stream of toxic substances that contaminated the Songhua River, which affected the whole of northeastern China, and eventually Russia, the Sea of Japan, and parts of the Pacific Ocean. As in food safety and fisheries management, these sectoral characteristics that currently prevail in environment protection in China present a challenging context in which to manage scale politics.

Similar to food safety and fisheries management, environmental regulation in China has thus far failed to define the appropriate scale of governance to deal with pollution due to unclear delegation of authority between the central and local scales. Since the 1980s, the implementation of environmental regulations has been decentralized to nearly 2,500 environmental protection bureaus (EPB) operating at the municipal and county levels (Tilt 2007; Zhu et al. 2014). However, while implementation has largely been delegated to local governments, the central government has often been involved in issuing broad directives and pollution targets from the top-down. For example, in 2001, the National Development Reform Commission specified targets for air, water, and solid waste pollutants. These targets were then broken down by province, and sub-provincial targets were then established by local authorities, with ambiguous effect (Cai et al. 2015). A similar example of a targeted, but poorly implemented, top-down policy in the field of environmental protection has been the establishment of the Energy Conservation Target Responsibility System, where targets for total energy reductions were set by the central government for all subnational governments to follow, with unclear direction (Lo 2015).

I suggest that the important issue regarding what scale of governance is best suited to identify environmental problems, devise solutions, and develop institutions for effective governance has not been resolved due to scale politics. One scholar notes that the environmental regulatory framework is a system of "command without control" in which an authoritarian center issues binding directives to local governments, but local governments are then provided with far too much flexibility to implement them faithfully or consistently (Lo 2015). An unresolved tension between the center and localities has emerged, with local actors claiming that policies do not comport with the local political economy, while the center blames weak implementation on local regulators (Tilt 2007). In other instances, local participants contend that central government targets are too uniform and do not account for important variations among localities. In this regard, studies have shown how provincial targets are set without consultation with provincial authorities, and how there is surprisingly little variation in provincial targets, notwithstanding significantly different conditions from province to province (Cai et al. 2015; Lo 2015). As a result, governments at different scales typically refuse to cooperate with one another.

In the field of environmental protection in China, lack of regulatory attention to how systems can scale down and scale up across multiple dimensions has also led to severe conflicts. For example, in terms of the managerial dimension of scale, air pollution and energy reduction targets set at the national scale have encountered significant impediments to compliance as they scale down. There is little direction as to how these broad national targets should be translated into local targets and it is not specified as to how local enterprises should be monitored under the target system (Lo 2015). In terms of network-related dimensions of scale, policies fail to take into account the cumulative or conflicting effects of the multiple networks (local, regional, national) in which polluters are situated (Zhu et al. 2014). In terms of the knowledge-related dimension of scale, problems have emerged regarding how monitoring information from the lowest scales should be aggregated and interpreted at each level of scale. Data collection includes a mix of self-reporting and crude measurement; significant loss of accuracy occurs as data is filtered, and reporting advances from one scale to the next (Cai et al. 2015). In order to overcome these problems in the area of air pollution, the central government has recently implemented a centrally controlled monitoring network of air pollution inspection stations.

The failure to address and manage scale externalities in environmental protection has also led to severe scale politics. First, numerous studies have highlighted how local pollution is rarely the simple consequence of the polluting behavior of industries in a locality, but is often a result of the accretion and aggregate effect of neighboring polluters. When jurisdictions fail to map onto the scale of a pollution problem in nested systems, subnational units can be incentivized to cheat and manipulate scale externalities to their advantage. For example, revealing research by Cai et al. (2015) shows that provinces adopt a "pollute-thy-neighbor" strategy with respect to water pollution, strategically placing dirtier industrial firms with relatively high levels of pollution downstream in waterways near borders with other provinces. The same study also highlights how enforcement of environmental regulations is less stringent in downstream areas. These cases tellingly demonstrate how scale politics operate to the detriment of good governance for the large-scale system as a whole.

Another scale externality that leads to scale politics is seen to arise when local air pollution policies cause local industries to relocate to other regions (Zhu et al. 2014). When numerous localities impose stringent emissions standards, this proscription can lead to a broader regional scale effect when the affected polluting firms migrate inland en masse. Scholars have also noted how scale externalities and ensuing scale politics can have an influence in the opposite direction, from the large to smaller scale, in ecosystem management, where larger scale infrastructure choices can result in problematic consequences for smaller scale ecosystems. For example, regional road and bridge construction can have severe consequences for local ecosystems (Grumbine & Xu 2013). When the costs of noncompliance or regulatory decision-making are borne by governing systems operating at other scales, significant political tensions emerge.

In direct contrast to fisheries management and environmental protection, China's aviation system is characterized by low levels of scale politics. China's aviation sector is a notable success in China's regulatory development history. Suttmeier (2008) explores how China's Civil Aviation authority developed into a high reliability organization (HRO). Prior to the late 1990s, China's aviation safety record was one of the worst in the world. In 1992 alone, 5 major crashes led to more than 300 fatalities. The regulatory system involved a patchwork of small, municipal airports. Planes were in disrepair and their pilots lacked formal training. However, beginning in 1998, China quickly managed to build a first-class aviation system, and now has the second largest aviation system in the world (Wall Street Journal 2013).

The aviation sector is characterized by its centralized management, high level of industrial concentration, and high level of interdependence among scales. Aviation standard setting and controls were vested in the central government's regulatory agency, the Civil Aviation Authority of China (CAAC). Also, the aviation sector was largely promoted and developed by national actors. The central government forcibly shutdown noncompliant companies and slowed the growth of the overall aviation sector to ensure that it would not outpace regulatory development. Airports in smaller cities were closed and excluded from the new system. The system involved a select number of international airline carriers and large national aviation companies. As a result, coordination of activities was far less complicated compared to food safety, fisheries management, and environmental protection. In terms of scalar interdependence, aviation safety requires the careful coordination of local airport authorities, regional airspace controllers, and international aviation authorities in order to prevent an aviation accident. As one former airline executive explained, "A single route from Detroit to Beijing required the coordination of four governments and fourteen agencies. If at any point someone did something wrong, a highly visible disaster could happen. If other executives were working at six *sigma*, we were working at ninety-nine *sigma*" (BJ 01).

In the aviation sector in China, a clear definition of the scale of governance, careful negotiation of multidimensional scale mismatches, and effective management of scale externalities have reduced scale politics. The national government worked hand in glove with authorities operating on the global scale. Participants were primarily oriented toward global aviation safety standards; municipal standards and local airport operating procedures were quickly removed. Those who opposed the new regulatory framework were no longer permitted to use the nation's airways. While large national aviation companies did initially resist new standards, international pressures eventually forced them to accede to the new safety regime (Pasztor 2007; Chung 2003).

Multidimensional scale conflicts in terms of knowledge and management were mitigated with the assistance from the Boeing group, Airbus, and the US Federal Aviation Authority. Global aviation participants did not only provide a standard for Chinese aviation authorities to meet, but were active participants in scaling down the system. For example, a former Boeing executive explained that international standards for aviation safety were carefully disaggregated into a system of manageable checklists used by individuals throughout the system (BJ 02). Northwest, Lufthansa, and United also established partnerships with major Chinese airlines to facilitate the transfer of information and knowledge and to help mediate international best practices with local conditions (BJ 01). A retired Boeing executive notes that Boeing did not simply lay out a plan for aviation safety, but took the time to provide Chinese regulators with multiple solutions, allowing them to "weigh alternatives and come to their own conclusions" (Pasztor 2007). Jurisdictionally, global governance processes were integrated with local inspection systems. After 2002, China permitted foreign inspectors access to crash sites in China, and the International Air Transportation Authority was invited to audit the safety records of Chinese airlines and make results public (Fuller 2010).

Scale externalities were quickly addressed because failures of authorities operating on the subnational or national scale could have global scale consequences for air traffic safety. As a result, it was well known and understood that the FAA would pressure US carriers not to affiliate with Chinese partners if China's aviation system was not up to acceptable FAA standards (Fuller 2010). And, when China's safety standards were seen as lacking, the FAA did not hesitate to prohibit new routings for Chinese carriers, as occurred, for example, in the case of China Southern Airlines in 2001 (BJ 02).

A caveat should be registered that the foregoing comparisons are not meant to be a comprehensive study of scale politics in each of the enumerated sectors but rather to illustrate how scale politics operates in sectors other than the food sector with similar, or distinctively different, underlying characteristics. We can expect scale politics to be most severe in sectors with a combination of high levels of decentralization, low levels of industrial concentration, and high interdependence of scales. In contrast, scale politics in sectors that are centralized, highly concentrated, and with a low level of interdependence among scales are likely to be more moderate, with better regulatory outcomes. While the aviation sector has a high level of interdependence among the various scales of governance involved, a careful coordination of all participants allowed for the smooth working of the overall system. I would invite other scholars to consider in more detail what combinations of the foregoing underlying sectoral characteristics are more problematic or beneficial. For example, a useful area of exploration would be to compare whether baseline levels of centralization, industrial concentration, and interdependence among scales affect scale politics equally or if one sectoral characteristic is more deleterious or benign, acting independently or in combination with other underlying baseline conditions.

While certain sectoral characteristics may make scale politics more or less likely to emerge, it has been the focus of this study that the governance processes used to manage scale politics determine regulatory outcomes. While governments have, indeed, attempted to institute measures to modify underlying characteristics to address scale politics, such as readjusting the concentration of industry to effect better regulatory outcomes, such undertakings to alter baseline sectoral characteristics are difficult. In the specific case of food safety, China cannot simply delimit the overall size of the food production sector to achieve better regulatory outcomes because of overriding food security concerns. Beyond the issue of food safety, China must secure an adequate food supply to feed its population. There are also other pressing concerns that limit government action to change baseline conditions in the food sector, such as transitioning from low concentration to high industrial concentration, because many of China's farmers depend on the sale of their agricultural produce for their livelihood. Denying small, widely dispersed farmers the ability to enter agricultural markets could lead to social unrest. Moreover, even if one is able to centralize management or increase industrial concentration through concerted action, the various sectors must still address the challenge of interdependence among scales (which I suggest is more difficult to change) to moderate scale politics and have better regulatory outcomes. While the aviation sector was shown to be far more centralized and highly concentrated, numerous mechanisms had to be put in place to address the high interdependence of scales.

PARTING THOUGHTS

John King Fairbank (1988) had it right: *the Chinese behemoth represents the ideal test case for how to govern scale.* While China's size and heterogeneity have long been its governance curse, how China chooses to reintegrate its fragmented system will prove instructive for other complex, multiscale polities. Mechanisms for ameliorating scale politics should be further explored and articulated. Studies on federalism, multilevel and adaptive governance, and democratic experimentalism can be expanded to include a framework of scale politics; solutions and the coordination costs, information asymmetries, and the political obstacles of possible solutions under such a framework should be assessed. The challenges of scale management need not be limited temporally to the present. Indeed, lessons on scale politics from other historical, large, and heterogeneous polities, such as the British Empire, Napoleon's France, and Imperial China, will be instructive. Technological innovation—how it has both increased the scales of governance while also providing tools to solve scale's attendant problems—should also be considered.

As China transitions to a risk society, as it inevitably must, along with the rest of the world, its inability to address its scale problem is likely to prove politically costly. According to Ulrich Beck (1992), our interlinked global society has now entered a new phase of postmodernity in which individuals are more concerned about the distribution of risk throughout existing economic, political, and social systems. Citizens expect the state to provide guarantees to minimize and fairly allocate risk, while at the same time they are less confident about those who are charged to ensure their safety.

China seems to be following a well-trodden path to the establishment of a risk society. The tragic irony of China's food safety problem is that many of its food safety failures are a direct consequence of the successful development of its food production industry. As China's food markets expanded, products from different areas began to circulate more broadly. The increased circulation of food also made traceability, refrigeration, and storage more difficult. As new producers gained access to a range of modern, but potentially dangerous, inputs, including pesticides and chemical fertilizers, many companies lacked the prerequisite monitoring capabilities to ensure even baseline compliance over a large and fragmented supplier base. Companies, in effect, exposed larger swaths of the population to the risk of contaminated food through their extensive distribution chains. The increased scale of production and distribution led directly to an increase in risk.

One cannot simply turn back the clock to a time when all food was produced and consumed at the local scale. China finds itself trapped in a developmental bind with regard to risk management in its food production and distribution system. Despite the increase in food safety risk, moving away from industrialized agriculture is impractical given food security pressures. Already, experts forecast that China will no longer be food-self-sufficient in the next decade. The state faces a challenging dilemma: it must industrialize agriculture and increase the risk of food scandal and crises, or adopt more limited and scale-controllable organic practices but face the prospect of severe food shortages.

As the scale of China's food system expanded, risks have not been evenly distributed throughout society, fueling social unrest. Food safety is increasingly viewed as a privilege of the rich and powerful rather than an inalienable right of every citizen. The state operates a special supply (特供 *tegong*) system that supplies safe food to major state-owned enterprises, government ministries, and the military. The CSA movement can be seen as a reaction by the wealthier members of society to manage risk on their own, which raises a politically salient issue. On the one hand, this behavior signals that social groups can and are willing to define and manage food safety risks irrespective of government action. On the other hand, opting out of the public regulatory system highlights a fundamental lack of faith in the government's ability to manage modern-day risks. Other researchers have pointed to significant disparities between rural and urban food safety systems, which raise similarly loaded political issues. Urban regulatory authorities are provided with more resources and personnel, whereas their rural counterparts remain severely underfunded. A national survey of food safety systems also highlights significant regional disparities between poorer regions in the west and wealthier eastern provinces of the country.

Thiers (2003) contends that the Chinese state's performance-based legitimacy is at stake as it transitions to a risk society. This somewhat alarmist suggestion is not without historical precedent. In Europe, trust in government plummeted following the BSE scandals, and led to serious losses at the polls by governing parties (Ansell & Vogel 2006; Kjaernes et al. 2007). The Chinese government has struggled to develop the information networks, traceability and recall systems, and monitoring facilities to adequately measure risks, not only in food safety but in other quality-of-life areas that are vital to the well-being of its citizens. It has also failed to rally the support of NGOs and other civic actors who can better provide information on emerging problems. Food safety, air pollution, air safety, and water safety frequently represented the top concerns of Chinese citizens in the 2013 and 2014 Pew surveys.

All interested China watchers hope that China solves its scale problem—and soon. A "real-world" consequence of China's integration with processes at the global scale is that whatever happens in China affects us all. Few could have predicted that China's infant formula crisis in 2008 would precipitate a global milk powder shortage, as hundreds of thousands of Mainland Chinese tourists hoarded cans of milk powder stripped from the shelves of foreign supermarkets in a frenzy of panic—buying on behalf of their children and loved ones.

With Chinese food exports constituting an ever-greater market share of foreign food supplies, China's food safety problems may quickly become a problem for the rest of the world. Even more significantly for China, the state's inability to provide its citizens with food that is safe to consume foreshadows a real crisis of governance. Corruption and inequality may constitute a longer-term challenge to the party's authority. But the lack of food safety, which threatens basic human survival, could be potentially explosive, confirming the basic truth of the old adage that "all nations are but seven meals from a revolution."

Appendix

I. A NOTE ON FIELD SITE SELECTION AND INTERVIEW STRATEGY

The book draws from more than 200 interviews with food safety regulators, food producers, and technical advisors gathered over 15 months of fieldwork and follow-on interviews between 2009 and 2016. My research on the CSA market utilizes more than 25 interviews and 15 site visits conducted over a three-month period. Research on the CSA market was conducted in Beijing, Chengdu, and Shanghai, which serve as the primary nodes of the CSA network. NGOs active in establishing CSA markets across the country also provided archival evidence of their activities including internal communications, op-eds, and journal articles.

Research on China's food export sector involved discussions with export producers, third-party auditors, and members of the diplomatic community involved in food safety: 30 interviews and 10 site visits were conducted over a five-month period. Most of the field research was conducted in Shandong province, one of China's largest exporting provinces for fruits and vegetables, and a select number of interviews were conducted in hejiang, Sichuan, and Ningxia. I selected Chinese, Japanese, European, and American exporters to observe variation in the effectiveness of food safety approaches employed by these firms. Japanese exporters are viewed as the most successful, Europeans moderately successful, and the Americans least successful. Diplomatic officials provided information on the safety of exports, the results of recent audits, and their general perceptions of China's export controls.

For the domestic sector, I conducted approximately 130 interviews and visited 4 counties to develop a broader view of food safety. The Chinese government does not permit researchers free rein to select research sites. Sites were selected purposively based upon the relationships of my sponsoring research institute with local county governments. I stratified counties to maximize variance on degree of regulatory risk and market development, which may have effects on food safety irrespective of scale. Scholars assert that areas with more advanced food markets are likely to have higher levels of food safety. Supermarkets, specialty stores, and global distribution chains have stronger monitoring capacities and are thus more likely to provide safe food. Consumers are also likely to be more willing to pay for higher quality food and to punish noncompliant firms in the market. In addition, advanced food markets are typically in areas in which government regulatory capacity is more developed. In terms of regulatory risks, some products are inherently more difficult to regulate than others due to the nature of the production process. Aquaculture and meat products are at high risk of microbial contamination. Processing procedures can be technical, complex, and capital intensive. Deviations from procedures can lead to significant food safety risks. By contrast, vegetable production is far less complicated. Pesticide residues may lead to chronic health problems but will only rarely lead to sudden death.

Level of food market development was approximated by GDP per capita in each county (high, medium, low). Level of regulatory risk was approximated by focusing on three different food types, each with a qualitatively differing level of risk: vegetables, which represent the lowest risk; pork, which represents moderate risk; and aquatic products, which represent the highest risk. The unit of analysis, therefore, is a county/food sector (e.g., Zhuguang county/aquaculture).

Studies of the domestic sector were conducted in "Zhuguang" county in Sichuan province, "Dingxian" county in Yunnan province, and "Antian" and "Dingming" counties in Zhejiang province.[1] Three types of food production were investigated in each county. The counties selected represent the range of market development from low to high: Dingxian county in Yunnan, a low level of market development; Zhuguang county in Sichuan, a moderate level; and Antian/Dingming county in Zhejiang, a high level. For each site/food sector, I conducted approximately 15 interviews with food producers, producer associations, distributors, and civic groups. In each county, officials from AQSIQ, the Husbandry Bureau, the Agricultural Bureau, the State Administration for Industry and Commerce, township food safety offices, and village food safety

---

[1] The names are fictional.

offices were interviewed. All interviews were conducted using pretested interview guides. Group observations were conducted at the farm level. Provincial-level interviews included officials from the Agricultural Bureau and Food Safety Commission in two provinces. At the central level, interviews were conducted with two food safety officials.

II. A NOTE ON THE SCALE INDEX

The study creates a Scale Index from several indicators: population, surface area, tiers of administration, level of biodiversity, and agricultural production. A country is scored from 1 (25th Percentile) to 4 points (100th Percentile) for each element of the Scale Index for a total of 20 points. Each individual element attempts to capture elements of size and heterogeneity relevant to food safety management and scale politics. In addition to population and surface area, I also add tiers of administration to capture the size of government and administrative complexity. The biodiversity measure is from a World Bank study that scores a country's ecological complexity from 1 to 100. Biodiversity seeks to capture the heterogeneity of the agricultural production system. The volume of agricultural production proxies for the length of supply chains and size of food markets in a country. Each of these measures themselves is negatively correlated with a country's Food Safety Index.

APPENDIX 1 *Index Components and Food Safety*

	Population		Tiers		Ag Prod.		Bio Diversity		Area	
Coefficient	−0.18	***	−0.3872	**	−0.12	*	−0.302	***	−0.234	***
	(0.05)		(0.12)		(0.05)		(0.090)		(0.053)	
Intercept	1.94	*	0.541		0.9034		−0.72	***	0.31	
Adjusted R Sq	0.08		0.07		0.72		0.25		0.12	
N =	142		125		137		139		132	

. = .1; * = .05; ** = .01; *** = .001.

III. ADDED VARIABLE PLOTS

The added-variable plots, also known as partial regression plots, show the effect of adding another variable to a model conditioned by other independent variables. The plots are particularly useful in identifying potential outliers, in this case, the EU.

APPENDIX 2 Added Variable Plots

Food Safety and GDPPC

Food Safety and Scale

IV. RELATIVE IMPORTANCE

The relative importance of two sets of predictors was determined by the relimp package in R. The output is as follows:

APPENDIX 4 *Relative Importance Summary Output*

Relative Importance Summary for Model:	
lm(formula = fsi.avg ~ scaleo5.08 + poly(gdppco5.08, 2) + poly(revo5.08, 2) + coro5.08 + polo5.08 + log(fdio5.08) + log(foodexpo5.08))	
Numerator Effects ("Set 1")	**Denominator Effects ("Set 2")**
Scaleo5.08	Poly(gdppco5.08, 1)
	Poly(gdppco5.08, 2)
Ratio of Effect Standard Deviations	1.455
Log (sd ratio)	0.375 (se 0.358)
Approximate 95% CI for log (sd ratio)	(−0.327, 1.077)
Approximate 95% CI for sd ratio	(0.721,2.936)

V. DATA SOURCES

*All data collected from 2005 to 2008 unless otherwise specified.

APPENDIX 5 *Data Sources*

Variable	Detail	Source
Population	Total	World Bank
Tiers	Levels of Government	Treisman (2008)
Ag Production	Million tons; 2004–2007	FAOSTAT
Biodiversity	Scored 0–100	World Bank; GEF
Surface Area	Sq km	Treisman (2008)
Food Safety Index (log)	DI/TI	Convertino et al. (2013)
Revenue	% GDP	World Bank
FDI	US $	World Bank
GDP per Capita	US $	World Bank
Corruption	Scored −2.5 to 2.5	World Bank; Worldwide Governance Indicators
Food Exports	% of Merchandise Exports	World Bank
Polity	Scored −10–10 (Rescaled to 0–20)	Polity Score
Trade w/Europe	Euros	EUROSTAT;UNCOMTRADE

Interviews

BJ01, Retired Airline Executive, Beijing, China, 9 May 2016.
BJ02, Former Aviation Cooperation Project Official, Beijing, China, 28 August 2013.
BJ03, Researcher, Beijing, China, 7 May 2016.
CC 1, SFDA Central Government Official, Beijing, China, 19 May 2009.
CSA 1, CSA Farmer, Chongming, Shanghai, 7 December 2011.
CSA 2, CSA NGO, Chengdu, Sichuan, 13 December 2011.
CSA 3, CSA Farmer, Haidian, Beijing, 21 November 2011.
CSA 3, CSA Farmer, Pudong, Shanghai, 7 December 2011.
CSA 4, CSA Farmer, Anlong, Sichuan, 14 December 2011.
CSA 5, CSA Farmer, Anlong, Sichuan, 14 December 2011.
CSA 6, CSA Farmer, Anlong, Sichuan, 14 December 2011.
CSA 8, CSA Farmer, Chongming, Shanghai, 7 December 2011.
CSA 9, CSA Farmer, Pudong, Shanghai, 8 December 2011.
CSA 10, CSA Farmer, Haidian, Beijing, China, 21 November 2011.
CSA 11, CSA Farmer's Market Organizer, Beijing, China, 22 November 2011.
CSA 13, CSA Farmer, Chongming, Shanghai, 7 December 2011.
CSA 14, CSA Corporate Consultant, Shanghai, 8 December 2011.
CSA 16, CSA Farmer, Pudong, Shanghai, 8 December 2011.
CSA 18, CSA Consultant, San Francisco, USA, March 2012.
EU Interview, EU Food Safety Official, Beijing, China, 13 April 2011.
EUCTP Interview, EUCTP Food Safety Staff, Beijing, China, 26 January 2011.
EX 1, Food Safety Auditor, Qingdao, Shandong, 28 November 2011.
EX 2, Government Official MOA, Jinan, Shandong, 30 November 2011.
EX 3, Exporter, Qingdao, Shandong, 22 September 2011.
EX 4, Laboratory President, Qingdao, Shandong, 23 September 2011.
EX 5, Chinese Export Producer, Qingdao, Shandong, 22 September 2011.
EX 6, Export-Import Food Producer, Qingdao, Shandong, 18 September 2011.
EX 7, Multinational Food Exporter, Qingdao, Shandong, 23 September 2011.
EX 8, Food Safety Auditor, Qingdao, Shandong, 21 September 2011.

EX 9, Exporter, Qingdao, Shandong, 22 September 2011.

EX 10, Food Safety Expert, Qingdao, Shandong, 18 September 2011.

EX 11, Export Grade Producer, Shouguang, Shandong, 27 November 2011.

EX 12, Government Agricultural Promotion Official, Shouguang, Shandong, 29 November 2011.

EX 15, Chinese Export Producer, Shouguang, Shandong, 20 May 2011.

EX 16, Export Company "F," Qingdao, Shandong, 19 September 2011.

EX 17, Lab, President, Qingdao, Shandong, 28 August 2013

EX 18, Food Safety Auditor, Qingdao, Shandong, 28 August 2013

HK 1, Academic, Polytechnic University, Hong Kong, 20 April 2016.

JS 1, Independent Producer, Jiangsu, 15 September 2011.

NX 1, SFDA, Ningxia, 16 November 2011.

NX 2, Provincial Level Officials Multiple Ministries, Ningxia, 16 November 2011.

NX 3, Dragonhead, Ningxia, 16 November 2011.

NX 4, Dragonhead, Ningxia, 15 November 2011.

NX 5, NGO, Ningxia, 14 November 2011.

NYT Interview, New York Times Correspondent, Shanghai, 1 June 2011.

SD 1, Agricultural Office Provincial Official, Jinan, Shandong, 1 December 2011.

USDA Interview, US Government Food Safety Officer, Beijing, China, 1 June 2009.

YL 3, Township Husbandry Chief, Yunnan, 15 July 2011.

YL 9, Association Leader, Yunnan, 18 July 2011.

YL 10, Township Official, Yunnan, 18 July 2011.

YL 11, County AQSIQ Official, Yunnan, 14 July 2011.

YL 16, Township Official, Yunnan, 19 July 2011.

YL 17, Township Official, Yunnan, 19 July 2011.

YL 21, Contract Farmer, Yunnan, 21 July 2011.

YL 22, Cooperative Farmer, Yunnan, 19 July 2011.

YL 23, Dragonhead, Yunnan, 20 July 2011.

ZJ 8, Township Official, Zhejiang, 27 October 2011.

ZJ 11, Former Export Pig Farmer,, Zhejiang, 28 October 2011.

ZJ 15, Agricultural County Bureau Official, Zhejiang, 12 October 2011.

ZJ 17, Chinese Export Food Company President, Zhejiang, 11 October 2011.

ZJ 19, Dragonhead/Exporter, Zhejiang, 12 October 2011.

ZJ 21, Farmer, Zhejiang, 13 October 2011.

ZJ 40, Researcher, Hangzhou, Zhejiang, 5 December 2010.

ZZ 1, Township Official, Sichuan, 6 March 2011.

ZZ 2, Cooperative Leader, Sichuan, 6 March 2011.

ZZ 3, Cooperative Member, Sichuan, 6 March 2011.

ZZ 10, Cooperative Leader, Sichuan, 5 March 2011.

ZZ 14, Cooperative Leader, Sichuan, 6 March 2011.

ZZ 17, Former Cooperative Leader, Sichuan, 4 March 2011.

ZZ 18, Large Independent Producer, Sichuan, 8 March 2011.

ZZ 19, Township Official, Sichuan, 8 March 2011.

ZZ 21, County Bureau Chief, Sichuan, 16 March 2011.

ZZ 30, Dragonhead, Sichuan, 9 March 2011.

ZZ 35, Dragonhead, Sichuan, 8 April 2011.

ZZ 36, Dragonhead, Sichuan, 8 April 2011.

ZZ 38, Township Official, Sichuan, 7 April 2011.
ZZ 39, Farmer, Sichuan, 7 April 2011.
ZZ 40, Farmer, Sichuan, 7 April 2011.
ZZ 42, Township Official, Sichuan, 7 April 2011.
ZZ 46, Cooperative Farmer, Sichuan, 6 April, 2011.
ZZ 49, Cooperative Farmer, Sichuan, 2 April 2011.
ZZ 50, Cooperative Member, Sichuan, 2 April 2011
ZZ 53, Township Official, Sichuan, 5 April 2011
ZZ 55, Agricultural County Bureau Chief, 2 April 2011.
ZZ 56, Fishery Bureau Chief, Sichuan, 4 May 2011.
ZZ 57, Fishery, Sichuan, 5 May 2011.
ZZ 58, Cooperative Leader, Sichuan, 4 May 2011.
ZZ 60, Cooperative Member, Sichuan, 4 May 2011.
ZZ FSC, County Official, Sichuan, 13 December 2011.

Bibliography

Alesina, A., & Spolaore, E. (2005). *The size of nations.* Cambridge, MA: MIT Press.

Agranoff, R. (2001). Managing within the matrix: Do collaborative intergovernmental relations exist? *Publius: The Journal of Federalism,* 31(2), 31–56.

Alemanno, A. (2009). Solving the problem of scale: The European approach to import safety and security concerns. In C. Coglianese, A. M. Finkel, & D. Zaring (Eds.), *Import safety: Regulatory governance in the global economy* (pp. 171–189). Philadelphia: University of Pennsylvania Press.

Andersson, K. P., & Ostrom, E. (2008). Analyzing decentralized resource regimes from a polycentric perspective. *Policy Sciences,* 41(1), 71–93.

Anderlini, J. (2011). Lipton tea faces safety scandal in China. *Financial Times.*Accessed July 28, 2017 at www.ft.com/content/378f686e-0c55-11e1-8ac6-00144feabdco

Ansell, C. & Torfing, J. (2015). How does collaborative governance scale? *Policy & Politics,* 43(3), 315–329.

Ansell, C. & Vogel, D. (2006). *What's the Beef? The Contested Governance of European Food Safety.* Cambridge, MA: MIT Press.

Asian Development Bank (ADB). (2005). Report: The food safety control system of the People's Republic of China. *Technical Assistance Product 1 (A) and (B).* Beijing: Asian Development Bank.

Asia Development Bank, State Food and Drug Administration, & WHO. (2007). *The food safety control system of the People's Republic of China.* Beijing: Authors.

Associated Press (AP). (2006, July 27). Japan lifts ban on the US beef imports. *Associated Press.* Accessed February 5, 2012, at www.msnbc.msn.com/id/14067330/ns/business-retail/t/japan-lifts-ban-us-beef-imports/#.T2Tp7RGPWrg

Auel, K. (2014). Intergovernmental relations in German federalism: Cooperative federalism, party politics and territorial conflicts. *Comparative European Politics,* 12(4), 422–443.

Bagumire, A., Todd, E., Muyanja, C. & Nasinyama, G. (2009). National food safety control systems in Sub-Saharan Africa: Does Uganda's aquaculture control system meet international requirements, *Food Policy*, 34(5), 458–467.

Baker, T. (2009). Bonded import safety warranties. In C. Coglianese, A. M. Finkel, & D. Zaring (Eds.), *Import safety: Regulatory governance in the global economy* (pp. 215–232). Philadelphia: University of Pennsylvania Press.

Balleisen, E. J., & Moss, D. A. (Eds.). (2010). *Government and markets: Toward a new theory of regulation*. New York: Cambridge University Press.

Balzano, J. (2012). China's Food Safety Law: Administrative Innovation and Institutional Design in Comparative Perspective, *Asian-Pacific Law & Policy Journal*, 13(2), 23–80.

Balzano, J. (2015). New layers of China's food safety regulation. *Forbes Online*. Accessed July 29, 2017 at www.forbes.com/sites/johnbalzano/2015/09/20/new-layers-of-chinas-food-safety-regulation/#4815c0483b8c

Balzano, J. (2016). Lingering food safety regulatory issues for China in 2016. *Forbes Online*. Accessed July 29, 2017 at www.forbes.com/sites/johnbalzano/2016/01/10/lingering-food-safety-regulatory-issues-for-china-in-2016/#7bee46ca5f5a

Bamberger, K. A., & Guzman, A. T. (2008). Keeping imports safe: A proposal for discriminatory regulation of international trade, *California Law Review*, 96(6), 1405–1447.

Bate, R. & Porter, K. (2009). The problems and potential of China's pharmaceutical industry: Health policy outlook, *American Enterprise Outlook*, 3, 1–10.

Barboza, D. (2010). Recycled cooking oil found to be latest hazard in China. *The New York Times*. Accessed March 6, 2017 at www.nytimes.com/2010/04/01/world/asia/01shanghai.html

Barclay, E. (2011). Tainted pork is latest food safety scandal in China. *National Public Radio*. Accessed on March 6, 2017 at www.npr.org/sections/health-shots/2011/04/29/135839397/tainted-pork-is-latest-food-safety-scandal-in-china

Baum, R., & Shevchenko, A. (1999). The state of the state. In M. Goldman & R. MacFarquhar (Eds.), *The paradox of China's post-Mao reforms* (Vol. 12, pp. 333–360). Cambridge, MA: Harvard University Press.

Beck, U. (1992). *Risk society: Towards a new modernity*, Vol. 17. London: Sage Publications.

Becker, G. (2005). *Japan-US Beef Trade Issues: CRS Report for Congress*. Congressional Research Service. RS22115.

Becker, G. (2009). *US Food and Agricultural Imports: Safeguards and Selected Issues: CRS Report for Congress*, Congressional Research Service. 7–5700.

Beijing Chenbao [BCB]. (2012, July 4). Guowuyuan Mingque jiang Shipin Anquan naru Difang Zhengfu Kaohe. *Beijing Chenbao*. Accessed July 15, 2012 at http://news.ifeng.com/mainland/detail_2012_07/04/15756564_0.shtml

Beijing Farmer's Market Guidelines. Handout.

Berkes, F. (2007). Community-based conservation in a globalized world. *Proceedings of the National Academy of Sciences*, 104(39), 15188–15193.

Bernstein, T. P. (2006). Mao Zedong and the Famine of 1959–1960: A Study in Wilfulness. *The China Quarterly*, 186, 421–445.

Bevir, M. (Ed.). (2007). *The encyclopedia of governance*. 2 volumes. London: Sage.

Bevir, M., & Rhodes, R. (2004). *Interpreting British governance*. London: Routledge.

Bevir, M. (2007). Hollow state. In M. Bevir (Ed.), *Encyclopedia of governance* (pp. 418–419). London: Sage.

BioFarm website. Brief on farm. Accessed August 10, 2011 at www.biofarm.cn/en/yj_ncjj.html

Biswas, A. & Hartley, K. (2015). India and food safety. *The Diplomat*. Accessed on July 29, 2017 at http://thediplomat.com/2015/09/india-and-food-safety/

Inocencio, R., & Ke, F. (2013). Maggots, bacteria allegedly plagued China's number one meat brand. *CNN News*. Accessed 6 March 2017 at www.cnn.com/2013/05/31/business/china-food-tainted-shuanghui-maggots/

Boix, C., & Posner, D. N. (1998). Social Capital: Explaining its Origins and Effects on Government Performance, *British Journal of Political Science*, 28, 686–693.

Borzel, T. A., & Hosli, M. O. (2003). Brussels between Bern and Berlin: comparative federalism meets the EU, *Governance*, 16(2), 179–202.

Bottemiller, H. S. (2010). USDA bans US organic inspector in China. *Food Safety News*. Accessed July 29, 2017 at www.foodsafetynews.com/2010/06/usda-bans-us-organic-inspector-in-china/#.WXoKpojyuUk

Bowles, S., & Gintis, H. (2002). Social capital and community governance, *The Economic Journal*, 112(483), 419–436.

Bradsher, K. (2011). Chinese city shuts down 13 Wal-Marts. *New York Times*. Accessed July 28, 2017 at www.nytimes.com/2011/10/11/business/global/wal-marts-in-china-city-closed-for-pork-mislabeling.html?mcubz=2

Braithwaite, J. (2008). *Regulatory capitalism: How it works, ideas for making it work better*. Cheltenham: Edward Elgar Publishing.

Bramall, C. (1995). Origins of the Agricultural "Miracle": Some Evidence from Sichuan, *The China Quarterly*, 143, 731–755.

Brewer, C. (2012). China takes steps to strengthen food safety. *FDA Voice*. Accessed February 10, 2013 at http://blogs.fda.gov/fdavoice/index.php/2012/12/china-takes-steps-to-strengthen-food-safety/

Brooks, N., Regmi, A., & Jerardo, A. (2009). US Food Import Patters, 1998–2007: A Report from the Economic Research Service. USDA, FAU-125.

Brown, C., & Miller, S. (2008). The impacts of local markets: A review of research on farmers markets and community supported agriculture. *American Journal of Agricultural Economics*, 90(5), 1298–1302.

Buckley, C. (2013). Rice tainted with cadmium is discovered in southern China. *New York Times*. Accessed March 6, 2017 at www.nytimes.com/2013/05/22/world/asia/cadmium-tainted-rice-discovered-in-southern-china.html

Buizer, M., Arts, B., & Kok, K. (2011). Governance, scale and the environment: The importance of recognizing knowledge claims in transdisciplinary arenas, *Ecology and Society*, 16(1), 1–18.

Burke, B. F. (2014). Understanding intergovernmental relations, twenty-five years hence. *State and Local Government Review*, 46(1), 63–76.

Cai, H., Chen, Y., & Gong, Q. (2015). Polluting thy neighbor: Unintended consequences of China's pollution reduction mandates. *Journal of Environmental Economics and Management*, 76, 86–104.

Calvin, L., Gale, F., Hu, D., & Lohmar, B. (2006). Food safety improvements underway in China. *Amber Waves*, 4(5), 17–21.

Cameron, D., & Simeon, R. (2002). Intergovernmental relations in Canada: The emergence of collaborative federalism. *Publius: The Journal of Federalism*, 32(2), 49–72.

Carter, C., & Rozelle, S. (2001). Will China become a major force in world food markets? *Applied Economic Perspectives and Policy*, 23(2), 319–331.

Cash, David, Adger, W. Berkes, F. Garden, P. Lebel, L. Olsson, P. Pritchard, L. & Young, O. (2006). Scale and Cross-Scale Dynamics: Governance and Information in a Multilevel World. *Ecology and Society*, 11, 1–12.

Certification and Accreditation Administration for China [CNCA]. (2009). CNAS Renke Fazhan Baogao. *CNAS Annual Report*.

Chen, J., Pan, J., & Xu, Y. (2016). Sources of authoritarian responsiveness: A field experiment in China. *American Journal of Political Science*, 60(2), 383–400.

Chen, K. Z., Chen, Y., & Shi, M. (2005). Globalization, pesticide regulation, and supply chain development: A case of Chinese vegetable export to Japan. In Z. Huang, K. Chen, & M. Shi (Eds.), *Food safety: Consumer, trade, and regulation issues* (pp. 106–127). Zhejiang University Press.

Chen, K., & Zhao, J. (2010). Development of Farmer Cooperatives With Chinese Characteristics: A Political Economic Lens. Unpublished Manuscript.

China Statistics Bureau. (2010). *China Statistics Yearbook 2010*.

Chongming Government. (2012). "Chongmingxian Renmin Zhengu Yinfa Guanyu Fuchi Choming Gaoxiao Shengtai Nongye Jiakuai Fazhan zhengce Yijian tongzhi." Accessed August 9, 2012 at www.cmx.gov.cn/html/DefaultSite/shcm_xxgk_zfgb_201202_zfwj/2012-05-31/Detail_28665.htm

Christmann, P., & Taylor, G. (2001). Globalization and the environment: Determinants of self regulation in China. *Journal of International Business Studies*, 32(3), 439–458.

Chung, J. H., & Lam, T. C. (Eds.). (2009). *China's local administration: Traditions and changes in the sub-national hierarchy*. New York: Routledge.

Chung, J. H., Lai, H., & Joo, J. H. (2009). Assessing the "Revive the Northeast" (zhenxing dongbei) programme: Origins, policies and implementation. *The China Quarterly*, 197, 108–125.

Chung, J. (2003). The political economy of industrial restructuring in China: The case of civil aviation. *The China Journal*, 50, 61–82.

Coglianese, C., Finkel, A. M., & Zaring, D. (2009). *Import safety: Regulatory governance in the global economy*. Philadelphia: University of Pennsylvania Press.

Coglianese, C., & Lazer, D. (2003). Management-based regulation: Prescribing private management to achieve public goals. *Law and Society*, 37(4), 691–730.

Conlan, T. (2006). From cooperative to opportunistic federalism: Reflections on the half-century anniversary of the commission on intergovernmental relations. *Public Administration Review*, 66(5), 663–676.

Convertino, M., & Liang, S. (2014). Probabilistic supply chain risk model for food safety. *Planet@ Risk*, 2(3), 191–195.

Dahl, R. A. (1994). A democratic dilemma: System effectiveness versus citizen participation. *Political Science Quarterly*, 109(1), 23–34.

Dan, W. (2011). Jianli Kechixushengtai Tixi, *Business China*, 9, 42–44.

Dasgupta, J. (2001). India's federal design and multicultural national construction. In A. Kohli (Ed.), *The success of India's democracy* (Vol. 6, pp. 49–77). New York: Cambridge University Press.

Davis, C. (2001). The west in flames: the intergovernmental politics of wildfire suppression and prevention, *Publius: The Journal of Federalism*, 31(3), 97–110.

Davison, N. (2013). Rivers of blood: The dead pigs rotting China's water supply. *The Guardian*. Accessed March 6, 2017 at www.theguardian.com/world/2013/mar/29/dead-pigs-china-water-supply

Day, A. (2008). The end of the peasant? New rural reconstruction in China, *Boundary* 2(35), 49–73.

De Oliveira, A., Croson, R., & Eckle, C. (2009). Are preferences stable across domains? An experimental investigation of social preferences in the field. CBEES Working Paper 2008–3.

DeLisle, J. (2009). The other China trade deficit. In C. Coglianese, A. M. Finkel, & D. Zaring (Eds.), *Import safety: Regulatory governance in the global economy* (pp. 22–49). Philadelphia: University of Pennsylvania Press.

Demick, B. (2011, September 16). In China, what you eat tells you who you are. *Los Angeles Times*. Accessed November 10, 2011 at http://articles.latimes.com/2011/sep/16/world/la-fg-china-elite-farm-20110917

DG SANCO. (2006). Memorandum of Understanding on Administrative Co-Operation Arrangements between The European Commission's Directorate General for Health and Consumer Protection (DG SANCO) and The General Administration of Quality Supervision, Inspection and Quarantine of the People's Republic of China (AQSIQ).

DG SANCO. (2008). Summary Record of the Standing Committee on the Food Chain and Animal Health held in Brussels on 25 September 2008. SANCO – D1(2008)D/411968.

Dhar, A. (2012). Food free from fear. *The Hindu*. Accessed May 22, 2014 at www.thehindu.com/news/national/food-free-from-fear/article3283640.ece

Diani, M. (1997). Social Movements and Social Capital: A Network Perspective on Movement Outcomes, *Mobilization: An International Quarterly*, 2, 129–147.

Dietz, T., Ostrom, E., & Stern, P. C. (2003). The struggle to govern the commons. *Science*, 302(5652), 1907–1912.

Dikotter, F. (2010). *Mao's Great Famine*. London: Bloomsbury.

Distelhorst, G. & Hou, Y. (2014). Constituency Service Under Nondemocratic Rule: Evidence from China. In APSA 2014 Annual Meeting Paper.

Dixit, V., Magni, M., St-Maurice, I., Süssmuth-Dyckerhoff, C., & Tsai, H. (2008). *Insights China, Annual Chinese Consumer Survey 08*, McKinsey and Company.

Donovan, J., Caswell, J., & Salay, E. (2001). The Effect of Stricter Regulations on Food Safety Levels in Developing Countries: A Study of Brazil, *Applied Economic Perspectives and Policy*, 23, 163–175.

Dressler, W., Büscher, B., Schoon, M., Brockington, D. A. N., Hayes, T., Kull, C. A., ... & Shrestha, K. (2010). From hope to crisis and back again? A critical history of the global CBNRM narrative. *Environmental Conservation*, 37(1), 5–15.

Dyer, G. (2007, October 29). China arrests 774 in crackdown. *Financial Times*. Accessed August 10, 2010 at www.ft.com/cms/s/0/1acf1f42–865f–11dc-b00e-0000779fd2ac.html#axzz2VYjmrM45

Echols, M. A. (1998). Food safety regulation in the EU and the United States: Different cultures, different laws. *Columbia Journal of European Law*, 4, 525–543.

Ecoland. Undated. Manifesto for Production.

Economist. (2016). Beware the Cult of Xi. *Economist Online*. Accessed July 29, 2017 at www.economist.com/news/leaders/21695881-xi-jinping-stronger-his-predecessors-his-power-damaging-country-beware-cult

Edin, M. (2003). State capacity and local agent control in China: CCP cadre management from a township perspective, *The China Quarterly*, 173, 35–52.

Egorov, G., Guriev, S., & Sonin, K. (2009). Why resource-poor dictators allow freer media: A theory and evidence from panel data. *American Political Science Review*, 103(4), 645–668.

Eijlander, P. (2005). Possibilities and constraints in the use of self-regulation and co-regulation in legislative policy: experience in Netherlands – Lessons to be learned for the EU? *Electronic Journal of Comparative Law* 9 (1), 1–8.

EIU. (2017). Global Food Security Index. Accessed July 29, 2017 at http://foodsecurityindex.eiu.com/Country/Details#United%20States

Elazar, D. J. (1993). International and comparative federalism, *PS: Political Science & Politics*, 26(2), 190–195.

Endres, A., & Johnson, N. R. (2011). Integrating stakeholder roles in food production, marketing, and safety systems: An evolving multi-jurisdictional approach. *Journal of Environmental Law and Litigation*, 26(1), 29–108.

EU-China Trade Project [EUCTP]. (2008). Organic Agriculture in China-Current Situation and Challenges. *EU-China Trade Project Report*. Beijing.

EU-China Trade Project [EUCTP]. (2009). The EU-China Trade Project: An Important Contribution to China's Integration into the World Trading System: Results and Achievements Report. *EU-China Trade Project*, Beijing.

European Commission, DG Trade, Bilateral Relations, Statistics, China, 2012 http://ec.europa.eu/trade/creating-opportunities/bilateral-relations/statistics/

EU SME Centre. (2013). The food and beverage market in China. EU SME Centre Report. Beijing.

Fackler, M. (2007, October 11). Safe food for Japan. *New York Times*.

Fackler, M. (2008, February 2). Insecticide-tainted dumplings from China sicken 175 in Japan. *New York Times*.

Fairbank, J. K. (1973). The early treaty system in the Chinese world order. In J. Fairbank (Ed.), *The Chinese world order: Traditional China's foreign relations* (pp. 276–288). Cambridge, MA: Harvard University Press.

Fairbank, J. (1988). The Chinese behemoth. *New York Review of Books*. Accessed July 28, 2017 at www.nybooks.com/articles/1988/01/21/the-chinese-behemoth/

Fan, H., Ye, Z., Zhao, W., Tian, H., Qi, Y., & Busch, L. (2009). Agriculture and food quality and safety certification agencies in four Chinese cities, *Food Control*, 20(7), 627–630.

Fan, S. (1997). Production and productivity growth in Chinese agriculture: New measurement and evidence. *Food Policy*, 22(3), 213–228.

Fewsmith, J. (1994). *Dilemmas of reform in China: Political conflict and economic debate*. New York: ME Sharpe/Armonk.

Food and Drug Administration [FDA MOU]. (2007). Agreement between the Department of Health and Human Services of the USA and AQSIQ of the PRC of the Safety of Food and Feed. Accessed October 25, 2011 at www.fda.gov/InternationalPrograms/Agreements/MemorandaofUnderstanding/ucm107557.htm

Food and Water Watch [F&W]. (2011). *A Decade of Dangerous Food Imports from China.*

Food Safety Documents (Internal Government) [FSDOC]. (2010–2011). County Food Safety Documents.

FoodDrink Europe. (2016). *Data & trends EU food and drink industry 2016: FoodDrink Europe Report*. Belgium: FoodDrink Europe.

Freidberg, S. (2004). *French beans and food scares: Culture and commerce in an anxious age*. New York: Oxford University Press.

FSIS. Slaughter Inspection 101. Accessed July 28, 2017 at www.fsis.usda.gov/wps/portal/fsis/topics/food-safety-education/get-answers/food-safety-fact-sheets/production-and-inspection/slaughter-inspection-101/slaughter-inspection-101

Fu, L. (2016). What China's Food Safety Challenges Mean for Consumers, Regulators, and the Global Economy. Brookings blog. Accessed July 29, 2017 at www.brookings.edu/blogs/order-from-chaos/posts/2016/04/21-food-safety-china-fu

Fukuyama, F. (1995). *Trust: The social virtues and source of prosperity*. London: Hamish Hamilton London.

Fuller, B. (2010). "China's Air Safety Overhaul." NYU Marion School blog. Accessed June 10, 2014 at https://marroninstitute.nyu.edu/content/blog/chinas-air-safety-overhaul

Gale, F. (2011). Building trust in food. *China Dialogue*. Accessed March 21, 2012 at www.chinadialogue.net/article/show/single/en/4207

Gale, F., & Buzby, J. (2009). Imports from China and food safety issues. *Economic Information Bulletin*, 52, Department of Agriculture, Economic Research Service.

GAO (U.S. Government Accountability Office). 2008. Food safety: Selected countries' systems can offer insights into ensuring import safety and responding to foodborne illness. GAO-08-794. Washington, DC: GAO.

Gavaravarapu, S. M., & Nair, K. M. (2015). From farm to plate & beyond: A culture & context sensitive perspective for food safety. *The Indian Journal of Medical Research*, 141(4), 377–379.

Gervasoni, C. (2010). A rentier theory of subnational regimes: Fiscal federalism, democracy, and authoritarianism in the Argentine provinces, *World Politics*, 62(2), 302–340.

Ghosh, A. (2012). Food authority to set standards for alcoholic drinks. *The Indian Express.*Accessed May 22, 2014 at http://archive.indianexpress.com/story-print/909852/

Gibson, C. C., Ostrom, E., & Ahn, T. K. (2000). The concept of scale and the human dimensions of global change: A survey. *Ecological Economics, 32*(2), 217–239.

Gibson, E. L. (2005). Boundary control: Subnational authoritarianism in democratic countries. *World Politics, 58*(1), 101–132.

GK News. (2012). Govt ignoring food safety act. *Greater Kashmir News Network.* Accessed May 22, 2014 at www.greaterkashmir.com/news/news/govt-ignoring-food-safety-act/111770.html

Gobel, C. (2011). Uneven Policy Implementation in Rural China. *The China Journal, 65,* 53–76.

Godfrey, M. (2012). "China Still Struggling to Manage Food Safety." *SeafoodSource.* Accessed October 5, 2012 at www.seafoodsource.com/newsarticledetail.aspx?id=14940

Goland, C. (2002). Community Supported Agriculture, Food Consumption Patterns, and Member Commitment, *Culture, Agriculture, Food and Environment, 24*(1), 14–25.

Goldstein, L. J. (2013). Chinese fisheries enforcement: Environmental and strategic implications, *Marine Policy, 40,* 187–193.

Green, S. (2004). *The development of China's stock market.* New York: RoutledgeCurzon.

Greenpeace. (2010). Greenpeace China gets action on food safety. Accessed June 21, 2011 at www.greenpeace.org/eastasia/news/stories/food-agriculture/2010/supermarkey-guide-china/

Greer, S. (2011). The weakness of strong polices and the strength of weak policies: Law, experimentalist governance, and supporting coalitions in EU healthcare policy. *Regulation and Governance, 5*(2), 187–203.

Grumbine, R. E., & Xu, J. (2013). Recalibrating China's environmental policy: The next 10 years. *Biological Conservation, 166,* 287–292.

Gunningham, N., & Sinclair, D. (2009). Regulation and the Role of Trust. *Journal of Law and Society,* 36:2, 167–194.

Haas, B., & Wang, J. (2013, March 10). China plans revamp of railways, energy, and food safety agencies. *Bloomberg News.* Accessed March 15, 2013 at www.bloomberg.com/news/2013-03-10/china-restructures-energy-regulation-in-government-overhaul.html

Han, J. (Ed.). (2007). *Zhongguo Shipin Anquan Baogao Report on Food Safety in China.* Beijing: Social Sciences Academic Press China.

Hassanein, N. (2011). Matters of scale and the politics of the Food Safety Modernization Act. *Agriculture and Human Values, 28*(4), 577–581.

Havinga, T. (2006). Private regulation of food safety by supermarkets, *Law & Policy* 28(4), 515–533.

Heilmann, S. (2005). Regulatory innovation by Leninist means: Communist Party supervision in China's financial industry, *The China Quarterly,* 181, 1–21.

Heilmann, S., & Perry, E. (2011). *Mao's invisible hand: The political foundations of adaptive governance in China.* Cambridge, MA: Harvard University Press.

Heilmann, S. (2009). Maximum tinkering under uncertainty: Unorthodox lessons from China. *Modern China*, 35(4), 450–462.

Henson, S., & Caswell, J. (1999). Food safety regulation: An overview of contemporary issues. *Food Policy*, 24, 589–603.

Henson, S., & Loader, R. (2001). Barriers to agricultural exports from developing countries: The role of sanitary and phytosanitary requirements, *World Development*, 29, 85–102.

Henson, S., & Mitullah, W. (2004). Kenyan exports of Nile Perch: Impact of food safety standards on an export-oriented supply chain. *World Bank Policy Research Working Paper 3349*, 1–86.

Henson, S., Brouder, A. & Mittullah, W. (2000). Food safety requirements and food exports from developing countries: The case of fish exports from Kenya to the EU. *American Journal Agricultural Economics*, 82, 1159–1169.

Herbst, J. (2000). *States and power in Africa: Comparative lessons in authority and control*. Princeton, NJ: Princeton University Press.

Heritier, A., & Lehmkuhl, D. (2008). The shadow of hierarchy and new modes of governance. *Journal of Public Policy*, 28(1), 1–17.

Hinrichs, CC. (2000). Embeddedness and local food systems: Notes on two types of direct agricultural market. *Journal of Rural Studies*, 16, 295–303.

Hobbs, JE, Fearne, Andrew, and John Spriggs. (2002). Incentive structures for food safety and quality assurance: an international comparison. *Food Control*, 13(2), 77–81.

Hobbs, J. E., & Young, L. M. (2000). Closer vertical co-ordination in agri-food supply chains: A conceptual framework and some preliminary evidence. *Supply Chain Management: An International Journal*, 5(3), 131–143.

Hochschild J. L. (2009). Searching for a politics of space. In G. King, K. L. Schlozman, & N. H. Nie (Eds.), *The future of political science: 100 perspectives* (pp. 249–251). New York: Routledge.

Hooghe, L., & Marks, G. (2003). Unraveling the central state, but how? Types of multi-level governance, *American Political Science Review*, 97(2), 233–243.

Howitt, R. (1998). Scale as relation: Musical metaphors of geographical scale. *Area*, 30(1), 49–58.

Hsing, Y. T. (2010). *The great urban transformation: Politics of land and property in China*. New York: Oxford University Press.

Hsueh, R. (2011). *China's regulatory state: A new strategy for globalization.* Ithaca, NY: Cornell University Press.

Hu, D. (2010). *Farmer-supermarket direct-purchase: A how-to guide.* Beijing: Chinese Academy of Agricultural Sciences Press. [Chinese]

Hu, Y. (2005, March 31). Red dye 'a food for thought' for Chinese. *China Daily*. Accessed March 11, 2011 at www.chinadaily.com.cn/english/doc/2005–03/31/content_429921.htm

Hu, Y., & Hou, L. (2009, March 9). Vice premier to head food safety commission. *China Daily*. Accessed March 5, 2011 at www.chinadaily.com.cn/china/2009–03/09/content_7554541.htm

Huang, J. et al. (2007). *Agrifood secto studies China: Restructuring agrifood markets in China – the horticulture sector.* London: Regoverning Market Program, IIED.

Huang, P. (2011). China's new-age small farms and their vertical integration: Agribusiness or co-ops? *Modern China*, 37(2), 107–134.

Huang, R. (2010, August 12). Jiakuai jianshe shengchan jidi cujin nongye zhuanx-ingshengji. *Changshu Ribao*. Accessed August, 5, 2011 at www.js.xinhuanet .com/zheng_fu_online/2010–08/12/content_20605818.htm

Huang, Y. (2012). China's worsening food safety crisis. *The Atlantic*. Accessed, July 28, 2017 at www.theatlantic.com/international/archive/2012/08/chinas-worsening-food-safety-crisis/261656/

Hurst, W. (2009). *The Chinese worker after socialism*. Cambridge: Cambridge University Press.

Ito, K., & Dyck, J. (2010). Fruit policies in Japan. A Report from the Economic Research Service. FTS, 341–01.

Jacoby, W. (2006). *The enlargement of the EU and NATO: Ordering from the menu in Central Europe*. Cambridge, MA: Cambridge University Press.

Japan Economic Trading Research Office [JETRO]. (2011). Japan's food imports by category (2009–2010). Accessed May 16, 2012 at www.jetro.go.jp/en/ reports/statistics/data/0910_import.pdf

Jarosz, L. (2000). Understanding agri-food networks as social relations, *Agriculture and Human Values* 17, 279–283.

Jessop, B. (1999). The changing governance of welfare: Recent trends in its primary functions, scale, and modes of coordination. *Social Policy & Administration*, 33(4), 348–359.

Jha, A. (2013). With food safety and standards act, India, scales a new food safety era. *FnB News*. Accessed on May 9, 2014 at www.fnbnews.com/Top-News/ With-Food-Safety-and-Standards-Act-India-scales-a-new-food-safety-era

Jia, X., Huang, J., & Xu, Z. (2010). Marketing of farmer professional cooperatives in the wave of transformed agrofood market in China, *China Economic Review*, 23(3), 665–674.

Jiang, C. (2011, December 20). CSA Shiyan: fenxiangshouhuo, gongdan-fengxian [The CSA Experiment: Shared Harvests, Shared Risks]. *Zhejiang Daily*. Accessed January 5, 2012 at http://zjdaily.zjol.com.cn/html/2011–12/20/ content_1260781.htm?div=-1

Jonker, T, Ito, H., & Fujishima, H. (2004). Food safety and quality standards in Japan: Compliance of suppliers from developing countries. *Agriculture and Rural Development Discussion Paper*. World Bank.

Kelemen, R. D. (2000). Regulatory federalism: EU environmental regulation in comparative perspective. *Journal of Public Policy*, 20(2), 133–167.

Kim, S. (2011). USDA Issues Public Notice of Fraudulent National Organic Program Certificate. *USDA Notice AMS No. 026–11*.

King, G., Pan, J., & Roberts, M. E. (2013). How censorship in China allows government criticism but silences collective expression, *American Political Science Review*, 107(2), 326–343.

Kipnis, A. (2006). Suzhi: A keyword approach, *The China Quarterly*, 186, 295–313.

Kjaernes, U., Harvey, M., & Warde, A. (2007). *Trust in food: A comparative and institutional analysis*. New York: Palgrave Macmillan.

Klijn, E. H. (2002). Governing networks in the hollow state: Contracting out, process management or a combination of the two? *Public Management Review*, 4(2), 149–165.

Kong, H., Xue, X., Mao, Z., Ngoran, S. D., & Yang, W. (2015). Towards integrated coastal governance with Chinese characteristics – A preliminary analysis of China's coastal and ocean governance with special reference to the ICM practice in Quanzhou, *Ocean & Coastal Management*, 111, 34–49.

Krapohl, S. (2007). Thalidomide, BSE, and the single market: A historical-institutionalist approach to regulatory regimes in the EU, *European Journal of Political Research* 46(1), 25–46.

La Vallee, J., & Charlebois, S. (2014). *2014 world ranking: Food safety performance*. Ottawa: The Conference Board of Canada.

LaFraniere, S. (2009). 2 executed in China for selling tainted milk. *New York Times*. Accessed March 6, 2017 at www.nytimes.com/2009/11/25/world/asia/25china.html

Lam, T. (2010). Central-provincial relations amid greater centralization in China, *China Information*, 24(3), 339–363.

Landry, P. (2008). *Decentralized authoritarianism in China: The Communist Party's control of local·elites in the post-Mao era*. Cambridge: Cambridge University Press.

Lau, M. (2005). Integrated coastal zone management in the People's Republic of China – An assessment of structural impacts on decision-making processes. *Ocean & Coastal Management*, 48(2), 115–159.

Lebel, L., Garden, P., & Imamura, M. (2005). The politics of scale, position, and place in the governance of water resources in the Mekong region. *Ecology and Society*, 10(2), 1–19.

Leitner, H. (2008). The politics of scale and networks of spatial connectivity: Transnational interurban networks and the rescaling of political governance in Europe. In E. Sheppard & R. McMaster (Eds.), *Scale and geographic inquiry: Nature, society, and method*. Malden, MA: Blackwell Publishing.

Li, J., & Shen, J. (2009). Study on food traceability system. In M. Tang (Ed.), *Study report on food and drug safety and regulatory policies (2009)*. Beijing: Social Sciences Academic Press (China). [Chinese]

Li, L. (2010). Central-local relations in the People's Republic of China, *Public Administration and Development*, 30(3), 177–190.

Liang, J. (2010, September 28). 4 major problems ail China's food industry. *People's Daily*. Accessed November 5, 2011 at http://english.people.com.cn/90001/90778/90860/7153465.html

Lieberman, E. S. (2005). Nested analysis as a mixed-method strategy for comparative research. *American Political Science Review*, 99(3), 435–452.

Lieberthal, K. & Lampton, D. (Eds.). (1992). *Bureaucracy, politics, and decision-making in post-Mao China*. Berkeley: University of California Press.

Lieberthal, K., & Oksenberg, M. (1988). *Policy making in China: Leaders, structures, and processes*. Princeton, NJ: Princeton University Press.

Liu, P. (2010). Tracing and periodizing China's food safety regulation: A study on China's food safety regime change. *Regulation and Governance*, 4(2), 244–260.

Liu, P., & McGuire, W. (2015). One regulatory state, two regulatory regimes: Understanding dual regimes in China's regulatory state building through food safety. *Journal of Contemporary China*, 24(91), 119–136.

Lo, K. (2015). How authoritarian is the environmental governance of China? *Environmental Science & Policy*, 54, 152–159.

Loader, R., & Hobbs, J. E. (1999). Strategic responses to food safety legislation. *Food Policy*, 24(6), 685–706.

Lorentzen, P. (2014). China's strategic censorship, *American Journal of Political Science*, 58(2), 402–414.

Lorentzen, P., Landry, P., & Yasuda, J. (2014). Undermining authoritarian innovation: The power of China's industrial giants. *The Journal of Politics*, 76(1), 182–194.

Lowder, S., Skoet, J., & Singh, S. (2014). What do we really know about the number and distribution of farms and family farms in the world? Background paper for The State of Food and Agriculture 2014. ESA Working Paper No. 14–02, April.

Lu, X. (2000). Booty socialism, bureau-preneurs, and the state in transition: Organizational corruption in China. *Comparative Politics*, 273–294.

Ma, C., Zhang, X., Chen, W., Zhang, G., Duan, H., Ju, M., & Yang, Z. (2013). China's special marine protected area policy: Trade-off between economic development and marine conservation. *Ocean & Coastal Management*, 76, 1–11.

MacLaren, D., Jayasuriya, S., & Mehta, R. (2006). Meeting Food Safety Standards in Export Markets: Issues and Challenges Facing Firms Exporting from Developing Countries. *Food Regulation and Trade: Institutional Framework, Concepts of Analysis and Empirical Evidence*. Paper Presented at IATRC Summer Symposium.

Macleod, C. (2011, January 23). China's organic farms rooted in food safety concerns. *USA Today*. Accessed January 24, 2012 at http://usatoday30.usatoday.com/news/world/2011-01-24-chinafood24_ST_N.htm

Mallory, T. G. (2013). China's distant water fishing industry: Evolving policies and implications, *Marine Policy*, 38, 99–108.

Mallory, T. G. (2016). Fisheries subsidies in China: Quantitative and qualitative assessment of policy coherence and effectiveness, *Marine Policy*, 68, 74–82.

Manor, J. (2001). Center-state relations. In A. Kohli (Ed.), *The success of India's democracy* (Vol. 6, pp. 78–102). New York: Cambridge University Press.

Marston, S. A. (2000). The social construction of scale, *Progress in human geography*, 24(2), 219–242.

Marston, S. A., Jones, J. P., & Woodward, K. (2005). Human geography without scale. *Transactions of the Institute of British Geographers*, 30(4), 416–432.

Martinez, M. G. et al. (2007). Co-regulation as a possible model for food safety governance, *Food Policy*, 32, 299–314.

McGinnis, M. (2005). Costs and Challenges of Polycentric Governance. *Workshop Paper Prepared for Discussion at the Workshop on Analyzing Problems of Polycentric Governance in the Growing EU, Humboldt University*, June 16–17.

McKenna, M. (2015). Is it time for a single food safety agency? *National Geographic*.Accessed July 28, 2017 at http://theplate.nationalgeographic.com/2015/02/05/budget-one-agency/

Meador, M., & Ma. J. (2013). The food safety management system in China. *FAIRS Subject Report*, Global Agricultural Information Network Report No. CH13020.

Meidinger, E. (2009). Private import safety regulation and transnational new governance. In C. Cogliances, A. M. Finkel, & D. Zaring (Eds.), *Import Safety: Regulatory Governance in the Global Economy* (pp. 233–253). Philadelphia: University of Pennsylvania Press.

Meng, T., Pan, J., & Yang, P. (2014). Conditional receptivity to citizen participation evidence from a survey experiment in China. *Comparative Political Studies*, 50(4), 399–433.

Merrill, R. A., & Francer, J. K. (2000). Organizing federal food safety regulation. *Seton Hall Law Review* 31(1), 61–173.

Mertha, A. C. (2005). China's 'soft' centralization: Shifting Tiao/Kuai authority relations. *The China Quarterly*, 184, 791–810.

Mertha, A. C. (2009). Fragmented authoritarianism 2.0: Political pluralization in the Chinese policy process. *The China Quarterly*, 200, 995–1012.

Ministry of Agriculture [MOA]. (2011). National Modern Agriculture Development Plan (2011–2015). Accessed March 10, 2012 at http://english.agri.gov.cn/hottopics/five/201304/t20130421_19482.htm

Ministry of Commerce. (2008). Chuangjian Shipin Anquan Shifanxian Shishi Fangan. Accessed May 4, 2012 at www.foods1.com/content/603513/

Ministry of Health, Labour and Welfare [MHLW]. (2011). *Statistics of imported food monitoring For FY2010*.Department of Food Safety, Pharmaceutical, and Food Safety Bureau.

Ministry of Health, Labour, and Welfare [MHLW]. (2010). Results of Monitoring and Guidance Based on the Imported Foods Monitoring and Guidance Plan for FY2009. Department of Food Safety, Pharmaceutical, and Food Safety Bureau.

Ministry of Health. (2004). Ministry of Health Statistical Yearbook.

Ministry of Health. (2009). Ministry of Health Statistical Yearbook.

Mitra, S. K. (2001). Making local government work: Local elites, Panchayati Raj and governance in India. In A. Kohli (Ed.), *The success of India's democracy* (Vol. 6, pp. 103–126). New York: Cambridge University Press.

Moncada, E., & Snyder, R. (2012). Subnational comparative research on democracy: Taking stock and looking forward. *Comparative Democratization Newsletter. American Political Science Association*, 10(1), 4–9.

Montinola, G., Qian, Y., & Weingast, B. (1995). Federalism, Chinese style: The political basis for economic success in China, *World Politics*, 48(1), 50–81.

More, A. (2012). Change to FSSR after consultation with govt, panels, indicates Chandramouli. *FnB News*. Accessed on May 22, 2014 at www.fnbnews.com/Top-News/Change-to-FSSR-after-consultation-with-Govt-panels-indicates-Chandramouli

Moustier, P., Tam, P. T. G., Anh, D. T., Binh, V. B., & Nguyen, T. T. L. (2010). The role of farmer organizations in supplying supermarkets with quality food in Vietnam, *Food Policy*, 35(1), 69–78.

Murdoch, J., & Miele, M. (1999). Culinary networks and cultural connections. In A. Hugues & S. Reimer (Eds.), *Geographies of commodity chains*. New York: Routledge.

Nair, P., & Antony, T. (2012). Food safety act hits roadblock. *IBN Live*. Accessed on May 22, 2014 at http://ibnlive.in.com/news/food-safety-act-hits-roadblock/234732-60-122.html

Nash, J., & Ehrenfield, J. (1996). Code Green: Business adopts voluntary environmental standards, *Environment* 38(1), 16–45.

Naughton, B. (2006). *The Chinese economy: Transitions and growth*. Cambridge, MA: MIT Press.

Naughton, B. J., & Yang, D. L. (Eds.). (2004). *Holding China together: Diversity and national integration in the post-Deng era*. New York: Cambridge University Press.

Nepusz, T., Petroczi, A., & Naughton, D. P. (2009). Network analytical tool for monitoring global food safety highlights China. *PLoS ONE, 4*, 1–7.

Neumann, W., & Barboza, D. (2010, June 13). US drops inspector of food in China. *New York Times*.

Newsdesk. (2014). US makes top 10 list of worst food safety violators. *Food Safety News*. Accessed July 29, 2017 at www.foodsafetynews.com/2014/08/u-s-in-top-ten-worst-food-safety-violators/#.WX4cVIjyuUl

Ni, H. G., & Zeng, H. (2009). Law enforcement is key to China's food safety. *Environmental Pollution*, 157(7), 1990–1992.

O'Brien, K., & Li, L. (1999). Selective policy implementation in rural China, *Comparative Politics*, 31(2), 167–186.

O'Brien, K., & Li, L. (2006). *Rightful resistance in China*. New York: Cambridge University Press.

Oi, J. (2004). *Rural China takes off: Institutional foundations of economic reform*. Berkeley: University of California Press.

Okello, J. J., & Swinton, S. M. (2007). Compliance with international food safety standards in Kenya's green bean industry: Comparison of a small-and a large-scale farm producing for export. *Review of Agricultural Economics*, 29(2), 269–285.

O'Lear, S., & Diehl, P. F. (2007). Not drawn to scale: Research on resource and environmental conflict, *Geopolitics*, 12(1), 166–182.

O'Lear, S. (2010). *Environmental politics: Scale and power*. New York: Cambridge University Press.

Oliver, J. E. (2000). City size and civic involvement in metropolitan America. *American Political Science Review*, 94(2), 361–373.

Ortega, D. L., Wang, H. H., Wu, L., & Olynk, N. J. (2011). Modeling heterogeneity in consumer preferences for select food safety attributes in China. *Food Policy*, 36(2), 318–324.

Ostrom, E. (2005). *Understanding institutional diversity*. Princeton, NJ: Princeton University Press.

Ostrom, E. (2006). *Governing the commons: The evolution of institutions for collective action*. New York: Cambridge University Press.

Ostrom, E. (2007). A diagnostic approach for going beyond panaceas. *Proceedings of the National Academy of Sciences*, 104(39), 15181–15187.

Ostrom, E. (2010). Beyond markets and states: Polycentric governance of complex economic systems. *Transnational Corporations Review*, 2(2), 1–12.

Ostrom, V., & Ostrom, E. (1965). A behavioral approach to the study of intergovernmental relations. *The Annals of the American Academy of Political and Social Science*, 359(1), 137–146.

Palthur, P., Palthur, S. S., & Chitta, S. K. (2009). The food safety and standards act, 2006: A paradigm shift in Indian regulatory scenario. *Pharmacological Review*, 7(5), 14–20.

Pape, S. M., Rubin, P. D., & Kim, H. (2004). Food security would be compromised by combining the food and drug administration and the U.S. Department of Agriculture into single food agency. *Food and Drug Law Journal*, 59(3), 405–416.

Parekh, J. (2012). FSSA licensing, registration for dairy industry. *FnB News*. Accessed on May 22, 2014 at www.fnbnews.com/Overview/FSSA-licensing-registration-for-dairy-industry

Parikh, S., & Weingast, B. R. (1997). A comparative theory of federalism: India. *Virginia Law Review*, 1593–1615.

Parker, G. (2005). Sustainable food? Teikei, co-operatives and food citizenship in Japan and the UK. Working Papers in Real Estate & Planning.

Pasztor, A. (2007). How China turned around a dismal air-safety record. *Wall Street Journal*. Accessed on July 29, 2017 at www.wsj.com/articles/SB119198005864354292

Pearson, M. (2005). The Business of Governing Business in China, *World Politics*, 57(2), 296–322.

Pearson, M. M. (2007). Governing the Chinese economy: Regulatory reform in the service of the state. *Public Administration Review*, 67(4), 718–730.

Pei, X., Tandon, A., Aldrick, A., Giorgi, L., Huang, W. & Yang, R. (2011). The China melamine milk scandal and its implications for food safety regulation, *Food Policy*, 36(3), 412–420.

Perkins, D. H., & Syrquin, M. (1989). Large countries: The influence of size. *Handbook of Development Economics*, 2, 1691–1753.

Peters, B. G., & Pierre, J. (2001). Developments in intergovernmental relations: Towards multi-level governance. *Policy & Politics*, 29(2), 131–135.

Pew Research Center. (2013). Growing Concerns in China about Inequality and Corruption. Global Attitudes Project. Accessed April 20, 2013 at www.pewglobal.org/files/2012/10/Pew-Global-Attitudes-China-Report-FINAL-October-10-2012.pdf

Phoenix Hills website. About Us. Accessed March 5, 2010 at www.phoenixcommune.com/EN/gywm.htm

Polansek, T. (2014). Meat supplier in China food scandal grew with McDonald's. *Reuters*. Accessed March 6, 2017 at www.reuters.com/article/us-china-food-lavin-idUSKBN0FT02M20140724

Prakash, A. (2000). Responsible care: An assessment, *Business and Society*, 39(2), 183–209.

Pretty, J. (2003). Social Capital and the Collective Management of Resources, *Science*, 302(5652), 1912–1914.

Provost, C. (2010). Governance and voluntary regulation. In D. Levi-Faur (Ed.), *The Oxford handbook of governance*. Oxford: Oxford University Press.

Qian, Y., & Weingast, B. R. (1997). Federalism as a commitment to preserving market incentives. *The Journal of Economic Perspectives*, 11(4), 83–92.

Qingdao Zaobao [QDZB]. (2006, April 27). Huangua Dudao Shang Bai Qingdao Shimin. *Qingdao Zaobao*.

Qiu, W., Wang, B., Jones, P. J., & Axmacher, J. C. (2009). Challenges in developing China's marine protected area system, *Marine Policy*, 33(4), 599–605.

Reardon, T., Timmer, P., & Berdegue, J. (2004). The rapid rise of supermarkets in developing countries: Induced organizational, institutional, and technological change in agrifood systems. *Electronic Journal of Agricultural and Development Economics*, 1(2), 168–183.

Rees, J. (1988). *Reforming the workplace: A study of self-regulation in occupational safety*. Philadelphia: University of Pennsylvania Press.

Renmin Ribao [RMRB]. (2012, August 15). Yi luse fazhan yinling anquan shipin shengchan jidi jianshe. *People's Daily*. Accessed September 1, 2012 at http://news.hexun.com/2012–08–15/144755593.html

Repnikova, M. (2015). Media oversight in non-democratic regimes. PARGC Paper 3. Project for the Advanced Study of Global Communication. University of Pennsylvania, Annenberg School.

Revell, B. (2008). An Analysis of Consumer Attitudes to Food Safety for Fresh Produce in Urban China. International Food and Agribusiness Management Association. Symposium Paper. Shanghai, China, June 11–12.

Roberts, D. (2012, July 20). On China's web, green activists grow bolder. *Bloomberg Businessweek*. Accessed September 2, 2012 at www.businessweek.com/articles/2012–07–20/chinese-protesters-see-greater-online-freedom-over-environment

Roberts, D. (2013, March 14). China sets up a food safety super-regulator. *Bloomsberg Businessweek*. Accessed April 1, 2013 at www.businessweek.com/articles/2013–03–14/china-sets-up-a-food-safety-super-regulator

Rodden, J. (2004). Comparative federalism and decentralization: On meaning and measurement. *Comparative Politics*, 481–500.

Rodrik, D. (2008). Second best institutions. *American Economic Review*, 98(2), 100–104.

Rothstein, B. (2011). *The quality of government: Corruption, social trust and inequality in a comparative perspective*. Chicago: University of Chicago Press.

Sharma, D. (2012). New food safety regulation could force many to close shop. *India Today*. Accessed on May 9, 2014 at http://indiatoday.intoday.in/story/new-food-safety-regulation-could-force-many-to-close-shop/1/209913.html

Schickler, E. (2001). *Disjointed pluralism: Institutional innovation and the development of the US Congress*. Princeton, NJ: Princeton University Press.

Schulman, P. (1975). Nonincremental policy making: Notes toward an alternative paradigm, *American Political Science Review*, 69(4), 1354–1370.

Scott, J. (1999). *Seeing Like a State: How Certain Schemes to Improve the Human Condition Have Failed*. New Haven, CT: Yale University Press.

Seawright, J., & Gerring, J. (2008). Case selection techniques in case study research: A menu of qualitative and quantitative options. *Political Research Quarterly*, 61(2), 294–308.

SFDA. (2007). Guanyu Gongbu Shoupi Guojiaji Shipin Anquan Shifan Xian de Tongzhi. Accessed February 10, 2010 at www.gov.cn/zwgk/2007–08/23/content_725541.htm

Shan, J. (2013, March 11). Shake up on the cards for food and drug safety. *China Daily*. Accessed April 1, 2013 at www.chinadaily.com.cn/china/2013npc/2013–03/11/content_16296447.htm

Shen, G., & Heino, M. (2014). An overview of marine fisheries management in China. *Marine Policy*, 44, 265–272.

Shi, Y., Cheng, C., Lei, P., Wen, T., & Merrifield, C. (2011). Safe food, green food, good food: Chinese community supported agriculture and the rising middle class. *International Journal of Agricultural Sustainability*, 9(4), 551–558.

Shue, V. (1988). *The reach of the state: Sketches of the Chinese body politic*. Palo Alto, CA: Stanford University Press.

Shukla, S., Shankar, R., & Singh, S. P. (2014). Food safety regulatory model in India. *Food Control*, 37, 401–413.

Silber, J. H., Rosenbaum, P. R., & Ross, R. N. (1995). Comparing the contributions of groups of predictors: Which outcomes vary with hospital rather than patient characteristics? *JASA*, 90, 7–18.

Sinclair, D. (1997). Self-regulation versus command and control? Beyond false dichotomies. *Law and Policy*, 19(4), 529–559.

Singh, A. (2014). FSSAI appellate tribunals in process of being set up in various states. *FnB News*. Accessed on May 9, 2014 at www.fnbnews.com/Top-News/FSSAI-Appellate-Tribunals-in-process-of-being-set-up-in-various-states

Sinha, A. (2003). Rethinking the developmental state model: Divided leviathan and subnational comparisons in India. *Comparative Politics*, 35(4), 459–476.

Sinha, A. (2005). *The regional roots of developmental politics in India: A divided leviathan*. Bloomington: Indiana University Press.

Skinner, G. W. (1964). Marketing and social structure in rural China, Part I. *The Journal of Asian Studies*, 24(1), 3–43.

Smil, V. (1995). Who will feed China? *The China Quarterly*, 143, 801–813.

Smith, N. (2008). Scale bending and the fate of the national, in E. Sheppard & R. B. McMaster (Eds.), *Scale and geographic inquiry: Nature, society, and method* (pp. 192–207). New York: Wiley.

Snyder, R. (2001). Scaling-down: The subnational comparative method. *Studies in Comparative International Development*, 36(1), 93–110.

Song, M., Gao, X., Liu, L., & Teruaki, N. (2010). Reducing Food Safety Risk: Experiences from the Adoption of Good Agricultural Practices in China, *Journal of the Faculty of Agriculture, Kyushu University*, 55(2), 379–385.

Srebrnik, H. (2004). Small island nations and democratic values. *World Development*, 32(2), 329–341.

State Council. (2004). Decision of the State Council about Further Strengthening Food Safety. Accessed November 10, 2011 at www.lawinfochina.com/display.aspx?lib=law&id=3739&CGid=

State Council. (2007). White Paper of Food Quality and Safety. Accessed October 5, 2012 at www.china.org.cn/english/news/221274.htm

State Council. (2012). Guowuyuan guanyu jiawiang shipinanquan gongzuo de jueding. *State Council Circular 20*. Accessed July 28, 2017 at www.gov.cn/zwgk/2012-07/03/content_2175891.htm

State Council. (2013). Guowuyuanbangongting Guanyu Jiaqiangnongchanpinzhiliang anquan jianguan gongzuo de tongzhi 2013 nian. http://politics.people.com.cn/n/2013/1211/c1001-23808412.html

State Council. (2015). Premier Li Keqiang: Zero tolerance for food safety failings. http://english.gov.cn/premier/news/2015/06/11/content_281475125300505.htm

State Food and Nutrition Consultant Committee [SFNCC]. (2010, April 7). Zhongrishipin anquan xieyi yiding 5 yue zhengshi qianding. Press Release.

Strauss, D. M. (2011). An analysis of the FDA Food Safety Modernization Act: Protection for consumers and boon for business. *Food and Drug Law Journal*, 66(3), 353–376.

Suttmeier, R. (2008). The 'Sixth Modernization'? China, Safety, and the Management of Risks, *Asia Policy*, 6(1), 129–146.

Sutton, P. (2007). Democracy and good governance in small states. In E. Kisanga & S. J. Danchie (Eds.), *Commonwealth small states: Issues and prospects* (pp. 201–217). London: Commonwealth Secretariat.

Tam, W. (2011). Organizational corruption by public hospitals in China. *Crime, Law and Social Change*, 56(3), 265–282.

Tam, W., & Yang, D. (2005). Food safety and the development of regulatory institutions in China. *Asian Perspective* 29, 5–36.

Tang, M. (Ed.). (2009). *Study report on food and drug safety and regulatory policies (2009)*. Beijing: Social Sciences Academic Press (China).

Taylor, M. R. (1997). Preparing America's food safety system for the twenty-first century: Who is responsible for what when it comes to meeting the food safety challenges of the consumer-driven global economy. *Food and Drug Law Journal*, 52(1), 13–30.

Teets, J. C. (2009). Post-earthquake relief and reconstruction efforts: The emergence of civil society in China, *The China Quarterly*, 198, 330–347.

Teets, J. C., & Hurst, W. (2014). *Local governance innovation in China: Experimentation, diffusion, and defiance*. New York: Routledge.

Termeer, C., Dewulf, A., & van Lieshout, M. (2010). Disentangling scale approaches in governance research: Comparing monocentric, multilevel, and adaptive governance, *Ecology and Society*, 15 (4), 1–15.

The Economist. (2011, October 29). In the gutter. *The Economist Online*. Accessed January 8, 2012 at www.economist.com/node/21534812

Thiers, P. (2003). Risk society comes to China: SARS, transparency and public accountability. *Asian Perspective*, 27(2), 241–251.

Thompson, D., & Hu, Y. (2007). Food safety in China: New strategies, *Global Health Governance* 1(2), 1–19.

Tilt, B. (2007). The political ecology of pollution enforcement in China: A case from Sichuan's rural industrial sector. *The China Quarterly*, 192, 915–932.

Tran, J. 2014. New laws in China to tackle rampant food safety problems. *Food Safety News*. Accessed March 6, 2016 at www.foodsafetynews.com/2014/04/draft-new-laws-in-china-to-tackle-rampant-food-safety-problems/#.WL1i2DvytPY

Treisman, D. (2007). *The architecture of government: Rethinking political decentralization*. New York: Cambridge University Press.

Treisman, D. (2008). Decentralization dataset. Available at www.sscnet.ucla.edu/polisci/faculty/treisman/

Trevaskes, S. (2002). Courts on the campaign path in China: Criminal court work in the "Yanda 2001" anti-crime campaign, *Asian Survey*, 42(5), 673–693.

Truex, R. (2017). Consultative authoritarianism and its limits. *Comparative Political Studies*, 50(3), 329–361.

Umali-Deininger, D., & Sur, M. (2007). Food safety in a globalizing world: Opportunities and challenges for India. *Agricultural Economics*, 37(S1), 135–147.

United Nations Comtrade Database [UN Comtrade]. Accessed February 10, 2012.

United Nations. (2008). *Occasional Paper: Advancing Food Safety in China*.

US Department of Agriculture [USDA]. (2010). China – Peoples Republic of, Organics Report. *GAIN Report 10046*.

US House of Representatives Committee on Energy and Commerce [USHRCEC]. (2007). Food from China: Can We Import Safely? Staff Report.

Uvin, P. (1995). Scaling-up the grassroots and scaling-down the summit: The relations between third world nongovernmental organisations and the United Nations, *Third World Quarterly*, 16(3), 495–512.

Van Rooij, B., Stern, R. E., & Fürst, K. (2016). The authoritarian logic of regulatory pluralism: Understanding China's new environmental actors. *Regulation & Governance*, 10(1), 3–13.

Van Rooij, B., & Lo, C. W. H. (2010). Fragile convergence: Understanding variation in the enforcement of China's industrial pollution law, *Law & Policy*, 32(1), 14–37.

Vogel, D. (2012). *The politics of precaution: Regulating health, safety, and environmental risks in Europe and the United States*. Princeton, NJ: Princeton University Press.

Vos, E. (2000). EU Food Safety Regulation in the Aftermath of the BSE Crisis, *Journal of Consumer Policy*, 23(3), 227–255.

Waldron, A. (1990). Warlordism versus federalism: The revival of a debate? *The China Quarterly*, 121, 116–128.

Wall Street Journal [WSJ]. (2007, October 10). How China turned around a dismal air-safety record. Accessed January 15, 2012 at http://online.wsj.com/article/SB119198005864354292.html

Wall Street Journal [WSJ]. (2011, August 5). China makes arrests over food. Accessed June 10, 2013 at http://online.wsj.com/article/SB10001424053111903885604576487780529072912.html

Wall Street Journal [WSJ]. (2013, May 15). China aviation industry analysis. Accessed June 11, 2013 at http://online.wsj.com/article/PR-CO-20130515-909065.html

Wang, H. (2012). Certified organic: New organic product certification rules in place to regulate market. *Beijing Review*. Accessed on July 29, 2017 at www.bjreview.com.cn/health/txt/2012-04/16/content_448772.htm

Wedeman, A. (2005). Anticorruption campaigns and the intensification of corruption in China. *Journal of Contemporary China*, 14(42), 93–116.

Weersink, A., & Rozelle, S. (1997). Marketing reforms, market development, and agricultural production in China, *Agricultural Economics*, 17(2–3), 95–114.

Wei, S. (2001, December 5). China's food industry reports healthy progress. *Beijing Youth Daily*. Accessed February 5, 2013 at www.china.org.cn/archive/2002–01/15/content_1025275.htm

Weisman, S. (2007, December 12). China agrees to post US safety officials in its food factories. *New York Times*.

Whiting, S. (2000). *Power and wealth in rural China*. Cambridge Modern China Series. New York: Cambridge University Press.

Wibbels, E. (2003). Bailouts, budget constraints, and Leviathans comparative federalism and lessons from the early United States. *Comparative Political Studies*, 36(5), 475–508.

Wike, R. (2013). What Chinese are worried about. *Pew Report*. Accessed on July 29, 2017 at www.pewglobal.org/2013/03/13/what-chinese-are-worried-about/

World Bank. (2006). *China-farm professional associations: Review and policy recommendations*. Washington, DC: The World Bank.

World Trade Organization [WTO]. (2015). *International trade statistics 2015*. Statistics Division.

Wright, T. (2004). The Political Economy of Coal Mine Disasters in China: 'Your Rice Bowl or Your Life.' *The China Quarterly*, 179, 629–646.

Wu, N. (2012, July 27). Guanzhu beijing nongfushiji [Focus on Beijing Farmer's Market]. *China Industry and Commerce News*. Accessed August 15, 2012 at www.cicn.com.cn/content/2012–07/25/content_115975.htm

Wu, L., Xu, L., & Gao, J. (2011). The acceptability of certified traceable food among Chinese consumers. *British Food Journal*, 113(4), 519–534.

Wu, L., & Zhu, D. (2014). *Food safety in China: A comprehensive review*. Chicago: CRC Press.

Xie, M., Gu, Z., & Liu, Y. (2009). Fulfilling scientific supervision to ensure meat safety of Shanghai. In M. Tang (Ed.), *Study report on food and drug safety and regulatory policies (2009)*. Beijing: Social Sciences Academic Press (China).

Xinhua. (2006, November 20). Shandong Bans Sales of Contaminated Turbot. *Xinhua*. Accessed March 10, 2013 at www.china.org.cn/english/health/189526.htm

Xinhua. (2011a, November 13). China steps up campaign on food safety awareness. *Xinhua*. Accessed June 10, 2013 at http://news.xinhuanet.com/english2010/indepth/2011-11/13/c_131244094.htm

Xinhua. (2011b). Moral education urged to ensure food safety. *China Daily Online*. Accessed July 29, 2017 at www.chinadaily.com.cn/china/2011–06/16/content_12714940.htm

Xinhua. (2012a, August 8). Beijing youji nongfushiji: mitudeshiji weilai nengzouduoyuan? [Beijing's Farmer Market: The Market Gone Astray, How Far

Can it Go?]. *Xinhua*. Accessed March 15, 2012 at http://news.xinhuanet.com/fortune/2012-08/08/c_123548631.htm

Xinhua. (2012b, April 3). Over 100 arrested for making new-type gutter oil. *Xinhua*. Accessed June 11, 2013 at http://news.xinhuanet.com/english/china/2012-04/03/c_131504678.htm

Xinhua. (2012c, October 11). More than 540,000 grassroots officials punished for discipline violations. Accessed June 11, 2013 at http://news.xinhuanet.com/english/china/2012-10/11/c_131900598.htm

Xinhua. (2013). One super ministry to oversee food and drug safety. Online Interview. Accessed July 29, 2013 at http://english.cntv.cn/program/china24/20130316/105289.shtml

Xiu, C., & Klein, K. K. (2010). Melamine in milk products in China: Examining the factors that led to deliberate use of the contaminant. *Food Policy*, 35(5), 463–470.

Xu, N. (2012, August 6). A decade of food safety in China. *China Dialogue*.

Yan, W. (2010, February 11). Japan, China discuss food safety. *China Daily*.

Yan, Y. (2012). Food safety and social risk in contemporary China, *The Journal of Asian Studies*, 71(3), 705–729.

Yang, C. (2006). The geopolitics of cross-boundary governance in the Greater Pearl River Delta, China: A case study of the proposed Hong Kong–Zhuhai–Macao Bridge. *Political Geography*, 25(7), 817–835.

Yang, C. (2011, June 1). Canzhuo "Zijiu." *Nanfang Dushibao*.

Yang, D. L. (2004). *Remaking the Chinese leviathan: Market transition and the politics of governance in China*. Palo Alto, CA: Stanford University Press.

Yang, D. (2008). Total recall. *The National Interest*, March/April.

Yang, D. (2009). Regulatory learning and its discontents in China: Promise and tragedy at the SFDA. Unpublished Manuscript.

Yang, G. (2013). Contesting food safety in the Chinese media: Between hegemony and counter-hegemony. *The China Quarterly*, 214, 337–355.

Yang, L., Qian, Y., Chen, C., & Wang, F. (2012). Assessing the establishment of agro-food control systems based on relevant officials' survey in China. *Food Control*, 26(2), 223–230.

Yao, P. (2012, July 3). Guanfang yaoqiu yanda shipin anquan weifa fanzui Jianchi zhongdian zhiluan. *China News Network*. Accessed July 29, 2017 at www.chinanews.com/jk/2012/07-03/4005579.shtml

Yeh, E. T., O'Brien, K. J., & Ye, J. (2013). Rural politics in contemporary China. *Journal of Peasant Studies*, 40(6), 915–928.

Young, O. R. (2003). *The institutional dimensions of environmental change: Fit, interplay, and scale*. Cambridge, MA: MIT Press.

Yu, D. (2011, April 16). Nongchang tansuo shipin anquan xin moshi [Farm explores a new model for food safety]. *Xinhua*. Accessed January 12, 2012 at http://news.xinhuanet.com/world/2011-04/26/c_121349030.htm

Yu, H., & Yu, Y. (2008). Fishing capacity management in China: Theoretic and practical perspectives. *Marine Policy*, 32(3), 351–359.

Yu, X. (2015). It's time to fix China's food safety conundrum. *Caixin Online*. Accessed June 6, 2015 at http://english.caixin.com/2015-04-28/100804427.html

Zachernuk, T. (2008). *Thematic report #6: The development of farmer organizations and the small farmers project. China-Canada small farmers adapting to global markets project.* Beijing: Beijing Project Office.

Zhang, L. (1999). Chinese central-provincial fiscal relationships, budgetary decline and the impact of the 1994 fiscal reform: An evaluation. *The China Quarterly*, 157, 115–141.

Zhang, Q. F. (2012). The political economy of contract farming in China's agrarian transition. *Journal of Agrarian Change*, 12(4), 460–483.

Zhang, Q. F., & Donaldson, J. A. (2010). From peasants to farmers: Peasant differentiation, labor regimes, and land-rights institutions in China's agrarian transition. *Politics & Society*, 38(4), 458–489.

Zhang, Y. (2014). Nanzichichoudoufu houwuzangqishuaijiehua15wanzhengzhengzhileyigeyue. *Wenzhou Shangbao*. Accessed March 6, 2017 at http://news.66wz.com/system/2014/08/07/104180187.shtml

Zhao, Ming. (2011). Shequzhichinongye (CSA) zaizhongguo de fazhan jiyu [CSA Development Prospects in China]. *Hope Springs Magazine*. Accessed March 10, 2012 at www.5xue.com/magazine/blog/?p=1392

Zhou, J., & Jin, S. (2009). Safety of Vegetables and the Use of Pesticides by Farmers in China: Evidence from Zhejiang Province, *Food Control*, 20(11), 1043–1048.

Zhou, J., & Jin, S. (2013). *Food safety management in China: A perspective from food quality control system.* Singapore: World Scientific Publishing.

Zhou, W. (2011, November 1). Food safety complaints more common. *China Daily*. Accessed March 10, 2012 at www.chinadaily.com.cn/business/2011-11/01/content_14012784.htm

Zhou, X. (2011). The autumn harvest: Peasants and markets in post-collective rural China. *The China Quarterly*, 208, 913–931.

Zhu, S., He, C., & Liu, Y. (2014). Going green or going away: Environmental regulation, economic geography and firms' strategies in China's pollution-intensive industries. *Geoforum*, 55, 53–65.

Laws

Food Safety Modernization Act of 2010, 111 U.S.C. 2751 (2010) (FSMA)

Food Safety Law of China, (2009).

Food Safety Law of China (revised), (2015)

Food Safety and Standards Act of India, (2006) (FSSAI)

Index

accountability
  food safety mechanisms, 15
  lack of transparency in authoritarian
    regimes, 18–20
agricultural production bases (APBs),
  107–113
  appropriate scale of production and
    distribution, 108–110
  contribution to regulatory confusion,
    111–113
  interprovincial standards and conflicts,
    111–112
  knowledge problems, 110–111
  local government investment in, 108
  one village, one product policy, 108
  unintended consequences of the APB
    model, 111–113
air pollution, 207, 209
aldicarb in cucumbers, 140
Anlong Village Project, Chengdu, 160–161
AQSIQ, 50, 138, 139
  licensing system, 69–70
  management of the export food sector,
    11
  organic production standards, 87
  regulation of the export food sector,
    61–62
AR food export company, 142
authoritarian regimes
  food safety regulation challenges, 18–20
  suppression of the media, 18–20
aviation sector in China, 210–211

Beck, Ulrich, 213
boundary of a scale, 21
Brazil
  domestic and export sectors, 148
  food export market, 77
BSE outbreak (1990s), 66, 173

carcinogens in turbot fish, 112
Cassis de Dijon case, 172–173
central government
  food safety accountability initiatives, 15
  motivation to improve food safety,
    15–16
  sandwich theory of Chinese politics,
    19–20
centralized federal food safety system (US),
  181–185
centralized, hierarchical governance, 31–33
  export food sector, 61–64
Chen Duxiu, 194
Chengdu Urban River Association
  (CURA), 160–161
China
  as a test case on governing scale,
    213–215
  challenges related to scale, 7–9
  emergence of severe food safety
    violations, 44–46
  failure of existing approaches to food
    safety, 192–194
  food production sectors, 44
  fragmented authoritarian system, 35–38